The Frontier
Years of
Abe Lincoln

The Frontier Years of Abe Lincoln

In the Words of His Friends and Family

Richard Kigel

Walker and Company
New York

Library of Congress Cataloging-in-Publication Data

Kigel, Richard.
   The frontier years of Abe Lincoln.

   Bibliography: p.
   Includes index.
   1. Lincoln, Abraham, 1809-1865. 2. Presidents--
United States--Biography. I. Title.
E457.15.K48 1986   973.7'092'4 [B]   86-19108
ISBN 0-8027-0921-4

Copyright © 1986 by Richard Kigel

First published in the United States of America in 1986 by the Walker Publishing Company, Inc.

Published simultaneously in Canada by John Wiley & Sons Canada, Limited, Rexdale, Ontario.

Frontispiece Courtesy of the Louis A. Warren Lincoln Library and Museum

Printed in the United States of America

10 9 8 7 6 5 4 3 2 1

This book is dedicated to my students in the evening classes at Malcolm-King College on 125th Street in Manhattan and to students everywhere who find themselves, as Lincoln did, mired in an atmosphere with "absolutely nothing to excite ambition for education." Still they come to school. A few find a way to excel. For these students I hold the highest respect.

"IN THE MIDST OF THIS, HOWEVER, HE FROM WHOM ALL
BLESSINGS FLOW MUST NOT BE FORGOTTEN."
—*Abraham Lincoln, from his final public speech*
April 11, 1865

Table of Contents

The Frontier
Years of
Abe Lincoln

"I have fancied, I say, some such venerable relic of this time of ours, preserved to the next or still the next generation of America. I have fancied on such occasion the young men gathering around; the awe, the eager questions. 'What! Have you seen Abraham Lindoln—and heard him speak—and touched his hand?' "

—**Walt Whitman**

Introduction

The Frontier Years: Digging Up the Story

"I have no confidence in biographies," Abraham Lincoln told his law partner William Herndon in their Springfield office one day. "You don't get a true understanding of the man." *(1)*

Least of all did he like biographies of Abraham Lincoln. "I know he thought poorly of the idea of attempting a biographical sketch," wrote journalist John Locke Scripps, who was preparing the candidate's life story on the eve of the 1860 Presidential campaign. "The chief difficulty I had to encounter," recalled Scripps, "was to induce him to communicate the homely facts and incidents of his early life."

" 'Why Scripps,' said Lincoln on one occasion, 'It is a great piece of folly to attempt to make anything out of my early life. It can all be condensed into a single sentence and that sentence you will find in Gray's Elegy: 'The short and simple annals of the poor.' That's my life and that's all you or anyone else can make of it.' " *(2)*

Billy Herndon saw his life—beyond the early years—differently. As the junior partner in the law firm of Lincoln & Herndon from 1844 until the day Lincoln died, he saw Lincoln's biography unfolding day by day. He was a major actor in the drama. He and Lincoln shared courtroom battles and ran political campaigns. Together they helped manage the birth of the modern day Republican Party. Billy was there, on stage, as Abe grew from an obscure country lawyer to a national figure and finally to President of the United States. He was Lincoln's friend, debating with him fine points of science, literature, philosophy—or whatever struck their nimble minds. He laughed at Abe's stories, listened to his whispered secrets and witnessed his inner suffering and personal struggle. "He was so good and so odd a man," wrote Herndon, "how in the hell could I help study him!" *(3)*

Herndon saw something in the Lincoln drama, a light of inspiration from beginning to end. It was a flame he vowed to keep alive for future generations. "Soon after Mr. Lincoln's assassination I determined to gather up all the facts of his life— truly, honestly and impartially, whatever it might cost in money or infamy—and to give the facts to the world as I understood them," he wrote. *(4)*

"Seeing Lincoln as I see him, he is a grand character. I see him in my mind from his cradle to his grave and I say Lincoln's life seems a grand march over the forces and resistances of nature and man. . . . *(5)* Many of our great men . . . have been self-made, rising . . . through struggles to the topmost round of the ladder. But Lincoln rose from a lower depth than any of them." *(6)*

Herndon wrote "dozens of letters weekly" *(7)* to folks in Kentucky and Indiana who may have known young Abe and his family. "Friend Hall"—began one letter to Levi Hall, husband of Matilda Johnston Hall, Abe's step-sister—"Please write to me at any time you may think of anything that is good or bad of Mr. Lincoln, truthfully, just as it happened and took place. . . . Hall, what is your honest opinion—Come, honest opinion—in reference to Mr. Lincoln's love for his kin and relations generally? Please friend, accommodate me." *(8)*

A month after Lincoln was shot, Herndon was out in the countryside, seeking old-timers who knew Lincoln when he lived in New Salem thirty years before. "When I met a man or woman who knew anything good or bad and was willing to tell it, I generally took notes then and there of what was said about Lincoln. . . . *(9)* I have been with the people, ate with them,

slept with them and thought with them—cried with them too."
(10)

On September 8, 1865, Herndon had his most important interview. He met the person who had the greatest impact on young Abe as he grew up—his beloved step-mother, Sarah Bush Lincoln. "When I first reached the home of Mrs. Lincoln and was introduced to her by Colonel A. H. Chapman, her grandson by marriage, I did not expect to get much out of her," said Herndon. "She seemed so old and feeble. She asked me my name two or three times and where I lived as often. . . . She breathed badly at first but she seemed to be struggling at last to arouse herself or to fix her mind on the subject.

"Gradually, by introducing simple questions to her about her age, marriage, Kentucky, Thomas Lincoln, her former husband (Daniel Johnston), her children, grandchildren . . . she awoke, as it were, a new being. Her eyes were clear and calm. . . . (11)

"She told me then that Mr. Lincoln, when a boy, used to keep an arithmetical copybook in which he put down his worked out sums. She likewise then told me that the boy Abraham was in the like habit of putting down in another copybook—his literary one—all things that struck him, such as fine oratory, rhetoric, science, art, etc. . . . Read them, looked at them over and over, analyzed them, thoroughly understanding them. He would translate them into his boyish language and would tell his schoolmates, friends and mother what they meant . . . and his schoolmates, friends and mother must hear or he would 'bust wide open.'

"The information thus given me by the good old lady, the kind and loving step-mother—God bless her—put me on nettles. . . . We commenced the search and found this, the arithmetical copybook. . . . We could not find the other book. It is lost and lost forever as our search was thorough. Mrs. Lincoln gave me the book with her own hands or by the hand of her grandson. . . . (12)

"Ate dinner with her," continued Herndon. "Ate a good hearty dinner, she did. When I was about to leave, she arose, took me by the hand, wept, and bade me good-bye, saying: 'I shall never see you again and if you see Mrs. Abraham Lincoln and family, tell them I send them my best and tenderest love. Good-bye my good son's friend. Farewell." *(13)*

A few days later, Herndon found Nat Grigsby, Abe's boyhood friend, in Gentryville, Indiana. Herndon listened and took notes as Nattie spoke of the days when he and Abe were young. On September 14, 1865, Herndon and Grigsby made a pilgrimage to the grave of Mrs. Nancy Hanks Lincoln, mother of Abraham.

"I started from Nat Grigsby's house with him as my guide and friend throughout the trip," related Herndon. "Started to find Mrs. Lincoln's grave. It is on a knob, hill or knoll about a half-mile south-east of the Lincoln house. . . . The grave is almost indistinguishable. It has sunk down, leaving a kind of hollow. There is no fence around the graveyard and no tomb, no headboard to mark where she lies.

"At her head, close to it, I pulled a dogwood bush and cut or marked my name on it. Mrs. Lincoln is buried between two or more persons, said to be Hall and his wife on the one hand and some children on her left hand. . . .

"God Bless her! If I could breathe life into her again, I would do it. Could I only whisper in her ear: 'Your son was President of the United States from 1861 to 1865,' I would be satisfied. I have heard much of his blessed good woman. I stood bareheaded in reverence at her grave. I can't say why, yet I felt in the presence of the living woman. . . . 'God bless her,' said her son to me once, and I repeat that which echoes audibly in my soul: 'God bless her.' " *(14)*

Herndon first met Dennis Hanks on June 13, 1865, at a Chicago Fair where Hanks was exhibiting the original Illinois Lincoln log cabin. Dennis Hanks could say more about the boyhood of Lincoln than any man.

Dennis was a likeable old codger who loved nothing more than reminiscing about the days of his youth with cousin Abe. ("My mother and Abe's mother's mother was sisters.") *(15)* In simple language that was pure country corn pone, he painted a lively, sharply detailed picture of growing up in the backwoods of Kentucky and Indiana. Hanks told his story to Herndon at the fair that day and he eagerly copied every word. They met again in September 1865 for another long interview and exchanged several letters.

"Want to know what kind o' boy Abe Lincoln was?" he drawled for interviewer Eleanor Atkinson years later. "Well, I reckon old Dennis Hanks is the only one livin' that knowed him that arly. Knowed him the day he was born an' lived with him most of the time till he was twenty-one an' left home fur good." *(16)*

Herndon knew that Dennis Hanks could provide a gold mine of priceless information. Yet he was wary. "You must watch Dennis," he warned. "Criticize what he says and how he says it. . . . *(17)* What he says about anything must be taken with much allowance. . . . *(18)* Dennis loves to blow." *(19)*

It is a rule of law that juries are permitted to disregard the entire testimony of a witness if he makes even one false statement. Lawyer Herndon mistrusted everything that Hanks said because he caught Dennis in a bit of deception.

"Dennis has got things mixed up," complained Herndon. "He purposely conceals all things that degrade the Hankses." *(20)* Loyal Dennis tried to hide from posterity the scandalous beginnings of Abe's mother, Nancy Hanks. Dennis loved Nancy like a sister. They were cousins, both removed from their mothers, the Hanks sisters, at an early age. They came to live with Aunt Betsy and Uncle Tom Sparrow. Dennis, ever the gentleman, tried to defend Nancy's honor by claiming that the Sparrows were her rightful parents. "If you call hir Hanks you make hir a Base born child which is not treu," *(21)* wrote Dennis to Herndon when his facts were challenged. "Hir Madin Name— Nancy Sparrow. So what is the use of all this." *(22)*

Dennis made a lame effort to hide the truth—that when the Sparrows were married in 1791, Nancy was already seven years old. Yet he stuck to his story offering explanations that Herndon found pitifully transparent. "Calling hir Hanks probily is my fault," Dennis claimed. "I always told hir she looked more like the Hankses than Sparrows . . . You know about families. They will always have Nick Names for one or another." *(23)*

Dennis Hanks had a sense of his place in history. He knew well that he had a starring role in the life of a man whose story would be told and retold for generations. Eager to make certain that his contribution was not overlooked, he may have been guilty of stretching his case. "I taught Abe his first lesson in spelling, reading and writing," he bragged. *(24)* "I no this," he continued. "I am the man that can tell all about it." *(25)*

"Now William," he prodded Herndon just in case he missed the point, "Be Shore and have my name very conspikus. . . . *(26)* I will say this much to you. If you don't have my name very frecantly in your book, it won't gaw of [go off] at all." *(27)*

Dennis was right. No man living could tell about Lincoln more convincingly. Even he wasn't sure that the whole story should be told. "I don't want to tell all the things that I know," he said. "It would not look well in history." *(28)*

Yet despite its major flaws, the testimony of Dennis Hanks is generally accepted as a reliable and finely drawn description of Lincoln's early life. Said Pulitzer Prize–winning biographer Albert Beveridge, "Dennis Hanks is watchful in the extreme in exalting the Hanks and Lincoln families. But aside from his boastfulness and championship of his clan, his statements are accurate. Luckily, it is easy to distinguish between fact and imagination in his letters and interviews." *(29)*

The surest source of information in any biography comes from the words of the subject himself. Lincoln loved to talk. In those moments when he was spinning yarns, sharing secrets or "argufyin' " someone was there listening. Later, each one could remember what he heard. "Herndon saw more of Lincoln and heard more from Lincoln's lips than any other human being, excepting Lincoln's wife," said Beveridge. *(30)*

Lincoln produced volumes of words. One historian observed that the sum of Lincoln's writings contains more words than the complete works of Shakespeare and the Bible combined. Yet, there are few words that tell of his childhood and growing up. Preparing for the Presidential election of 1860, Lincoln obliged a newspaperman who needed some information on his background. "Herewith is a little sketch, as you requested," wrote Lincoln. "There is not much of it, for the reason, I suppose, that there is not much of me." *(31)*

He wrote several pages of autobiographical notes. A few months later Lincoln wrote another autobiographical sketch, adding a few more details about his life, which he wrote impersonally, referring to himself as "Abraham" or "Mr. Lincoln." These two brief accounts, totaling less than a dozen pages, make up the only autobiography Lincoln left the world.

Since Lincoln did not tell his story, Herndon would. "If Mr. Lincoln could speak to me this day," Herndon wrote, "he would say 'Tell the truth. Don't varnish me.' " (32) This became Herndon's cherished goal. He used the highest standard of discrimination in his acceptance of evidence. Throughout his research, lecturing and writing about Lincoln, Herndon's lawyer-like skepticism about the reliability of witnesses helped to weed out what was false. He tried to avoid unsubstantiated statements. He always looked for witnesses who could support the testimony of others. He used his reason to piece together as truthful a picture as he could. "I think I knew Lincoln well," he said. "Thousands of stories about the man I rejected because they were inconsistent with the nature of the man." (33)

Yet he made mistakes. Herndon has been criticized by Lincoln historians for shrouding the man in a number of myths. Herndon believed sincerely that his explicit and personal analysis of the inner workings of the man's mind was absolute truth. "I know Lincoln better than I know myself," declared Herndon. (34) "My opinions are formed from the evidence before you and in a thousand other things, some of which I heard from Lincoln, others are inferences springing from his acts, from what he said and from what he didn't say." (35)

This is not history. Herndon's "opinions" and "inferences" based on what Lincoln "said" and "didn't say" are nothing more than erroneous conclusions drawn from partial facts. When Herndon avoids rampant hypothesizing and "armchair psychoanalysis" and presents the simple observations of what people saw and heard, then he becomes a true biographer. "In all my investigation his (Herndon's) character shines out clear and stainless," Beveridge wrote. "He was almost a fanatic in his devotion to truth. Wherever he states a fact as such, I accept it—unless other indisputable and documentary proof shows that his memory was a little bit defective." (36)

Finally, in 1889, when Herndon collected all his interviews, statements and personal observations and completed his *Hern-*

don's Lincoln: The True Story of a Great Life, he was satisfied that he had made a fair portrait of his friend. "I felt it my religious duty to tell all that I knew about Lincoln. . . . I did this to benefit my fellow-man. . . . *(37)* I drew the picture of Mr. Lincoln as I saw him and knew him. I told the naked God's truth and I'll stand by it. . . . *(38)* Pay or no pay, as to my book, I shall give to the world the facts of Lincoln's life, truly, faithfully, and honestly. The great future can then write its own book." *(39)*

For Abraham Lincoln, the future blooms with books. These days there are about 5,000 books on Lincoln, according to Lincoln scholar Herbert Mitgang. *(40)* Still they keep coming. "Of making many books there is no end," it says in Ecclesiastes. More books have been written about Abraham Lincoln than any other American. Almost every book relies on the pioneering research, the eyewitness reporting of William Herndon to make the story authentic.

Authenticity comes from being actual, true to life. In the tradition of Herndon's high-principled quest for truth-telling comes *The Frontier Years of Abe Lincoln,* an authentic portrait of a living man in words spoken by those who knew him. Here are the voices from Lincoln's past, mother, step-mother and father, cousins and friends, co-workers and rivals, all gathered from letters and interviews more than a century old, telling their story as they saw it and knew it.

This is their "biography," presented word for word, just as it flowed out of the pen or spilled from the lips. Since most of the letter writers were barely literate and cheerfully ignorant of the communication techniques required to reach a reading audience in the next century, they paid scant attention to such fine points as punctuation, sentence structure and paragraph organization. I've taken the liberty to make small corrections here and there for the sake of readability. A few periods were inserted at natural points in the conversation and new paragraphs were started when the focus changed, all to clarify the narrative and give the words an easy flow. Most of the original spelling errors and backwoods dialect have been left intact; clarifications have been made [in brackets, where needed] when the old frontier style wordricide seemed to brutalize an idea beyond recognition. For example: "cyards" [cards].

8

Perhaps this sort of biography would appeal to Abraham Lincoln. He always had a fascination for the way we could "exchange thoughts with one another . . . enabling us to converse with the dead, the absent and the unborn, at all distances of time and space." *(41)*

Here, in *The Frontier Years of Abraham Lincoln* are his own words and the words of his family and friends. It is real history—a true biography. "History," said Lincoln, "is not history unless it is the truth . . . *(42)* For people who like that sort of book," he added, "that is the sort of book they would like." *(43)*

1.

"Injuns!"

The new Americans were cocky and headstrong, confident as conquerors. Their battle cry ringing—"E Pluribus Unum" (Out of Many, One)—blacksmiths and carpenters, farmers and woodsmen, pioneers and gentlemen, all stood together against an Empire. Proclaiming a time for new ideas on the rights of men to life, liberty and the pursuit of happiness, these bold Americans announced to the world the birth of a nation. In 1781, the War for Independence was over. The mighty forces of King George III were chased from American soil forever.

From the beginning, this new American nation held a promise of greatness. Beyond the settlements on the eastern shore, a vast continent was yet to be explored. It seemed endless, this glorious wonderland of natural beauty. Raw, untouched, ever-new, the land was as fresh as the day it was made. Men heard the call of this lavish land in the song of Isaiah the prophet: "For ye shall go out with joy, and be led forth with peace: the mountains and the hills shall break forth before you into singing and all the trees of the field shall clap their hands."

Adventuresome Americans began to carve their way through thick walls of timber into the heart of the virgin land. Daniel Boone-said goodbye to the civilized parts of Virginia and headed west into the unknown forest. Colonel Boone and his men hacked out a pathway through the trees and the mountains and called it "Wilderness Road." They chiseled a little settlement out of the woods and watched it grow.

It was called "Kaintuckee," the "dark and bloody ground." Peaceful Cherokee Indians had roamed the woods as rightful heirs to the land, until, alarmed at the destruction of the forest stillness and their Mother Earth, they rose in anger to make the white men pay for their boldness in blood. Still, the Americans came—from warm homes in friendly towns. They came to the rough borders of their world to look into the dark eye of danger and daily toil. They came to the outer edge of man's rule of law and government and there set out to build a nation.

When Daniel Boone returned to the civilized world he was a genuine American hero, a valiant soldier in the battle to tame a wild country. He had been to another world and back, preparing the way for others to follow. He was calling it "a second paradise," (1) blue grass shimmering over the moist black earth, clear winding streams jumping with fish, wild game running everywhere. He moved his family to Kentucky and kept urging his friend Abraham Lincoln to sell his Virginia homestead and follow along.

This Abraham Lincoln was never to know that his namesake would become an enduring legend for unborn generations, a symbol for honor and freedom and decency among men. His grandson-to-be would become the most celebrated of all Americans. This Abraham Lincoln was a captain in the Virginia Militia during the Revolution. His brother, Jacob Lincoln, fought with Washington at Yorktown and saw the British surrender. Captain Abraham fought no battles with the British. Instead, he led patrols into the Virginia countryside to defend the community from the terror-attacks of angry Cherokee warriors.

Grandfather Abraham Lincoln put a lot of stock in the words of Daniel Boone. The Lincolns and the Boones had been friends for generations. When the Boone family came to America from England and settled in Pennsylvania, their first neighbors were Lincolns. Over the years, they became as close as family. The Boones and the Lincolns even united in matrimony. When Abraham Lincoln spoke to Daniel Boone, he felt as though he were speaking to a kinsman.

In 1782, the first full year of a growing young nation, restless families began looking to the west for new beginnings. Abraham

Lincoln sold his Virginia farm, packed up his belongings, and with his wife, Bathsheba and their five children, Mordecai, Josiah, Mary, Nancy and baby Thomas, they followed the moving stream of new American pioneers through the Wilderness Road to that "second paradise" in Kentucky.

"The first inhabitants of Kentucky, on account of the hostility of the Indians, lived in what were called forts," (2) wrote an early Kentuckian. Abraham Lincoln moved his family to a settlement known as Hughes Station on Floyd's Creek. The cabins were set together, side by side, forming a large closed-in courtyard. Here, the children could romp with the chickens, goats and pigs while the men practiced their military drills.

Abraham Lincoln filed claims for nearly two-thousand acres of open Kentucky land. One of his claims was found in the office of the Surveyor, Jefferson County:

"Surveyed for Abraham Linkhorn, 400 acres of land in Jefferson County, by virtue of a Treasury warrant No. 3334 on the fork of Floyd's fork, now called the Long Run, beginning about two miles up the said fork . . . at a sugar tree standing on the side of the same marked D S-B and extending there East 300 poles to a Poplar and Sugar Tree, North 213⅓ poles to a Beech and Dogwood, West 300 poles to a White Oak and Hickory, South 213⅓ poles to the beginning, May 7th, 1785." (3)

Daniel Boone, himself, surveyed another 500 acres for his friend. The name "Abraham Linkhorn," or "Abraham Linkern" often appeared on the official documents of the day. "They were called Linkhorn," an old friend said. "That proves nothing as the old settlers had a way of pronouncing names as they pleased." (4)

Frontier living was hard. What food and clothing they had came from the creatures of the forest. Chores were never-ending. Great forests had to be cleared and the soil plowed and prepared for bearing fruits. Dark surprises lurked in every new morning. Would a rainstorm wash the crops off the ground? Would drought wither them? Would fever weaken the family and maybe take one of the children? Would the livestock survive ravaging bears and mountain lions? Would they hear the savage war whoops of rampaging Indians?

One day in May of 1786 a bloody surprise knocked at the door of the Lincoln family. The pioneer father and his three boys were working to clear a plot of land just outside the fort. A rifle shot rang out and Abraham Lincoln fell dead.

"Injuns!" (5) the boys screamed in terror, and lit out in different directions. Mordecai ran back toward the cabin to get his father's gun. Josiah hid out in the woods. Young Tom was left behind, kneeling beside his father's bleeding body.

The story of the death of Grandfather Abraham became legend in the Lincoln home for generations. It was told over and over again, by the crackling fireplace on lonely evenings when the men swapped Indian tales. Dennis Hanks, close cousin and playmate of the future President, must have heard Tom Lincoln relive the death scene as often as Abe himself did. Years later, Dennis retold the story:

"Then the Indian ran out from his hiding place and caught Thomas, the father of Abraham. Mordecai, the oldest brother of Thomas and uncle of Abraham, jumped over the fence, ran to the post, shot the Indian through the pivot holes in the post. The Indian dropped Thomas, ran and was followed by the blood the next day and found dead. Mordecai said the Indian had a silver half-moon trinket on his breast at the time he drew his 'bead' on the Indian, that silver being the mark he shot at. He said it was the prettiest mark he held a rifle on." (6)

Tom Lincoln, father-to-be of the sixteenth President of the United States, was himself fatherless at the age of eight. He received no inheritance from his father. By law, the eldest son, Mordecai, received all the Lincoln property. Mordecai grew up to become a well-to-do Kentucky farmer. He never lost his hatred for Indians and was known as one of the most ruthless Indian fighters of his day.

Of his father, Abe Lincoln wrote: "Thomas, the youngest son . . . by the early death of his father, and very narrow circumstances of his mother, even in childhood was a wandering labor boy, and grew up literally without education. He never did more in the way of writing than to bunglingly write his own name." (7)

Tom grew into a strong, sturdy man, taking odd jobs wherever he could and doing them honestly and ably. "Thomas Lincoln was not a lazy man," wrote one of Abe's friends from boyhood, "but . . . a piddler, always doing but doing nothing great. (He) was happy, lived easy and contented. . . . He wanted few things and supplied them easily." (8)

Tom made a name for himself at the neighborhood general store where the men gathered, sharing the news, spinning yarns and gossip. "He didn't drink," says Dennis, "or swear, or play cards or fight; an' them was drinkin' and cussin', quarrelsome days. Tom was popylar, an' he could lick a bully if he had to." (9) Once, a fellow talked about a lady in a way that got to Tom. They squared off in a furious backwoods brawl—no holds barred, anything goes. In that brutal scrap, Tom set his teeth into the man and chewed off the tip of his nose.

Tom was eighteen when he came to stay with a cousin in Elizabethtown, Kentucky. "E-town," they called it, was a thriving frontier town, the largest settlement in the county. There were three stores in town. One of them was run by a young Frenchmen named John James Audubon, later to become famous for his natural paintings of birds.

Tom made some friends in Elizabethtown and found steady work. His brother Mordecai shared some of his inheritance with him so that he could buy a little farm, settle down, and gain some respectability. In 1805, the County Court appointed Tom and three other young men as Patrollers. Their job was to capture any slave travelling without a permit. On orders from the captain, Patrollers could administer ten lashes upon the bare back of any slave. At that time there were few slaves in the county, so the Patrollers protected the settlers from hostile Indians and strangers who happened to ride through those parts of Kentucky.

The Captain of the Patrollers was Christopher Bush, head of one of the leading families of Elizabethtown. He had six sons and three daughters, all built from sturdy stock. "There was no backout in them," (10) neighbors said. Tom became friendly with the Bush family, especially Isaac Bush and his young sister Sally. Tom was sweet on Sally Bush though he was older by ten years. Tom thought she was the marrying kind.

In March of 1806, Tom and Isaac Bush were hired to build a flatboat and make the dangerous journey down the Mississippi to New Orleans to sell a load of goods. While the boys were away, Sally Bush got married to Daniel Johnston. When they re-

14

turned, Tom and Isaac brought special wedding gifts for the bride.

Elizabethtown was swelling with new settlers. Homes, stores, and churches had to be put up from hewn logs. Joseph Hanks was the only carpenter in town. He had all the construction work he could handle from that busy community. When he went looking for a reliable assistant, he found a good man in Tom Lincoln. Learning the trade under Joseph Hanks, Tom became a craftsman in wood.

Now with a steady, respectable job, and a small place of his own, Tom was looking for a good wife, a wily Kentucky woman who could "toss a pancake off a skillet up through the top of a chimney and run outdoors and catch it coming down." *(11)* He found his woman the day he met Mr. Hanks' young niece, Nancy Hanks.

2.

"Purty as a Pitcher"

Two years after Grandfather Abraham Lincoln staked his claim to the black Kentucky earth, another caravan of hearty pioneer Americans left Virginia for Kentucky, among them a teenage mother and her suckling babe. The baby's father, a well-bred Virginia gentleman, made it plain that he wanted no part of a life together. So mother and daughter joined the sweeping tide of westward movers, looking to make a new life for themselves in the second paradise.

Baby Nancy Hanks was barely a few months old, a bundle in her mother's arms when she was carried through the Indian country along the Wilderness Road. Mother Lucy Hanks, a high-spirited nineteen-year-old, was coming to stay with her older sister Rachel, who had the good sense to marry a wealthy farmer named Richard Berry. The Berry plantation was a mile and a half from the home of Bathsheba Lincoln, Grandfather Abraham's widow.

Young Lucy Hanks was "not very much of a talker, very religious and her disposition was very quiet." (1) Yet soon after she arrived at her new Kentucky home the young mother found herself at the center of a storm of gossip. Folks accused her of being loose and shameless with men, wild in her ways. A suit was filed in court charging Lucy Hanks with the crime of displaying immoral tendencies.

Lucy was in love with a kind and gentle man, a Revolutionary War veteran named Henry Sparrow. When Lucy and Henry

16

decided to get married, she boldly stated her intentions in a note and presented it to the court:

"I do sertify and I am of age and give my approbation freely for Henry Sparrow to git out Lisons this or enny other day. Given under my hand this day. April 26, 1790.
                    Lucey Hanks" (2)

The suit against her was soon discontinued, and on April 3, 1791, they married. Together, Lucy and Henry Sparrow brought eight children into the world. Lucy was one of the few women of the time who could read and write, and she took care to see that this skill was passed to her children. Her deep religious worship was passed on to three of her sons, who later became travelling Ministers of God's Church.

Family played an important role when it came to raising children on the frontier. When Ma and Pa were broken by the everyday struggles of backwoods living, when there were too many hungry bellies, too many small bodies to clothe, clean and care for, loving aunts and uncles would open their hearts and homes for their own blood. Family was family—your brother's son was your son, your aunt was like a mother, your cousins like brothers.

So it was that Lucy's firstborn, Nancy Hanks, passed the first years of her childhood with the Berry family. It was a pleasant and comfortable place for a young pioneer girl to grow up. Richard Berry was well respected in the community, and owned a large plantation with a stock of cattle, horses, and a few slaves. He even owned a few feather beds.

While Nancy was growing up with the Berrys, a cousin of hers came there to live. Sarah Mitchell was the daughter of another of Lucy's sisters. She was twelve years old when Indians ambushed her family on their way to Kentucky. They tomahawked her mother to death and carried Sarah along with them to Canada. Sarah's father led a search party for her and was drowned in the Ohio River. After five years, the Indians finally released her under the terms of a peace treaty. Orphaned, homeless, she came to live with her aunt.

"Sarah Mitchell and Nancy Hanks were first cousins . . . and were reared and educated by Uncle Richard Berry. These two girls grew up together, went to school together and became known as sister cousins," (3) Sarah's grand-daughter later wrote. Nancy tried to help Sarah make up for her lost years. Nancy was particularly talented at spinning flax and Sarah was her pupil.

When Nancy was a teenager, Tom and Betsy Sparrow took her under their wing. Tom was Henry's brother, Betsy was Lucy's sister—another Sparrow-Hanks love match. They loved Nancy as their own daughter and she became known in the neighborhood as Nancy Sparrow.

Young Dennis Hanks, born out of wedlock in 1799 to another of Lucy's sisters, came to live with them. So, cousins Nancy and Dennis Hanks grew up with the Sparrows as brother and sister. He was a boy when Nancy was a flowering young woman. They rose together in the morning and he watched how she greeted each new day. They did their chores side by side and had their little tiffs and spats. They passed their young days together and told each other goodnight. Dennis Hanks could tell the world about the mother of Abraham Lincoln:

"She was purty as a pitcher an' smart as you'd find 'em anywhar. . . . (4) Mrs. Lincoln, Abraham's mother, was five feet eight inches high, spare made, affectionate—the most affectionate I ever saw—never knew her to be out of temper. . . . She seemed to be immovably calm. . . ." (5)

So it was that in a wild country where a civilization was being carved out of the woods, a son and a daughter of two hearty pioneer families—decent, God-loving folks in a savage land—found each other. For Tom Lincoln and Nancy Hanks, it may have been their faith in God that brought them together. They were both drawn to backwoods cabin revival meetings. They sat together in dim candle-lit log huts to hear the travelling preachers shout, wail, cry, quiver and sing in praise of the Creator.

Religious revival meetings were a big event on the frontier. When a travelling preacher came to town, folks flocked to hear him. Bible readings brought great comfort, a faith to hold them in the midst of fear. They were reminded that their trials as well as their blessings came from God, and that the supreme satisfaction to be found on this earth was to do God's will. The preachers moved them, opened their hearts, excited them. They gave them theater, entertainment, drama. "When I hear a man preach," said Abe of his early revival meeting roots, "I like to see him act as if he were fighting bees." *(6)*

Tom Lincoln's favorite preacher was the Reverend Jesse Head, a fiery disciple of decency and justice, well-known for his bold and passionate sermons on the evils of slavery. He was a carpenter like Tom, and he would not stand for any guff. Drunken or disorderly worshipers who were moved to disrupt the word of God soon found themselves face to face with the good Reverend, who would not hesitate to grab a ruffian by his coat and put him out. Children had a rhyme about him:

> "His nose is long and his hair is red
> And he goes by the name of Jesse Head."*(7)*

It was the Reverend Jesse Head who joined Tom Lincoln and Nancy Hanks in holy matrimony on June 12, 1806. They were married in the Berry home. Sarah Mitchell was Nancy's maid of honor and Tom's brother Mordecai was his best man. Richard Berry Jr. signed the legal papers as Nancy's guardian and gave her away. A wild Kentucky-style celebration lasted all day and into the night. A wedding guest remembered the party:

"We had bear-meat, venison, wild turkey and ducks, eggs wild and tame, maple sugar lumps tied on a string to bite off for coffee or whiskey, syrup in big gourds, peach-and-honey, a sheep that the two families barbecued whole over coals of wood burned in a pit, and covered with green boughs to keep the juices in, and a race for the whiskey bottle." *(8)*

The newlyweds made their home in Elizabethtown, in a log cabin close to the courthouse. Tom worked diligently at his trade, building cabinets, door and window frames, and coffins. He had a hand in putting up many of the cabins, stores and churches in the area. His reputation as an honest, reliable craftsman grew. A friend said that "Tom had the best set of tools" *(9)* in the county.

One of Tom's jobs was to build a new sawmill for the town. When the job was nearly finished, the owner tried to back out of his contract and refused to pay Tom for his services. He brought Tom to court, claiming that he didn't have to pay because the timbers Tom put up were not cut square and true. The judge threw out the suit and Tom won his pay and the respect of the community who began to look to him as a man whose word was his bond.

The Lincoln family was growing. On February 10, 1807, Nancy had a little girl. They named her Sarah in honor of Nancy's "sister-cousin." Tom bought a piece of land from his friend Isaac Bush about 14 miles outside of Elizabethtown on the Big South Fork of Nolin's Creek. They moved to their new home in the fall of 1808. By then, Nancy was growing bigger again, and before the winter was out the Lincolns had their second child.

3.

"Nancy's Got a Boy Baby"

February 12, 1809. A cold Sabbath Sunday in the dead of winter. A fine day for great souls to appear in the world. On this day, across a great ocean, a baby boy came into the home of a physician in a well-to-do English village. He would become a giant among men, his name celebrated into the next century. He would be well remembered for a backward look, millions of years into the wheels of time. The baby, born to Dr. and Mrs. Darwin, was named Charles.

That same morning in the backwoods of Kentucky, Tom Lincoln was poking at logs in the fireplace to keep the flame crackling. He made sure Nancy was tucked tightly into bed under some warm bearskins, then headed out toward the Sparrow's place to tell Nancy's sister Betsy the news. Dennis Hanks, now nine, opened the door.

"I ricollect Tom comin' over to our house one cold mornin' in February an' sayin' kind o' slow an' sheepish: 'Nancy's got a boy baby.' "

"Mother got flustered an' hurried up her work to go over to look after the little feller, but I didn't have nothin' to wait fur, so I jist tuk an' run the hill two miles to see my new cousin. . . ." (1)

"You bet I was tickled to death. Babies wasn't as plenty as blackberries in the woods o' Kaintucky. Mother come over an' washed him an' put a yaller flannen petticoat an' linsey shirt on him, an' cooked some dried berries with wild honey fur Nancy, an' slicked things up an' went home. An' that's all the nuss'n either of em' got. . . ." *(2)*

" 'What you goin' to name him, Nancy?' I asked her."

" 'Abraham,' she says, 'after his gran'father that come out to Kaintucky with Dan'l Boone.' " *(3)*

The Lincoln baby was born "in a hunter's hut not fit to be called a home," *(4)* wrote a man who knew them. Tom cut the timber for the house from the woods around it. There was one small window and a chimney made of packed-down clay. The earth was their floor.

On Abraham's first night, Dennis Hanks stayed with him, huddling under a bearskin by the fireplace. That night he could hear baby Abraham cry in the darkness and the gentle footsteps of the new father coming to comfort him.

In the morning, Dennis asked if he could hold the baby. "Well, now," said Dennis, "he looked jist like any other baby at fust, like a red cherry-pulp squeezed dry in wrinkles. An' he didn't improve none as he growed older. Abe was never much fur looks." *(5)*

Nancy eased the baby into Dennis's arms. "Be keerful, Dennis," she said, "fur you air the fust boy he's ever seen." *(6)*

Dennis swung the baby, and laughed and chattered and cooed to him. Little Abraham only bawled. Dennis had a feeling about his new cousin. "He'll never come to much," he declared solemnly. *(7)*

This cabin on Nolin's Creek was home for the Lincoln family for three years. Nearby was the Rock Spring, a high moss-covered ledge that folks liked to stand under for shade. A cool, flowing spring ran beneath the ledge. Nancy often climbed the ledge with baby Abraham and his sister Sarah. Here they listened to the bubbling song of the stream as Nancy sweetly chanted her favorite hymns and lullabies.

> "Come thou fount of every blessing.
> Tune my hear to sing Thy praise" *(8)*

> "Praise the mount, O, fix me on it!
> Mount of God's unchanging love." *(9)*

The land at Nolin's Creek was hard, stubborn land, mostly clay and stones beneath the thick underbrush. Every season

Tom's crops were poor and withered. Folks said the land had "the barrens."

Dennis remembered those difficult times: "Pore? We was all pore, them days. But the Lincolns was poorer than anybody. Choppin' trees, an' grubbin' roots, an' splittin' rails, an' huntin' an' trappin' didn't leave Tom no time to put a . . . floor in his cabin. It was all he could do to git his family enough to eat and kiver 'em." (10)

In the spring of 1811 the Lincolns moved ten miles northeast to Knob Creek, "one of the prettiest streams I ever saw," remarked one long-time resident. "You can see a pebble in ten foot of water." (11)

Little Abraham was just beginning to talk. For this young cub of two, words were everywhere. The air around him resounded with rough Kentucky voices—his father and the neighbors in home-spun conversation, his mother patiently explaining things and giving everything a name.

Abe listened to their jabbering, the way they formed their words. A family without money was "pore." You went to school to "larn" and get an "eddication." When you ran an errand you "brung" things back. During the summer you swam in the "crick." Sometimes a stray dog "follered" you home. If you acted against your better judgement, you were "hornswoggled." When you met your friends you said "howdy." If your friend was over "yonder," you might ask him "whar" he'd been.

Abe grew up hearing the voices of the old Kentucky sages, the backwoods wisdom of everyday folks telling little tales of gypsy magic to help them pass through unknown dangers and uncertain days. If you kill the first snake you see in the spring, you will defeat all your enemies that year. If your right foot itches, you will be going on a journey. If a dog crosses your path, it is bad luck, unless you hook your two little fingers together and pull till the dog is out of sight. If you feel your ears burning, it is a sign that someone is spreading gossip about you. If you can make your first finger and your pinkie meet over the back of your hand, you will get married some day.

Life in the woods was a drama of bitter surprises. Nature's round of birth and death followed its own secret rhythm. Nancy became pregnant again not long after the Lincolns arrived at

Knob Creek. A baby boy was born and she named him Thomas for his father. The baby lived for three days. Tom whipsawed some logs into a little coffin and laid the doll-like body to rest on a grassy hilltop near the cabin. A flat stone marked the grave, chiseled with the letters TL.

Abe learned to be at home in the woods. It was his playground. The little creatures darting along the tangled forest floor were his playmates. Dennis remembered:

"Abe was right out in the woods, about as soon's he was weaned, fishin' in the crick, settin' traps fur rabbits an' muskrats, goin' on coon-hunts with Tom an' me an' the dogs, follerin' up bees to find bee-trees, an drappin' corn fur his pappy. Mighty interestin' life fur a boy, but thar was a good many chances he wouldn't live to grow up."(12)

He was a shirt-tail boy. During the warmer months, his only covering was a long prickly woolen shirt. As soon as he was able, his father had him helping with the chores. He carried water buckets, filled the woodbox, cleaned the fireplace and gathered nuts and berries. He helped his father hoe the ground and plant the seeds. He learned the feel of the cold earth between his toes and of burning blisters on his hands.

One of the first memories Abe could recall was out in the fields. One Saturday he was helping his father with the spring planting. "I dropped two seeds every other hill and every other row," Abe remembered. "The next Sunday morning there came a big rain in the hills. It did not rain a drop in the valley, but the water coming down through the gorges washed ground, corn, pumpkin seeds and all clear off the field."(13)

The main road from Louisville to Nashville ran by the Lincoln cabin. It was a well-traveled road. Abe and Sarah could watch a daily procession of wayfarers in their comings and goings. Pioneer trains drove by with caravans of covered wagons. Peddlers came by pushing their wares. Travelling preachers, circuit judges and soldiers passed by. Gangs of black men and women shuffled along in chains, prodded by rifle-waving "slave-ketchers" on high horses. Abe could watch backwoods America parade before him and disappear into the far-off dust of the road.

Abe remembered a small incident that happened on that road. "I had been fishing one day and caught a little fish which I was taking home. I met a soldier in the road and, having been always told at home that we must be good to soldiers, I gave him my fish."(14)

Even before young Abe could read, Nancy interested him in Bible stories. The upright, magical men and women of the Old and New Testament stirred his boyish imagination. "Lincoln's mother learned him to read the Bible, study it and the stories in it . . . repeating it to Abe and his sister when very young," Dennis wrote. "Lincoln was often and much moved by the stories."(15)

"It was her custom on the Sabbath when there was no religious worship in the neighborhood—a thing of frequent occurrence—to employ a portion of the day in reading the Scriptures aloud to her family," his campaign biographer wrote during the Presidential election. "After Abraham and his sister had learned to read, they shared by turns in this Sunday reading. This practice, continued faithfully through a series of years, could not fail to produce certain effects. . . . There are few men in public life so familiar with the Scriptures as Mr. Lincoln."(16)

Said Abe: "The fundamental truths reported in the four gospels as from the lips of Jesus Christ that I first heard from the lips of my mother are settled and fixed moral precepts with me."(17)

There was plenty of talk about Indians to fire his dreams. They listened to stories of Daniel Boone—how he was chased by Indians and how he once swung forty feet on a grapevine so they would lose his trail; how he ran backwards in the woods so the Indians would follow his tracks and think he was going to where he'd already been. Nancy spoke of her cousin Sarah, how her family was massacred, how she lived with the Indians for five years before coming home.

One story that cut deeply into the boy's heart was told time and time again by Tom Lincoln—the story of the ambush-murder of Grandfather Abraham. Lincoln later confided that "The story of his death by the Indians and of Uncle Mordecai, then fourteen years old, killing one of the Indians, is the legend more strongly than all others imprinted upon my mind and memory."(18)

Abe lived on the Knob Creek farm until he was seven years

old. His best friend in the whole world was Austin Gollaher. They made a rowdy bunch—Austin, Sarah, Dennis and Abe. Dennis was the chief rascal and mischief-maker but Austin and Abe were all too happy to follow along.

One time, young Abe was in a playful mood. Reaching into a tree, he picked off a soft piece of fruit and mashed it around the inside of Austin's cap. That foxy Austin was too quick for Abe. He had already switched his cap for Abe's. It was a neat trick—on Abe—making him smear mash into his own cap.

Once, their antics were nearly tragic. Austin recalled: "One Sunday my mother visited the Lincolns, and I was taken along. Abe and I played around all day. Finally, we concluded to cross the creek to hunt for some partridges young Lincoln had seen the day before. The creek was swollen by a recent rain and in crossing on the narrow footlog, Abe fell in.

"Neither of us could swim. I got a long pole and held it out to Abe, who grabbed it. Then I pulled him ashore. He was almost dead and I was badly scared. I rolled and pounded him in good earnest. Then I got him by the arms and shook him, the water meanwhile pouring out of his mouth. By this means, I succeeded in bringing him to and he was soon all right.

"Then a new difficulty confronted us. If our mothers discovered our wet clothes, they would whip us. This we dreaded from experience and determined to avoid. It was June, the sun was very warm, and we soon dried our clothing by spreading it on the rocks about us. We promised never to tell the story. . . ."(19)

Austin had a crush on Abe's sister, Sarah. "She was a very pretty girl," he remembered. "Sallie Lincoln was about my age. She was my sweetheart. I loved her and claimed her, as boys do. I suppose that was one reason for my warm regard for Abe. When the Lincoln family moved to Indiana, I was prevented by circumstances from bidding goodbye to either of the children, and I never saw them again."(20)

The memory of his good friend filled a warm spot in Abe for the rest of his life. Nearly fifty years later, in the midst of his fiery trial as Commander-in-Chief of a bleeding nation, his troubled heart found a moment's rest in thoughts of the Kentucky backwoods country where he grew up and in memories of the innocent frolic of a childhood long gone. When the President took time out for an audience with an old Kentucky neighbor, he was sure to ask particularly about "my old friend and playmate Austin Gollaher," a man whom he would "rather see than any man living."(21)

4.

"It Was a Wild Region"

Pioneer Americans had gypsy blood in them. Their roots were never deep. The dark uncertainties of life on the edge of civilization drove them from one safe haven to the next. Tom and Nancy Lincoln, now married ten years, found themselves packing their worldly belongings four times to move to sunnier soil.

"Every man must skin his own skunk," (1) Tom used to say. He knew it was time to move on again. When a neighbor asked him why he was working so hard to fix up his place when he would soon be leaving it, he answered, "So I do. But I ain't going to let my farm find it out." (2)

The Knob Creek farm proved to be as disappointing as the others. "From this place," wrote Abe, referring to himself in the third person, "he removed to what is now Spencer County, Indiana, in the autumn of 1816, Abraham then being in his eighth [actually seventh] year. This removal was partly on account of slavery, but chiefly on account of the difficulty in land titles in Kentucky." (3)

In the early days, when Daniel Boone and his band of adventurers began carving out space for themselves in the Kentucky forest, they needed a way to set apart each man's claim. They made boundaries between one man's land and his neighbor's, carving letters into trees and marking large stones and meandering creeks as borders. Soon, new bark grew over the letters, rainstorms and mudslides slipped the stones out of place, creeks dried up. Boundaries became vague and confusing. "In the unskillful hands of the hunters and pioneers of Kentucky . . .," wrote one historian, "surveys . . . were piled upon each other, overlapping and crossing in endless perplexity." (4)

Tom Lincoln had seen dozens of acres taken away from his two previous farms due to faulty surveying. Now, a wealthy Philadelphia family was bringing Tom and nine of his neighbors to court, claiming rightful ownership of the entire Knob Creek valley.

Another of the undercurrents of life in the border states was a raging debate over the institution of slavery. Kentucky was a state where one man could keep others as property. Some defended this practice as natural and right. Others were deeply offended by its brutality. It was a hot issue. Passionate arguments spread like wildfire, setting neighbor against neighbor. The South Fork Baptist Church, where the God-fearing folks of Knob Creek came to worship, was forced to close its doors because the congregation could not meet in peace. Church records said that fifteen members "went off from the church on account of slavery." (5) The Reverend William Downs, who gave Tom his Christian Baptism in Knob Creek, was prohibited from preaching his anti-slavery sentiments at any Church meeting or at the home of any of its members. Reverend Downs led several families, including the Lincolns, in establishing the Little Mount Church, where they could damn the evils of slavery in a nation that would later sacrifice the blood of her children to bring slavery to its death.

Many Kentucky families whose consciences could not bear the sight of chained men and women crossed the Ohio River to settle in Indiana, a heavily wooded territory that was then applying to the United States Congress for statehood. The citizens of Indiana drew up a constitution that firmly declared that "no alteration of this constitution shall ever take place so as to introduce slavery or involuntary servitude in the state." (6)

Tom's brother Josiah Lincoln brought his family across the river into Indiana and sent back glowing reports of his prosperity. In the fall of 1816, Tom sold his Knob Creek farm for twenty dollars in cash and 400 gallons of whiskey. Tom wasn't a drinking man but he was taking advantage of this valuable commodity as a wise investment. Whiskey was used as a kind of money on the frontier.

Tom cut down some trees and fashioned a flatboat out of the logs. He set his "crazy craft" (7) into Knob Creek and young Abe helped his father load it with household goods and tools and all that whiskey. Abe and Sarah waved goodbye to their pa as he poled his way down Knob Creek to the Salt River and into the great waters of the Ohio. Tom's crude boat could not handle the river's rough currents and she turned over, spilling everything into the drink. Fighting desperately against the swift whirlpools, he managed to fish up most of the whiskey, his precious tools and some of the household goods. Undaunted, he righted the boat and determined to press on, sailing across the wide river to the shores of Indiana.

He left the cargo, with a friend near the river bank, and carrying only an ax and a hunting knife, he headed into the woods on foot. "Indiana is a vast forest," (8) an early explorer wrote in his diary. Giant trees—sycamore, oak, elm, willow, poplar, maple, ash, hickory, beech, walnut—all grew together, tightly placed, some twenty feet around and a hundred feet high. A thick layer of brush wove the trees together in an impenetrable net along the forest floor. Tom followed a narrow trail as far as he could. Then the way became impassable.

Tom "cut his way to his farm with an ax, felling the forest as he went," wrote a family friend. (9) He hacked and sliced a new trail, covering sixteen miles through the dense underbrush until he came upon a clearing near Little Pigeon Creek that he decided to call home.

As required by government land laws, he notched the trees, cleared out some brush and piled it in the four corners of his claim. Then he set up a small temporary shelter, a pole shed or a hunter's "half-faced camp" near where the cabin was to be built. It was a small shed, about fourteen feet square, made of log poles. The roof was dry bush and packed leaves and it had three sides with one side left open.

After a week, Tom was back home in Kentucky, loading up a borrowed wagon with pots, pans, kettles, blankets, a spinning wheel, farm tools, the family Bible and their good feather bed.

Cupboards, bureaus, tables and chairs were left behind since Tom could easily fashion new ones from the forest wood once they settled in.

On December 11, 1816, Indiana became the nineteenth state of the United States. About this time, the Lincoln family paid a solemn final visit to the grave of their departed son, baby Thomas, then said goodbye to their Kentucky friends and neighbors.

Dennis Hanks went along with the Lincolns and later wrote about the journey. "I went myself with them, backwards and forwards to Indiana and back to Kentucky and back to Indiana and know the story and all the facts well," said Dennis. *(10)*

In four days the travelers reached the ferry that carried them across the Ohio River. It was an awesome sight. The French explorers who first laid eyes on it years before called it "La Belle Riviere." Its shimmering beauty reminded them of their lovely French women. It was nothing like the Knob Creek Abe could cross on a log or wade in to find bullfrogs. The great Ohio was like a vast ocean, busy with boat traffic and new fangled steamboats, whose distant shores seemed to stretch into a blue eternity.

On the Indiana side, Tom retrieved their belongings and the whiskey and the rugged pioneer family pressed on through some of the roughest terrain any traveler could face. "I will jest say to you that it was the brushest country that I have ever seen. . . .," Dennis said later, "all kinds of undergrowth . . . matted together so that as the old saying goes you could drive a butcher knife up to the handle in it." *(11)*

They followed the narrow trail Tom blazed through the woods but it was not nearly wide enough for their wagon. The menfolk ripped through the tangle of vines to make an opening large enough for the wagon to squeeze through. Those gallant wooden wheels, scraping through layers of forest brush, carried the family through flowing streams and mounds of mud, across gullies and over rocks and stumps until they reached the little parcel of land in the woods that would be home to the Lincolns for the next fourteen years.

"We reached our new home about the time the state came

into the Union," Abe wrote. "It was a wild region, with many bears and other wild animals still in the woods. There I grew up." *(12)*

Frigid winter winds stung their faces as they came upon Tom's pole shed. The men piled logs and brush in front of the open side of the shed and kept a big bonfire alive day and night to keep the family warm and to frighten away the bears and panthers who hovered around the edge of their camp. Here they passed an Indiana winter, rough even for a pioneer family. Soaking rains and driving blizzards blasted into their home through the open wall. Nasty winds whipped choking smoke from the bonfire into their eyes and chased them out into the wintry air.

The pole shed was "not much better'n a tree," said Dennis. "I've seen Injun lodges that'd beat pole-sheds all holler fur keepin' out the weather. I don't see how the women folks lived through it. Boys are half wild anyhow, an' me 'n Abe had a bully good time. . . ." *(13)*

5.

"I Am Going Away From You, Abraham"

"We, Lincoln's family, including Sally and Abe and myself, slept and lodged in this cabin (the pole-shed) all winter and till next spring," Dennis recalled. "We, in the winter and spring cut down brush, underwood trees, cleared ground, made a field of about six acres on which we raised our crops. We all hunted pretty much all the time, especially when we got tired of work, which was very often, I will assure you. We did not have to go more than four or five hundred yards to kill deer, turkeys and other wild game. . . . Wild game and meat were our food." (1)

The woods around the Lincoln homestead were teeming with creatures of the forest. Raccoons, squirrels, opposum, skunks, deer, bears, wolves, wildcats, panthers—all came to the salt-lick near their cabin to rub their tongues against the salty rocks. Honking ducks and geese flew over their heads. Wild Carolina parakeets lined the treetops and brightened the forest with their bright yellow and green feathers and their shrill cries. Millions of passenger pigeons darkened the sky, whipping up powerful windstorms with their fluttering wings. Flocks of wild turkeys often came right upon them, almost into their cabin.

That winter, young Abe killed his first creature. He used his "fathers Riffle" [rifle] to bag a turkey more by accident than skill, since turkeys were too "numerous to mention," according to

Dennis. *(2)* The shooting incident left a lasting impression on the boy and he included it in his third-person autobiographical sketch:

"At this place Abraham took an early start as a hunter, which was never much improved afterward. A few days before the completion of his eighth year, in the absence of his father, a flock of wild turkeys approached the new log cabin, and Abraham with a rifle-gun, standing inside, shot through a crack and killed one of them. He has never since pulled a trigger on any larger game." *(3)*

Hunting was an everyday part of frontier living. The pioneers needed wild game for food and clothing. Some wild beasts were a worrisome menace to livestock and to human life. In Indiana, the men of the community often banded together to hunt down herds of wild beasts. It was necessary for their safety and they enjoyed it as great sport.

"There was a great many deer licks," said friend David Turnham, "and Abe and myself would go to these licks sometimes and watch . . . to kill deer, though Abe was not so fond of a gun as I was." *(4)*

Abe had no enthusiasm for taking the lives of animals, even for food. But the sporting hunts fascinated him. Thirty years after the Lincolns first set foot in Indiana, his stirred-up memory found vivid words to describe a bear hunt that he had witnessed:

A wild-bear chase, didst never see?
    Then hast thou lived in vain.
Thy richest bump of glorious glee,
    Lies desert in thy brain.

When first my father settled here,
    'Twas then the frontier line;
The panther's scream filled night with fear
    And bears preyed on the swine.

But woe for Bruin's short lived fun,
    When rose the squealing cry;
Now man and horse, with dog and gun,
    For vengeance, at him fly.

A sound of danger strikes his ear;
    He gives the breeze a snuff.

Away he bounds with little fear,
   And seeks the tangled rough.

On press his foes, and reach the ground,
   Where's left his half munched meal;
The dogs, in circles, scent around,
   And find his fresh made trail.

With instant cry, away they dash,
   And men as fast pursue;
O'er logs they leap, through water splash,
   And shout the brisk halloo.

Now to elude the eager pack,
   Bear shuns the open ground;
Through matted vines, he shapes his track
   And runs it, round and round.

The tall fleet cur, with deep-mouthed voice,
   Now speeds him as the wind;
While half-grown pup and short-legged fice,
   Are yelping far behind.

And fresh recruits are dropping in
   To join the merry corps;
With yelp and yell—a mingled din—
   The woods are in a roar.

And round and round the chase now goes,
   The world's alive with fun;
Nick Carter's horse, his rider throws,
   And more, Hill drops his gun.

Now sorely pressed, bear glances back,
   And lolls his tired tongue;
When as, to force him from his track,
   An ambush on him sprung.

Across the glade he sweeps for flight,
   And fully is in view.
The dogs, new-fired, by the sight,
   Their cry and speed renew.

The foremost ones, now reach his rear.
   He turns, they dash away;

And circling now, the wrathful bear,
    They have him full at bay.

At top of speed, the horse-men come,
    All screaming in a row
"Whoop! Take him, Tiger. Seize him Drum."
    Bang—bang—the rifles go.

And furious now, the dogs he tears,
    And crushes in his ire.
Wheels right and left, and upward rears,
    With eyes of burning fire.

But leaden death is at his heart,
    Vain all the strength he plies.
And, spouting blood from every part,
    He reels, and sinks, and dies. *(5)*

There was plenty of work to be done to make their little homestead liveable. It was, according to Abe, an "unbroken forest, and the clearing away of surplus wood was the great task ahead. Abraham, though very young, was large for his age, and had an ax put into his hands at once, and from that till within his twenty-third year he was almost constantly handling that most useful instrument." *(6)*

He helped Tom and Dennis chop logs for a new cabin to be built about forty yards from the pole shed. He trimmed the branches off the logs, hacked away piles of brush from the ground, and dug up the soil for planting. It was up to Abe and Sarah to fetch water from the spring a mile away.

Their days were long and filled with endless chores. They lived simply. "We wasn't much better off'n Injuns," said Dennis, "except we tuk an interest in religion and polytics. We et game an' fish an' wild berries an' lye hominy an' kep' a cow. Sometimes we had corn enough to pay fur grindin' meal an' sometimes we didn't. . . . When it got so we could keep chickens an' have salt pork an' corn dodgers . . . an' molasses an' have jeans pants an' cowhide boots to wear we felt as if we was gettin' along in the world. . . .

"Abe was runnin' 'round in buck skin moccasins an' breeches, a tow-linen shirt an' coonskin cap. Yes, that's the way we all dressed them days. . . . Most of the time we went b'arfoot. . . .

Them moccasins wasn't no putection against the wet. Birch bark with hickory bark soles stropped on over yarn socks beat buckskin all holler fur snow. Me 'n Abe got purty handy contrivin' things thataway." (7)

Evenings when the family gathered at the dinner table "dog-tired and hog-hungry," Tom would lead the family in a simple prayer: "Fit and prepare us for humble service, we beg for Christ's sake. Amen." (8) Once, during particularly tough times, there were only potatoes on the table for dinner. In thanksgiving, Tom offered a blessing for the potatoes. "Dad," complained Abe, "I call these mighty poor blessings." (9)

The land was not always so miserly toward them and soon they had a healthy crop of corn and other vegetables. The corn had to be ground into flour for use in baking bread. One of Abe's greatest pleasures was the day-long visit to the mill, some sixteen miles away. It was a chance to get away from the farm, a welcome break in the day-to-day routine. The mill was a place to see new faces, hear fantastic tales and learn the latest news.

"When we got there, the mill was a poor concern," recalled Dennis. (10) It was "pulled by a bag-o'-bones hoss. Abe used to say his hound could eat meal faster'n that mill could grind it an' then go hungry for supper. But it was a good place fur visitin' an swappin' yarns. Other men'd be comin' in an' have to wait all day, mebbe, an' they'd set on a rail fence . . . crackin' jokes or argyin' polytics. Abe'd come home with enough news an' yarns to last a week." (11)

It was at the mill, Abe later recalled, that he was "kicked by a horse and apparently killed for a time." (12) On that day, he rode to the mill by himself atop an old flea-bitten gray mare. He arrived late in the day and had to wait till it was nearly dark for his turn.

Customers had to provide their own horsepower so Abe hitched up his tired old beast to the mill machinery. The gears cracked up and spun around slowly. The old mare was in no hurry. Abe grew impatient. "Get up, you old hussy! Get up . . ." (13) In anger the old horse let a hoof fly, which landed square on the boy's forehead. He went sprawling to the ground, and laid there motionless. The miller sent for Tom Lincoln and they carried the bleeding, senseless boy to a wagon for the trip home.

All night, Abe lay unconscious; Tom and Nancy thought he was dying.

Morning came. Abe began to stir. His body twitched. His tongue began to roll. Suddenly, his body jerked upright for an instant and he was wide awake, blurting out the words "you old hussy." It was the unfinished part of the sentence he started the moment he was hit.

Years later, Abraham Lincoln's law partner, William Herndon, recounted how deeply this mishap impressed Abe. "Mr. Lincoln considered this one of the remarkable incidents of his life. He often referred to it and we had many discussions in our law office over the psychological phenomenon involved in the operation." (14)

"Just before I struck the old mare," Abe explained, "my will through the mind had set the muscles of my tongue to utter the expression ("Get up, you old hussy"), and when her heels came in contact with my head the whole thing stopped half-cocked, as it were, and was only fired off when mental energy or force returned." (15)

By the fall of 1817, the Lincolns took up residence in their new cabin. Nancy was overjoyed when her Uncle Tom and Aunt Betsy Sparrow joined their adopted son Dennis Hanks in the move from Kentucky to Indiana. "Lived on Thomas Lincoln's place," said Dennis, "in that darn little half-face camp." (16)

The summer of 1818 was hot and dry. Much of the grass in the cow pastures was parched and brittle, scorched by a searing sun. Cattle, ravenously hungry for fresh greens, discovered a tall white-flowered weed called snakeroot flourishing in the shadows of the trees. The cows would flock to the cool comfort of the shade, graze on the moist plant, and amble away satisfied. Soon, these same cows would be stricken with a severe case of trembling. Within three days, the cows would be dead.

Anyone who drank the milk of a sick cow would soon come down with the same disease. There would be dizziness, nausea, vomiting, stomach pains, cold hands and feet and a ghoulish white coating to the tongue and mouth. The patient would slip into a coma. In a week or less, the siege would be over. Most victims did not survive.

The discovery of a case of milk sickness, or even trembling in the cows, was enough to fill a pioneer community with dread. The toll on human life and livestock of this horrible disease was staggering. When a family was relocating, as when the Lincolns did, the first question they would ask the folks in their new neighborhood was if milk sickness had been there. If there was the slightest suspicion that the disease was still alive, the family would quickly move on.

In the fall of 1818, one of Tom Lincoln's cows began to tremble. Within days, Tom Sparrow came down with the disease. On September 21, he wrote his last will and testament, giving all his worldly belongings to his wife "Elizabeth Sparrow so she can do as she pleases with it until her death." Then, the "whole property is to fall to Dennis Hanks when he comes of age." (17) A healthy Nancy Lincoln signed the document as a witness by making an X. A week later, both Tom and Betsy Sparrow were dead from milk sickness.

Nancy was at the Sparrow home every day, nursing them, comforting them in their final days. When a neighbor, Mrs. Brooner, came down with a white mouth, Nancy was at her bedside, easing her misery until the end. It was a busy season for the local carpenter, Tom Lincoln. " 'Pears to me," said Dennis, "like Tom was always makin' a coffin fur some one." (18)

The dreaded milk sickness came to Nancy Lincoln. She became weak and had to take to her bed. The gallant soul who nursed others with unfailing generosity now took her turn to receive care. Nancy sank rapidly. "She struggled on day by day," remembered Dennis, "a good Christian woman. . . . She knew she was going to die and called the children to her dying side. . . ." (19)

"I am going away from you, Abraham," she whispered to him, "and I shall not return. I know that you will be a good boy, that you will be kind to Sarah and to your father. I want you to live as I have taught you and to love your Heavenly Father." (20)

. On October 5, 1818, just two weeks after the dread disease infected her beloved uncle, Nancy Lincoln died. "O Lord, O Lord," wailed Dennis. "I'll never furgit the mizry in that little green log cabin in the woods when Nancy died." (21)

Whenever death was a guest in a one-room frontier cabin, the mood was particularly grim. The body laid in the cabin until it was ready for burial while the family tried to get on with the routine of life. Tom Lincoln, who built so many coffins for his neighbors that season, now had to make one for his beloved wife.

"Me 'n Abe helped Tom make the coffin," Dennis remembered. "He tuk a log left over from buildin' the cabin, an' I helped him whipsaw it into planks an' plane 'em. Me 'n Abe held the planks while Tom bored holes an' put 'em together with pegs Abe'd whittled. . . . We laid Nancy close to the deer-run in the woods. Deer was the only wild critters the women wasn't afeerd of." (22)

The coffin traveled by sled up the side of a little hill near the Lincoln cabin, and was lowered into the ground beside the graves of the Sparrows and Mrs. Brooner. Mrs. Brooner's son was at the burial, just days after he had watched his mother laid to rest. "I remember very distinctly that when Mrs. Lincoln's grave was filled, my father, Peter Brooner, extended his hand to Thomas Lincoln and said, 'We are brothers now.' " (23)

An elder of the Little Pigeon Baptist Church spoke a simple Christian prayer, and Tom followed the custom of the day by laying stones at the head and the foot of the grave. On the headstone he carved the initials N. L.

"Abe was some'ers 'round nine years old, but he never got over the mizable way his mother died," lamented Dennis. "I reckon she didn't have no sort 'o keer [care]—pore Nancy!" (24)

Young Abe was not satisfied with the meager ceremony his mother received on the day of her burial. The boy scrawled a letter to an old family friend, the pastor at the Lincoln's old church in Kentucky, Reverend David Elkin, and asked him to give a proper sermon at his mother's grave. When the Reverend Elkin came the following spring, it was an occasion for the whole community to turn out. One of the neighbors recalled the scene:

"On a bright sabbath morning, the settlers of the neighborhood gathered in. Some came in carts of the rudest construction . . . some came on horseback, two or three upon a horse, others came in wagons drawn by oxen, and still others came on foot.

"Taking his stand at the foot of the grave, Parson Elkin lifted his voice in prayer and sacred song and then preached a sermon. He spoke of the precious Christian woman who had gone, with warm praise, which she had deserved, and held her up as an example of true womanhood." *(25)*

Abe never spoke much about his mother. Whatever secret feelings her memory stirred remained locked in his heart. He loved his mother dearly. Yet her image was veiled. A long hushed family scandal obscured her cherished memory. Not until thirty years had passed could he bear to pour his heart out, even to a friend. Billy Herndon recalled the moment when a brooding, sensitive Abraham Lincoln let the truth spill about his mother.

"This is a substantial statement made to me by Lincoln just on a hot overlapping spring creek on the road to Petersburg, two and a half miles west of this city [Springfield] about 1851. . . . Lincoln and I had a case in the Menard circuit court, which required a discussion on hereditary qualities of mind, natures, etc. Lincoln's mind was dwelling on his case, mine on something else.

"Lincoln all at once said: 'Billy, I'll tell you something. But keep it a secret while I live. My mother was a bastard, was the daughter of a nobleman, so called, of Virginia. My mother's mother was poor . . . and she was shamefully taken advantage of by the man. My mother inherited his qualities and I hers. All that I am or hope ever to be I get from my mother. God bless her.' " *(26)*

Years later, just after Abraham Lincoln died, Billy Herndon stood beside the grave of Nancy Hanks Lincoln and those words from her son's lips came to mind—"God bless her." His head solemnly bowed, he meditated in silence, offering his own tribute to a woman Dennis Hanks called "one of the very best women in the whole race known for kindness, tenderness, charity and love to the world." *(27)*

6.

"Here's Your New Mammy"

That winter of 1818-19 brought loneliness and despair into the Lincoln cabin. A hardened woodsman and carpenter, now forty, a youngster of nineteen, a girl going on twelve and a boy near ten struggled to hold together as a family in that dark season of misery inside their unfinished, windowless, floorless, cheerless hut deep in the woods of Indiana.

Winter doldrums used to pass merrily for the Lincolns. There was plenty to celebrate. First Christmas. Then the new year. Tom's birthday came on the sixth of January. But there was one special week they waited for all year long, a time for parties and for singing. It was a whole week of birthdays. Nancy's came on February sixth, Sarah's on the tenth, and Abe's two days later.

Now they could only busy themselves with their winter chores, hustling after the simple necessities of daily living. Dennis complained that they had "to work very hard . . . for to keep soul and body to geather [together] and every spare time that we had we picked up our rifle and fetched in a fine deer or turkey." (1)

Even the coming warmth of spring brought little comfort. Without the gentle guiding light of a caring womanly presence, their home became squalid. They went the whole winter without bathing. Their clothing, worn day in, day out for months, became tattered and worn. They ate poorly cooked flesh without knives or forks. They slept on piles of twigs, leaves and skins.

Their cabin went untended, reeking from filth and vermin, the scent of disarray.

Young Sarah did what she could to fill her mother's role, cooking, cleaning, sorting, mending, but her young shoulders faltered under the weight of her new burdens. Grief appeared to hit Sarah harder than the others. Tom, Dennis, and Abe—they were all boys. They had each other. They went out every day to do the things menfolk do. They didn't have to be alone.

"She was the only woman in the cabin that year, an' no neighbors fur miles," recalled Dennis. "Sairy was a little gal, only 'leven, an' she'd git so lonesome, missin' her mother, she'd set by the fire an' cry. Me 'n Abe got 'er a baby coon an' a turtle and tried to git a fawn but we couldn't ketch any." (2)

Abe felt the loss deeply. A neighbor, Arminda Rankin, remembered how he spoke of his mother during one of his frequent visits to her home: "He said he was nine years old when his mother died, that his instruction by her in letters and morals, and especially the Bible stories, and the interest and love he acquired in reading the Bible through this teaching of his mother had been the strongest and most influential experience of his life. He referred with evident sadness to the lonely months after his mother's death, and said that the Bible she had read and had taught him to read was the greatest comfort he and his sister had after their mother was gone." (3)

"Tom, he moped 'round," remembered Dennis. "Wasn't wuth shucks that winter." (4) His long nights were filled with curious dreams. He'd see himself strolling along a path to a strange house. He'd step inside and look around at the walls, a table and some chairs. There would be a woman sitting by the fireplace, paring an apple. Her face would be clear, eyes bright. He knew that face. He knew it was the face of the next Mrs. Lincoln. Night after night the dream came haunting. It would keep coming back until he walked that path, stepped inside that house, and found that woman.

Above all, Tom was a family man. He could not bear to see his children live through another desperate winter. He resolved to do something about it. "He put the corn in the spring an' left us to 'tend to it, an' lit out fur Kaintucky," said Dennis. "Yes, we knowed what he went fur, but we didn't think he'd have any luck, bein' pore as he was, and with two children to raise." (5)

Backtracking through the same forest trails he cut three years before, Tom crossed the Ohio River into Kentucky and headed straight for his old friends in Elizabethtown. Isaac Bush still owed him $200 as part of a land deal they made ten years earlier. Tom may have heard the news about Isaac's sister Sarah. It was this same Sally Bush whom Tom favored years ago and who married Daniel Johnston while Tom and Isaac were away in New Orleans.

After Tom married Nancy, the Lincolns and the Johnstons became friends. Nancy and Sally had a lot to talk about. They became pregnant at about the same time and gave birth to two of the prettiest baby girls in Elizabethtown.

Sally's life with Daniel Johnston did not go well. They were married on March 13, 1806. Three months later he was borrowing money from the well-off Bush family. He ran up a sum of debts to the merchants in town and was unable to pay his taxes. Finally, in 1814 Daniel Johnston was appointed as jailor of Hardin County. The jailor's family lived in one part of the stone prison and his wife was expected to serve as caretaker. Sally cooked for the prisoners and cleaned the cells, including the grim basement dungeon. She struggled to make a cheery home for her three young children among whipping posts and cursing criminals. Then, in 1816, her husband died.

Saddled by her husband's debts, Sally and her children were taken into the home of Samuel Haycraft, the County Clerk, where she worked hard to earn her keep and made a reputation for herself around town as "an honest poor widow." (6)

It was the path to the Haycraft cabin that Tom followed one day, and when he went inside, there was Sally, her eyes bright, her face still youthful.

"He made a very short courtship," Haycraft wrote. "He came to see her on the first day of December 1819, and in a straight forward manner told her that they had known each other from childhood. 'Miss Johnston,' said he, 'I have no wife and you no husband. I came a-purpose to marry you. I knowed you from a gal and you knowed me from a boy. I've no time to lose, and if you're willin', let it be done straight off.' She replied that she could not marry him right off as she had some little debts which she wanted to pay first. He replied, 'Give me a list of them.' He got the list and paid them that evening. Next morning, I issued the license and they were married within sixty yards of my house." (7)

A few weeks before Christmas, a tough teen-age boy and his two young cousins, eeking out a bare existence for themselves on Little Pigeon Creek, were in for a surprise. They heard a wagon approaching one morning and saw their father jump off, helping a large, kindly looking woman, a young lady the same age as Sarah, a boy about like Abe, and a little girl.

"Here's your new mammy," Tom told the family. (8)

"We was all nigh about tickled to death when Tom brung a new wife home . . . ," recalled Dennis. "She had three children of 'er own, an' a four-hoss wagon-load o' goods—feather pillers an' homespun blankets, an' patchwork quilts an' chists o' drawers, an' a flax-wheel an' a soap kittle, an' cookin' pots an' pewter dishes—lot o' truck like that 'at made a heap o' diffrunce in a backwoods cabin. . . . (9)

"Yes, Aunt Sairy was a woman o' propputy, an' could a' done better, I reckon, but Tom had a kind o' way with the women, an' maybe it was somethin' she tuk comfort in to have a man that didn't drink an' cuss none." (10)

Sarah Bush Lincoln was a fine woman, made of sturdy pioneer stock. Her granddaughter later remembered her as "a very tall woman, straight as an Indian, fair complexion and was when I first remember her, very handsome, sprightly, talkative and proud. Wore her hair curled till gray. Is kind hearted and very charitable and also very industrious." (11)

The new Mrs. Lincoln, born and raised in a buzzing village community, knew nothing of the hardships of life on the frontier. She was used to neighbors just across the road, shops and stores nearby, and interesting travelers passing through. She was in for a rude awakening. "When we landed in Indiana," she later recalled, "Mr. Lincoln had erected a good log cabin— tolerably comfortable. . . . The country was wild and desolate." (12)

She brought her feisty, industrious nature into the wilderness and immediately got down to moving and shaking and molding that woeful bunch into a respectable family again. Dennis Hanks: "I reckon we was all purty ragged and dirty when she got thar. The fust thing she did was to tell me to tote one o' Tom's carpenter benches to a place outside the door near the hoss-trough. Then she had me 'n Abe n' John Johnston, her boy, fill the trough with spring water. She put out a big gourd full o' soap an' another one to dip water with an' told us boys to wash up fur dinner. . . . *(13)*

"She soaped, rubbed and washed the children clean so that they looked pretty, neat, well and clean. She sewed and mended their clothes and the children once more looked human as their own good mother left them. . . . *(14)*

"You jist naturally had to be somebody when Aunt Sairy was around. . . . *(15)* She made a heap more o' Tom, too, than pore Nancy did. Before winter he'd put in a new floor, he'd whip-sawed an' planed off so she could scour it, made some good beds an' cheers an' tinkered at the roof so it couldn't snow in on us boys 'at slep' in the loft. Purty soon we had the best house in the kentry. . . . *(16)*

"She had Tom build 'er a loom, an' when she heerd o' some lime burners bein' 'round Gentryville, Tom had to mosey over an' git some lime, an' whitewash the cabin. An' he made 'er an ashhopper fur lye an' a chicken-house nuthin' could git into. Then—te he he he!—she set some kind of a dead fall trap fur him an' got him to jine the Baptist Church! Cracky, but Aunt Sairy was some punkins!" *(17)*

By spring of 1820, the new Lincoln family had been completely remade. Broken remnants of three families now shared that one room cabin and called it home. There was Tom Lincoln, forty-two years old, and Sarah Bush Lincoln, thirty-two. Dennis Hanks was twenty-one. Sarah Lincoln and Elizabeth Johnston were both thirteen. Abe was eleven, John Johnston was ten and Matilda Johnston was nine.

Mrs. Lincoln, somehow, made everyone feel at home in their cramped quarters. Abe, Dennis and John climbed the wall pegs each night and slept in the loft with the rain and snow seeping in through the cracks. Sarah, Elizabeth and Matilda slept together in a big bed Tom built for them. At bedtime, the men undressed first, then the ladies, and by the frontier code of decency, no one was embarrassed.

"Thar was eight of us then to do fur, but Aunt Sairy had faculty an' didn't appear to be hurried or worried none," observed Dennis. "Little Sairy just chirked right up with a mother an' two sisters fur comp'ny. Abe used to say he was glad Sairy had some good times." *(18)*

Abe and Sarah, old hands at wilderness living, must have had a grand time showing their city sisters and new brother all the surprises in the woods. The forest was like a store full of delicious treats. Candy bars came from sweet maple sap. Sassafras bark and roots mixed in water made a tangy, sparkling drink. Sweet and juicy berries, in patches so plentiful their clothing would be stained red all over from the juice, melted on their tongues— juneberries, mulberries, strawberries, dewberries, blackberries and raspberries. All through the summer and fall the children could just about reach out anywhere, pick some sweet fruits or delectable nuts from the trees and pop them into their mouths. The men, out hunting all the time, brought back deer, rabbit, squirrels, turkey, quail, pigeons and wild ducks.

Abe and Sarah taught the Johnston children some games, backwoods style. They made a ball by wrapping some of Mrs. Lincoln's yarn around a pebble and covering it with a piece of buckskin. They played games like "hare and hounds," "wet and dry stones," "prisoner's base," and "hide and seek." They twisted some long hickory saplings and fastened the ends together to make hoops. Grapevines made excellent jump ropes.

The Johnstons had a lot to tell the Lincolns about town life, especially Sally, who brought Tom up to date on all the gossip in Hardin County since he moved away. Abe and Sarah heard wonderful stories about circuses and travelling shows that passed through Elizabethtown. The Lincoln children could only gape in amazement as the Johnstons told them about the elephants, the lions, the tigers they saw with their own eyes.

They loved to hear Sally's stories about her family, especially the time her brother Isaac was shot in the back, without warning, by a coward. The doctors wanted to tie him down while they cut him open to take out the bullet. He told them he didn't need to be tied down. He put two steel musket balls between his teeth and bit and chewed and ground them down as the doctors sliced into his body. He never let out a moan or a whimper. In the end, when the slug was removed, he spat out the musketballs, chewed flat, and got up to thank the doctors.

Meanwhile, Abraham and his step-mother were forming a close, loving bond. Mrs. Lincoln later spoke of how much he seemed like a blood-son: "Abe never gave me a cross word or look and never refused in fact or even in appearance to do anything I requested of him. I never gave him a cross word in all my life. . . . His mind and mine, what little I had, seemed to run together more in the same channel. . . . He was dutiful to me always. He loved me truly, I think. I had a son John who was raised with Abe. Both were good boys, but I must say, both now being dead, that Abe was the best boy I ever saw or ever expect to see." (19)

Tom Lincoln loved his new wife, and always remained devoted to her. He was known for his sense of humor, and Sarah could take a joke. Once, Sarah asked her husband: "Thomas, you never yet told me who you like best, your first wife or me." Tom answered, "Sarah, that reminds me of old John Hardin down in Kentucky who had a fine-looking pair of horses and a neighbor came in one day to look at them and said, 'John, which one of these horses do you like the best?' John said, 'I can't tell. One of them kicks and the other bites and I don't know which is worst.' " (20)

7.

"Land O' Goshen, That Boy Air A' Growin' "

Throughout the 1820's, settlers from Kentucky continued to cross the Ohio River to build their homes in the new state of Indiana. The community around Little Pigeon Creek grew—some fifty families lived within five miles of the Lincoln cabin. Nine families with forty-nine children were just a mile away. Yet there was plenty of frontier space. The cabins were spread too far apart to form a village or community center.

Their main gathering place was two miles from the Lincoln home at Gentryville. The Gentrys were the wealthiest family in the county. James Gentry came to Little Pigeon Creek a few years after the Lincolns and bought over a thousand acres of land. He began to keep a small stock of goods for sale at his farmhouse. A blacksmith set up shop nearby and soon there were a few more cabins. That was the beginning of the town of Gentryville.

The Gentrys had eight children. Abe became friendly with the boys near his age, Matthew, Allen and Joseph. Abe, Joseph Gentry and Nattie Grigsby went to school together and formed a close friendship that was to last until Abe moved to Illinois.

The Grigsby family lived three miles from Abe. They had been there about a year when Tom Lincoln came to Little Pigeon Creek to build his "half-faced" camp. Reuben Grigsby and his seven sons helped Tom clear the land to build his cabin.

They owned a whiskey still. During that first brutal Indiana winter, Reuben Grigsby paid Tom to make wooden casks to hold his liquor.

Both Reuben Grigsby and Tom Lincoln had their own childhood stories to tell about bloody Indian raids. Tom was eight when his father was shot in an Indian ambush. When Reuben Grigsby was about four, a band of Indians broke into his home, massacred his whole family, and carried him away. When they tired of his crying, they threw him in the river. He was rescued by an old squaw. The Indians didn't want him around so they threw him in again. The squaw swam out again to save him. Finally, they decided to let the old woman keep the child. He stayed with the Indians for seven years, learning their language, following their customs, practicing their religion. Even as an old man he was known in the territory as a white man who followed the ways of the Indian.

His new family was growing together, as Abe Lincoln himself continued to grow at the start of adolescence. The juices and glands churned inside him, stretching his muscles and bones. Long and lean he grew. He found he could see over the heads of the other boys. Soon, he could look down at their fathers. When he was seventeen, they measured him—six foot four from his heels to his head. The neighbors said, "Land o' Goshen, that boy air a' growin.' " (1)

"He was as tall as he was ever goin' to be, I reckon," said Dennis. "He was the ganglin'est, awkwardest feller that ever stepped over a ten-rail snake fence. He had to duck to git through a door an' appeared to be all joints. Tom used to say Abe looked as if he'd been chopped out with an ax an' needed a jackplane tuk [took] to him." (2)

Abe grew up handling the ax. From the day he set foot on the Lincoln homestead in Indiana as a boy of seven, the sinews of his hands were molded around the wooden grip of an ax. The inside skin of his hands toughened with calluses thick as leather. He learned how to make artful use of his ax. Measuring by eye, he could pinpoint a spot on a log and slice into it. Swaying his hips and shoulders behind his swing, he learned how to throw the full weight of his body into each blow. By the time he approached the fullness of his size, those long, wiry arms could

50

hold the ax straight out in front of him and let it rest there, easy and steady, as if it were a twig.

His companions remembered his skill as an axman:

"He was a master woodsman and could size up a tree that would work up well into rails at almost a glance." *(3)*

"He can sink an ax deeper into wood . . . than any man I ever saw." *(4)*

"My how he could chop. His ax would flash and bite into a sugar tree or sycamore—down it would come. If you heard him felling trees in a clearing, you would say there were three men at work the way the trees fell." *(5)*

Abe was about sixteen when he accidentally gored his step-sister Matilda with his trusty ax. Matilda told the story of how she and Abe "grew up together loving one another as brother and sister." *(6)* On this morning, Abe started down the road, ax on his shoulder, to begin a long day's work in the woods. Matilda trailed him playfully, even though she knew she was forbidden by her mother to go into the woods. She wanted to give Abe a big surprise. Suddenly, she "bounced on his back like a panther." *(7)* Abe was thrown off balance. Falling backward, he let the ax slip, nipping Matilda's flesh. Abe tore off part of his shirt and tried to soak up the blood as best as he could.

"Now what are you going to tell your good mother, 'Tilda?" Abe asked her.

"Why Abe," she said, "I'll tell my mother that I cut myself badly on the ax and that will be the truth about it."

"Yes, that will be the truth but it won't be the whole truth, 'Tilda," Abe said. " 'Tilda, the very best thing you can possibly do is to tell your mother the whole truth and nothing but the truth and risk your mother. This I advise you to do." *(8)*

Once, Abe was sharpening his ax when it slipped and nearly sliced off his thumb. It left a jagged white scar that became his badge as an axman. There was a saying in the backwoods country: "You never cuss a good ax."

As folks in the Little Pigeon Creek community saw Abe take on the body of a man, they put him to task doing man's work. He was hired out as a farm hand, driving teams of oxen and horses to plow the fields, cutting down trees to clear the land, splitting logs to build cabins, pigpens and fences.

Building fences was Abe's specialty. Settlers on the frontier said that a fence had to be "horse high, bull strong and pig tight"—high enough so a horse can't jump it, strong enough so a bull won't topple it and tight enough so a pig won't slip through it. Each fence rail was about ten feet long and four inches wide. Abe could make 400 of them in a day. For that labor he was paid twenty-five cents.

Years later, when Abe was running for President, there was a great demand for rails actually split by him. The grandson of Josiah Crawford recalled that "Grandfather employed young Abe to make rails for pens. These rails were longer than the ordinary ten-foot rails and larger. Abe notched the rails at the ends to make them fit closer together." In 1860 he went "over the farm with grandfather . . . searching for these rails. They were easily identified by their length and size and notches in the ends." (9)

Abe often worked alongside his father, who tried to teach Abe his craft. "Thomas Lincoln was a carpenter by trade. Relied on it for a living, not on farming," one of the neighbors related. (10) As the finest carpenter in the area, Tom Lincoln was chosen by the congregation to supervise the construction of a new meeting house for the Little Pigeon Creek Baptist Church. Abe was his father's right-hand man, working along with the crew. When it was finished, Abe was given the job of sexton of the church, taking care of all church property.

"Thomas Lincoln often and at various times worked for me," recalled William Wood. "Made cupboards . . . other household furniture for me. He built my house, made floors, ran up the stairs, did all the inside work for my house. Abe would come to my house with his father and romp with my children." (11)

Once, Lincoln father and son worked together to build a wagon for James Gentry. It was constructed "entirely out of wood, even to the hickory rims to the wheels." (12)

When the neighborhood boys found some time on their hands, they whooped and frollicked like frisky kittens, holding contests of strength, agility and endurance. They threw the maul, they ran dashes, they wrestled, they played "knocking off hats," they raced horses, chased foxes, swam and fished. Abe found that he could beat all the boys his own age, and just about everyone else.

His great strength became legendary. One of his friends said that he "could carry what three ordinary men would grunt and swear at. Saw him carry a chicken house made of poles pinned together and carried that weight, at least six hundred [pounds], if not much more." (13)

"He wouldn't take no sass, neither," recalled Dennis. "If a feller was spoilin' fur a fight, an' nothin' else'd do him, Abe'd accomydate him all right. Generally, Abe could lay him out so he wouldn't know nothin' about it fur a spell. . . . When he was fifteen he could bring me down by throwin' his leg over my shoulder. I always was a little runt of a feller." (14)

James and Joseph Gentry and Redmond Grigsby told of the time Abe and William Grigsby quarrelled over who owned a certain spotted pup. It came down to a fist fight. Grigsby dared Abe to a contest. Abe smiled down at him and said that it would not be a fair fight since Grigsby was too small for him. If Grigsby wanted to fight someone, he should take on his step-brother, John Johnston, offered Abe. The winner could keep the pup.

The day for the big fight was set. Johnston and Grigsby faced each other, stripped to the waist, their seconds rooting them on. The crowd that formed a ring around them was so large and boisterous that one man claimed that he "climbed a tree that he might see over the heads of the people who gathered around." (15)

The two men lit into each other, punching, mauling, bruising with bloody fists as the crowd yelped and hollered. Green Taylor was there—his father was a second for Johnston. "They had a terrible fight," relates Taylor, "and it soon became apparent that Grigsby was too much for Lincoln's man Johnston. After they had fought a long time without interference—it having been agreed not to break the ring—Abe burst through, caught Grigsby, threw him some feet away." (16) "Bodily hurled him over the heads of the crowd," said another witness. (17)

"There he stood," recalled Green Taylor of Lincoln, "proud as Lucifer, and swinging a bottle of liquor over his head, swore he was 'the big buck of the lick. If anyone doubts it,' he shouted, 'he has only to come on and whet his horns.' (18) Being a general invitation for a general fight they all pitched in and had quite a general fight." (19) There was a wild, bone-smashing brawl and for months they argued about who got the biggest whipping.

Those long legs of Abe's just kept on growing. Nattie Grigsby remembered that "between the shoe and sock and his britches made of buckskin, there was bare and naked six or more inches of Abe Lincoln's shin bone." (20) Someone said that "he looked as if he were made for wading in deep water." (21)

"Aunt Sairy often told Abe 'at his feet bein' clean didn't matter so much because she could scour the floor, but he'd better wash his head, or he'd be a rubbin' dirt off on her nice whitewashed rafters," Dennis remarked.

"That put an idy in his head, I reckon . . . thar was always a passel o' youngsters 'round the place. One day Abe put 'em up to wadin' in the mud-puddle by the hoss trough. Then he took 'em one by one, turned 'em upside down, an' walked 'em acrost the ceilin', them ascreamin' fit to kill.

"Aunt Sairy come in, an' it was so blamed funny she set down an' laughed, though she said Abe'd oughter be spanked. I don't know how far he had to go fur more lime, but he whitewashed the ceilin' all over agin." (22)

While his limbs were abruptly filling out, mysterious changes came simmering into his heart. Many quiet moments he spent looking deep within himself. "As he shot up," said one of his friends, "he seemed to change in appearance and action. Although quick witted and ready with an answer, he began to exhibit deep thoughtfulness and was so often lost in studied reflection we could not help noticing the strange turn in his actions. He disclosed rare timidity and sensitiveness, especially in the presence of men and women, and although cheerful enough in the presence of boys, he did not appear to seek our company as earnestly as before." (23)

Lincoln's greatest biographer, Carl Sandburg, came to know his subject from the inside and wrote with a lyric eloquence that earned him a Pulitzer Prize. Sandburg could almost breathe with Lincoln, follow his heartbeat. He knew the forces that shaped Lincoln's soul as he grew up in backwoods America. Sandburg wrote of the food that nourished him and that ripened him into a giant:

"Growing from boy to man, he was alone a good deal of the time. Days came often when he was by himself all the time except at breakfast and supper hours in the cabin home. In some years more of his time was spent in loneliness than in the company of other people. . . .

"It was the wilderness loneliness he became acquainted with. . . . He rested between spells of work in the springtime when the upward push of the coming out of the new grass can be heard, and in autumn weeks when the rustle of a single falling leaf lets go a whisper that a listening ear can catch. . . .

"And so he grew. Silence found him; he met silence. In the making of him as he was, the element of silence was immense." (24)

8.

"A Real Eddication"

Some mornings, when Abe was six years old, his mother would get him up early, scrub his face and hands extra clean, slick his hair back, and march him two miles down the road with eight-year-old Sarah. They were going to school.

"Nancy kep' urging Abe to study," recalls Dennis. " 'Abe,' she'd say, 'you l'arn all you kin an' be some account.' " (1)

Tom said he wanted Abe to have "a real eddication. . . . You air a-goin' to larn readin', writin' and cipherin' (arithmetic)." (2)

"My father," said Abe, "had suffered greatly for the want of an education and he determined that I should be well educated. And what do you think he said his ideas of a good education were? We had an old dog-eared arithmetic in our house and Father determined that somehow or somehow else, I should cipher clear through that book." (3)

A school appeared in a community when a number of parents showed an interest in education for their children. The classroom opened for a season and families sent their children whenever household chores were not pressing. Each family paid the teacher for this privilege in deer meat, ham, corn, animal skins or produce—items more valued than paper money on the frontier.

They were known as "blab schools." Students were called "scholars." Scholars were made to recite their lessons aloud, all at once, so the teacher could be sure each student's mind would not wander from his work. To anyone passing by, the chorus of mixed voices in unison sounded like "blabbing." Scholars who misbehaved were handed a dunce cap to wear and were shown to a seat in the corner. The master had only to wave his whip to fire the seat of ambition in an unruly scholar.

"There were some schools, so called." said Abe. "But no qualification was ever required of a teacher beyond readin', writin' and cipherin' to the Rule of Three. If a straggler supposed to understand Latin happened to sojourn in the neighborhood, he was looked upon as a wizard. There was absolutely nothing to excite ambition for education." (4)

By the time Abe started school at Knob Creek, he knew the alphabet and could read some. "About Abe's early education and his sister's education, let me say this," relates Dennis. "Their mother first learned them ABC's. She learned them out of Webster's old spelling book. It belonged to me and cost in those days 75 cents, it being covered with calfskin. . . . I taught Abe to write with a buzzard's quill which I killed with a rifle, and having made a pen, put Abe's hand in mine and moving his fingers by my hand to give him the idea of how to write." (5)

"Well, me 'n Abe spelled through Webster's spellin' book twict before he got tired. Then he tuk to writin' on the . . . floor, the fence rails and the wooden fire shovel with a bit o' charcoal.

"We got some wrappin' paper over to Gentryville, an' I made ink out o' blackberry brier root an' copperas. Kind o' ornery ink that was. It et the paper into holes. Got so I could cut good pens out o' turkey-buzzard quills. . . .

"When Tom got mad at his markin' the house up, Abe tuk to markin' trees 'at Tom wanted to cut down, with his name, an' writin' it in the sand at the deer-lick. He tried to interest little Sairy in l'arnin' to read, but she never tuk to it. . . .

"It pestered Tom a heap to have Abe writin' all over every-thing thataway, but Abe was jist wropped up in it.

" 'Denny,' he sez to me many a time, 'look at that, will you? ABRAHAM LINCOLN! That stands fur me. Don't look a blamed bit like me!' An' he'd stand an' study it a spell. 'Peared to mean a heap to Abe." (6)

Abe's first teacher at Knob Creek was Zachariah Riney. There Abe learned mostly from a book called Dilworth's Speller.

When Mr. Riney left town, the school was taken over by a neighbor of the Lincoln's, Caleb Hazel.

"Young Abraham commenced trudging his way to school to Caleb Hazel, with whom I was well acquainted and could perhaps teach spelling, reading, and indifferent writing and perhaps could cipher to the rule of three," recounts Samuel Haycraft. "But he had no other qualification of a teacher except large size and bodily strength to thrash any boy or youth that came to his school." (7)

"With this standard of an education," a friend wrote, "he started to school in a log-house in the neighborhood and began his educational career. He had attended this school but about six weeks, however, when a calamity befell the father. He had endorsed some man's note in the neighborhood for a considerable amount and the prospect was he would have it to pay and that would sweep away all their possessions. His father, therefore, explained to him that he wanted to hire him out and receive the fruits of his labor and his aid in averting this calamity." (8)

When the Lincolns moved to Indiana, many of their neighbors wanted to write letters to family and friends back in Kentucky. Word got around that young Abe could read and write and suddenly his skill was in great demand. They came to him with their personal messages and he listened, writing them down as best he could. Seeing a boy so young reading and writing surprised a lot of people. "He set everybody a wonderin' to see how much he knowed and he not mor'n seven," a neighbor said. (9)

By the time his mother died in Abe's ninth year, he hadn't been to school for four years. "I reckon it was thinkin' o' Nancy an' things she'd done said to him that started Abe to studyin' that next winter," said Dennis. (10)

"Abraham Lincoln and Sally and myself all went to school," recalled Abe's friend Nattie Grigsby. "We first went to school to Andy Crawford in the year 1818 in the winter, the same year that Mrs. Lincoln died, she having died in October. Abe went to school nearly a year, say nine months. I was going to school all this time and saw Lincoln there most, if not all, the time. (11)

"The house was built of round logs just high enough for a man to stand erect under the ruff (roof). The floor was split logs or what we called puncheons. The chimney was made of poles and clay. The window was constructed by chopping out a part of two logs and placing pieces of split boards at proper distance and then we would take our old copy books and grease them and paste them over the window. This give us light. In this school room Abraham Lincoln and myself entered school. (12)

"When we went to Crawford's," Nattie continued, "he tried to learn us manners. . . . He would ask the scholars to retire from the schoolroom, come in, and then some scholar would go around and introduce him to all the scholars, male and female." (13)

His friends remembered Abe as a student:

"He was always at school early and attended to his studies. He was always at the head of his class and passed us rapidly in his studies. He lost no time at home and when he was not at work, was at his books. He kept up his studies on Sunday and carried his books with him to work so that he might read when he rested from labor." (14)

"Whilst other boys were idling away their time, Lincoln was studying his books. . . . He read and thoroughly read his books whilst we played." (15)

"Lincoln had a strong mind. I was older than he was by six years and further advanced but he soon outstripped me. . . ." (16)

"He always appeared to be very quiet during playtime, never was rude, seemed to have a liking for solitude, was the one chosen in almost every case to adjust difficulties between boys of his age and size and, when appealed to, his decision was an end of the trouble. He was also rather noted for keeping his clothes clean longer than any of the others. . . ." (17)

Nattie Grigsby remembered how one day Abe "came forward with an awkward bow and a deprecative smile to read an essay on the wickedness of being cruel to helpless animals." (18)

Every Friday, Master Crawford lined the scholars up against the wall for a spelling bee. Kate Roby told of the time she was stuck on a word and how Abe gallantly came to her rescue. "I was to spell," she recalled. "The word I was to spell was DEFIED.

Crawford said that if we did not spell it he would keep us in school all day and night. We all missed the word. Couldn't spell it. We spelled the word every way but the right way. *(19)*

"Abe stood on the opposite side of the room and was watching me. I began D-E-F . . . and then I stopped, hesitating whether to proceed with an I or a Y. Looking up, I beheld Abe, a grin covering his face and pointing with his index finger to his eye. I took the hint, spelled the word with an I and it went through all right." *(20)*

Kate Roby was Abe's special friend. "I knew Mr. L. well," she remembered. "He and I went to school together. I was fifteen years old. Lincoln about the same age. . . .

"He often and often communicated or talked to me about what he knew. . . .," she confided. "One evening, Abe and myself were sitting on the banks of the Ohio. . . . I said to Abe that the sun was going down."

"That's not so," he insisted. "It don't really go down. It seems so. The earth turns from west to east and the revolution of the earth carries us under. We do the sinking, as you call it. The sun, as to us, is comparatively still. The sun's sinking is only an appearance."

Kate was amused. "I replied—'Abe, what a fool you are!' "

Years later, Abe's discourse got Kate to thinking. "I know now that I was the fool, not Lincoln," she admitted. "I am now thoroughly satisfied that he knew the general laws of astronomy and the movements of the heavenly bodies. He was better read then than the world knows or is likely to know exactly. No man could have talked to me as he did that night unless he had known something of geography as well as astronomy."*(21)*

Abe told a story of how each of the scholars took a turn reading aloud from the third chapter of the *Book of Daniel*. They read:

"Nebuchadnezzar the king made an image of gold, whose height was threescore cubits and the breadth thereof six cubits. . . . Thou, O king, hast made a decree that every man . . . shall fall down and worship the golden image. And whoso falleth not down and worshippeth, that he should be cast into the midst of a burning fiery furnace. . . .

"There are certain Jews whom thou hast set over the affairs of the province of Babylon, Shadrach, Meshach and Abednego; these men, O king, have not regarded thee; they serve not thy gods, nor worship the golden image which thou hast set up." *(22)*

The reading went smoothly, until verse twelve, when a small boy named Bud took his turn. "Little Bud stumbled on Shadrach, floundered on Meshach, and went all to pieces on Abednego," recalled Abe. "Instantly the hand of the master dealt him a cuff on the side of the head and left him wailing and blubbering as the next boy in line took up the reading. But before the girl at the end of the line had done reading, he had subsided into sniffles and finally become quiet. His blunder and disgrace were forgotten by the others of the class until his turn was approaching to read again. Then, like a thunderclap out of a clear sky, he set up a wail which even alarmed the master, who with rather unusual gentleness inquired, 'What's the matter now?'

"Pointing with a shaking finger at the verse which a few moments later would fall to him to read, Bud managed to quaver out the answer: 'Look there marster,' he cried. 'There comes them same damn three fellers again.' " *(23)*

A story is told about the time Squire Crawford got up to leave the room and Abe felt the urge to do a little mischief. Above the door, hanging within a leap's reach, were the Squire's prize buck antlers. Abe was in a mood to show off, so he sauntered up to the doorway, jumped up, grabbed the antlers, and swung merrily back and forth. There was a sharp crack and suddenly, Abe tumbled flat on his back with a jagged piece of buck horn in his hand.

He scurried to his seat and buried himself in his book, not even blinking an eye when Squire Crawford came back and loudly demanded to know who did the damage.

The master looked straight at Abe and asked him if he knew who was responsible. "Yes sir," said Abe. "I did it sir, but I didn't mean to. I just hung on it and it broke." Abe earned a stern tongue lashing for that prank. *(24)*

When Abe left Crawford's classroom he didn't go to school again for two years. He had done plenty of reading on his own when James Swaney opened a school on Hoskins farm. Swaney was just twenty-one and could barely read, write and cipher himself. Abe's attendance was irregular. According to John Hoskins, the young scholar "had to travel four and a half miles—and this going back and forth so great a distance occupied entirely too much of his time. His attendance was therefore only at odd times and was speedily broken off altogether." (25)

Two years later, Abe studied briefly with Azel Dorsey, one of the most prominent citizens in the county. Dorsey served as tax commissioner, treasurer, and coroner and his cultural background was rich and varied. Dorsey recalled his student, Abraham Lincoln: "One of the noblest boys I ever knew. . . . Certain to become noted if he lives. . . . (26) Marked for the diligence and eagerness with which he pursued his studies. . . . Came to the log cabin schoolhouse arrayed in buckskin clothes, a raccoon skin cap and provided with an old arithmetic which had somewhere been found for him to begin his investigation into the higher branches." (27)

That was the end of formal education for Abraham Lincoln. He once wrote: "Abraham now thinks that the aggregate of all his schooling did not amount to one year." (28)

By this time, Abe had penetrated deeply into the world of books. Books became his passion. His teachers were books. As he passed into his fifteenth year, there was no reason for him to sit in a backwoods classroom. Said Kate Roby: "[It] could do him no further good. He went to school no more." (29)

9.

"Mighty Darned Good Lies"

"Seems to me now I never seen Abe after he was twelve 'at he didn't have a book some'ers 'round," says Dennis. "He'd put a book inside his shirt an' fill his pants pockets with corn dodgers, an' go off to plow or hoe. When noon come, he'd set down under a tree, an' read an' eat. An' when he come to the house at night, he'd tilt a cheer back by the chimbly, put his feet on the rung, an' set his backbone and read. Aunt Sairy always put a candle on the mantel-piece fur him, if she had one. An' as like as not, Abe'd eat his supper thar, takin' anything she'd give him that he could gnaw at an' read at the same time.

"I've seen many a feller come in an' look at him, Abe not knowin' anybody was 'round, an' sneak out ag'in like a cat, an' say: 'Well, I'll be darned!' It didn't seem natural, nohow, to see a feller read like that." *(1)*

"He worked for me," recalls John Romine. "Was always reading and thinking. [I] used to get mad at him. . . . I say Abe was awful lazy. He would laugh and talk and crack jokes and tell stories all the time. Didn't ever work but did dearly love his pay. He worked for me frequently, a few days only at a time. . . . Lincoln said to me one day that his father taught him to work but never learned him to love it." *(2)*

"Abe was not energetic except in one thing—he was active and persistent in learning. Read everything he could," said his step-sister Matilda. *(3)*

"He kept the Bible and Aesop's always within reach, and read them over and over again," his friend, David Turnham remembered. *(4)*

"I feel the need of reading," Abe explained. "It is a loss to a man not to have grown up among books." *(5)*

He was nine when he read Aesop's Fables. He was wonderstruck at the little tales of wise and foolish animals—*The Lion and the Four Bulls, The Cat and the Mice, The Crow and the Pitcher, The Mule, the Ape and the Fox.* There was a short biographical sketch of Aesop and he read how this revered sage began life as a humble slave.

His next book was *Pilgrim's Progress* by John Bunyan, found often in pioneer homes next to the Bible. As he lost himself in its pages, his fancy transported him to far-off places—the Slough of Despond, the Wicket Gate, Hill Difficulty, Delectable Mountain, Enchanted Ground, the City of Destruction, Celestial Country, Dead-Man's Lane and Doubting Castle. He met many strange and improbable characters—Mr. Moneylove, Mr. Hold-the-World, Mr. Save-All, Mr. Feeblemind, Mr. Greatheart, Mr. Honest, Mrs. Lightmind, Madam Wanton, Mr. Lechery, Mrs. Bats-Eyes, Mrs. Inconsiderate, young Mercy, and Hopeful, Atheist, Faint-Heart, Mistrust, and the wandering pilgrim, Christian.

When Abe was buried in the grief of his own "Slough of Despond" after his mother died, he turned to these books for relief. That winter, he lived inside his books and they gave him refuge.

When things brightened, Abe found *Robinson Crusoe* by Daniel Defoe and suddenly he found himself in the midst of a violent shipwreck. He saw a lone survivor thrown unconscious on the beach of a deserted island. He followed the man, watching as he made his clothing from animal skins, hunted for food, or scouted cautiously for signs of wild creatures or dangerous cannibals. Abe could grin knowingly as Crusoe hoisted the crippled ship's sails in front of a cave, trying to build a home in the jungle wilderness. Abe thrilled to the exciting discovery of a mysterious footprint that led to the capture of a friendly cannibal that the man called "Friday." Finally, just when the pages were running out, a dramatic rescue.

"Abe'd lay on his stummick by the fire an' read out loud to me 'n Aunt Sairy," recalls Dennis. "An' we'd laugh when he did, though I reckon it went in at one ear an' out at the other with her, as it did with me. . . ." (6)

" 'Denny,' he'd say, 'the things I want to know is in books. My best friend's the man who'll git me one.' Well, books wasn't as plenty as wild-cats, but I got him one by cuttin' a few cords o' wood. It had a lot o' yarns in it. One I ricollect was about a feller that got near some darned fool rocks 'at drawed all the nails out o' his boat an' he got a duckin'. Wasn't a blamed bit o' sense in that yarn. (7)

" 'Abe,' sez I, many a time,' them yarns is all lies.'

" 'Mighty darned good lies,' he'd say, an' go on readin' an' chucklin' to hisself, till Tom'd kiver up the fire fur the night an' shoo him off to bed." (8)

Dennis was thinking of an exciting collection of legends from the east, *The Arabian Nights*. It was about a Persian Sultan who was heartbroken at the treachery of his wife. He knew he could never trust a woman again, and in retribution he vowed to marry one beautiful woman every day and have her strangled the next morning.

There was a woman of beauty, courage and wit named Scheherazade who sought to put an end to this barbarity. She offered herself to the Sultan in marriage, knowing full well that she had less than a day to live.

An hour before dawn on the day she was to die, her sister came to pay a final visit. Scheherazade had instructed her sister to make one final innocent request.

"My dear sister," she said to Scheherazade, " 'ere I leave you, which will be very shortly, I pray you to tell me one of those pleasant stories you have read. Alas! This will be the last time that I shall enjoy that pleasure." (9)

The Sultan allowed Scheherazade to proceed with one final story. The tale was so packed with danger, adventure and mystery, that the Sultan would not allow her to stop. The stories of Scheherazade continued and Abe read each one. He read "The Seven Voyages of Sinbad the Sailor," and followed raptly as Sinbad and his men touched on a small island that looked like a giant green meadow. As the sailors enjoyed their meal, the island suddenly trembled and shook them terribly. To their horror, they realized they were on the back of a giant sea creature. Sinbad escaped by clinging to the back of the monster as he dived underwater, then by desperately grabbing hold of a piece of firewood.

Abe confronted the Roc, a huge white bird with legs as big as tree trunks. The Roc could snatch an elephant or a rhinocerous in the jaws of her horrible beak and carry it off to her nest to feed her young. When the giant bird took to the sky, her shadow darkened the sun.

Abe felt the thrills and chills of coming face to face with unspeakable, unearthly creatures. He read:

"We advanced into the island on which we were, and came to a palace, elegantly built, and very lofty, with a gate of ebony of two leaves, which we forced open. We entered the court, where we saw before us a large apartment, with a porch, having on one side a heap of human bones, and on the other a vast number of roasting spits. Our fears were not diminished when the gates of the apartment opened with a loud crash and out came the horrible figure of a black man as tall as a lofty palm tree. He had but one eye, and that in the middle of his forehead, where it looked as red as a burning coal. His fore-teeth were very long and sharp and stood out of his mouth, which was as deep as that of a horse. His upper lip hung down upon his breast. His ears resembled those of an elephant and covered his shoulders; and his nails were as long and crooked as the talons of the greatest birds. At the sight of so frightful a giant, we became insensible and lay like dead men." *(10)*

Abe loved to lose himself in far-off lands of mystery and adventure. Yet he was also intensely curious about the land of his birth, this new nation called the United States of America, and its founding fathers. He grew up hearing their names in awed tones—Washington, Jefferson, Madison, Franklin—and he longed to know what made them great. He turned the pages of Franklin's *Autobiography* and the man's own words engrossed him. Here was a boy, a lot like himself, an inquisitive, restless boy, who loved books more than anything else.

"My early readiness in learning to read, which must have been very early, as I do not remember when I could not read. . . .," *(11)* were Franklin's words to a wide-eyed Abe Lincoln.

"From my infancy I was passionately fond of reading, and all the money that came into my hands was laid out in the purchasing of books. . . . *(12)*

"An acquaintance with the apprentices of booksellers enabled me sometimes to borrow a small one, which I was careful to return soon and clean. Often I sat up in my chamber reading the greatest part of the night when the book was borrowed in the evening and to be returned in the morning, lest it should be found missing." *(13)*

The book that had the greatest impact on Abe, and caused him the most trouble, was *A History of the Life and Death, Virtues and Exploits of General George Washington* by Mason Weems.

"I know he read Weems's *Washington* when I was there," recalled his cousin John Hanks. "Got it wet—it was on a kind of bookshelf close to the window—the bookshelf was made by two pins in the wall and a clapboard on them." *(14)*

Abe borrowed the book from Josiah Crawford. Mrs. Crawford remembered the episode. "Lincoln, in 1829, borrowed this book (Weems's *Life of Washington*) and by accident got it wet. L. came and told honestly and exactly how it was done. . . . My husband said: 'Abe, as long as it is you, you may finish the book and keep it.' Abe pulled fodder a day or two for it." *(15)* It was a lesson Abe didn't soon forget.

Abe was taught how to be honest by his father. In Weems's *Washington* the boy discovered how powerfully his great hero loved the truth. He read how young George came to value honesty:

"Never did the wise Ulysses take more pains with his beloved Telemachus than did Mr. Washington with George to inspire him with an early love of truth. 'Truth, George,' said he, 'is the loveliest quality of youth. I would ride fifty miles, my son, to see the little boy whose heart is so honest and his lips so pure that we may depend on every word he says. . . .'

"When George . . . was about six years old, he was made the wealthy master of a hatchet, of which, like most little boys, he was immoderately fond, and was constantly going about chipping every thing that came in his way. One day, in the garden, where he often amused himself hacking his mother's pea-sticks, he unluckily tried the edge of his hatchet on the body of a beautiful young English cherry tree. . . .

"The next morning, the old gentleman, finding out what had befallen his tree, which, by the way, was a great favourite, came into the house and with much warmth asked for the mischievous author. . . . Nobody could tell him anything about it. Presently, George and his hatchet made their appearance. 'George,' said his father, 'do you know who killed that beautiful little cherry tree yonder in the garden?'

"This was a tough question, and George staggered under it for a moment, but quickly recovered himself, and looking at his father with the sweet face of a youth brightened with the inexpressible charm of all-conquering truth, he bravely cried out, 'I can't tell a lie, Pa. You know I can't tell a lie. I did cut it with my hatchet.'

" 'Run to my arms, you dearest boy,' cried his father in transports, 'run to my arms. Glad am I, George, that you killed my tree. For you have paid me for it a thousand fold. Such an act of heroism in my son is more worth than a thousand trees, though blossomed with silver and their fruits of purest gold.' "
(16)

Sometime after Abe finished *The Life of Washington*, a book came into his hands that caught the attention of the American public. It became something of a best-seller in the 1820's. The exact title was: *An Authentic Narrative of the Loss of the American Brig Commerce, Wrecked on the Western Coast of Africa in the Month of August, 1815—With an Account of the Sufferings of Her Surviving Officers and Crew, Who Were Enslaved By the Wandering Arabs on the Great African Desert or Zahahrah, and Observations Historical, Geographical . . . Made During the Travels of the Author While a Slave to the Arabs and in the Empire of Morocco.* The author was James Riley.

When Riley was fifteen, he was tired of the hard work on land and longed to go to sea. With his parents' consent, he went to work on a ship and learned the fine art of navigation. Soon, he rose to become captain of his ship. His story was a chilling tale of how his ship was wrecked, and of how he and his crew were taken into slavery. They were rescued after a time, and returned home. This was Abraham Lincoln's first serious encounter with the evils of slavery.

James Riley, a simple American seaman, had learned a searing lesson on the degradation and humiliation of slavery. He wrote to his fellow Americans:

"Unerring wisdom and goodness has since restored me to the comforts of civilized life, to the bosom of my family, and to the blessings of my native land, whose political and moral institutions are in themselves the very best of any that prevail in the civilized portion of the globe, and ensure to her citizens the greatest share of personal liberty, protection and happiness. And yet, strange as it must appear . . . my proud-spirited and free country-men still hold a million and a half nearly of the human species in the most cruel bonds of slavery. . . . Adversity has taught me some noble lessons. I have now learned to look with compassion on my enslaved and oppressed fellow-creatures." (17)

Abe was not above using his talent for reading for the riotous entertainment of his friends. Nattie Grigsby remembers: "There was another book that we boys got a lot of fun out of. Lincoln would read it to us out in the woods on Sundays. . . . It was the King's Jester—it was a book of funny stories." (18)

Actually, it was a volume of bawdy, vulgar humor called *Quinn's Jests* by an English actor named James Quinn. It was just the kind of book that teenaged boys had to sneak into the woods to read. And Heaven help them if their parents found out.

10.

"Somethin' Peculiarsome"

"Hey! Is that the only way Abe l'arnt things—out o' books?" mused Dennis in an interview years later. "You bet he was too smart to think everything was in books. Sometimes a preacher 'r a circuit-ridin' jedge 'r lawyer 'r stump-speakin' polytician 'r a school teacher'd come along. When one o' them rode up, Tom'd go out an' say: 'Light, stranger,' like it was polite to do. Then Abe'd come lopin' out on his long legs, throw one over the top rail and begin firin' questions. Tom'd tell him to quit but it didn't do no good so Tom'd have to bang him on the side o' his head with his hat. Abe'd go off a spell an' fire sticks at the snow-birds an' whistle like he didn't keer.

" 'Pap thinks it ain't polite to ask folks so many questions,' he'd say. 'I reckon I wasn't born to be polite, Denny. Thar's so darned many things I want to know. An' how else am I goin' to git to know 'em?' " *(1)*

Dennis said that Abe was "a good listener to his superiors— bad to his inferiors. That is, he couldn't endure jabber." *(2)*

As a young boy, visitors fascinated him. Each caller was an unopened book, full of unending surprises and useful ideas. Mrs. Lincoln spoke of how Abe studied their houseguests: "Abe . . . was a silent and attentive observer, never speaking or asking questions till they were gone and then he must understand everything—even to the smallest thing, minutely and exactly. He would then repeat it over to himself again and again, sometimes in one form and then in another and when it was fixed in his mind to suit him, he became easy and he never lost the fact or his understanding of it. Sometimes he seemed pestered to give expression to his views and got mad almost at one who couldn't explain plainly what he wanted to convey." (3)

Shyness did not remain long in Abe Lincoln's personality. Growing more and more cocksure of himself, he challenged the adults around him to explain, defend and clarify their ideas. "The Baptist preachers always stopped at the house," recalled Dennis. "Onct [Once] Abe tried to git a preacher to 'count fur them miracles about Jonah an' the whale an' the others an' got him so worked up that when Abe asked him who was the father of Zebedee's children, blamed if he could tell." (4)

Dennis always said there was "somethin' peculiarsome" about Abe. (5) "Abe had a powerful good mem'ry. He'd go to church an' come home an' say over the sermon as good as the preacher. He'd often do it fur Aunt Sairy when she couldn't go an' she said it was jist as good as goin' herself. He'd say over everything from 'beloved brethern' to 'amen' without crackin' a smile, pass a pewter plate fur a collection an' then we'd all jine him in singin' the Doxology." (6)

Abe loved to make speeches. He would go around and collect any children who happened along and sit them around a tree stump. Then, solemnly mounting the stump, he would begin to talk their ears off. "I have seen Lincoln—Abraham—make speeches to his step-brother, step-sisters and youngsters that would come to see the family," states John Hanks. (7)

"He made other speeches such as interested him and the children . . . ," said Mrs. Lincoln. "His father had to make him quit sometimes as he quit his own work to speak and made the other children as well as the men quit their work." (8)

Abe would talk a subject up in one direction, turn it on its head, spin it, bounce it, pinch it, pull it and bring it back down to where he began.

"I recollect some of the questions they spoke on," said Elizabeth Crawford. "The Bee and the Ant. Water and Fire. Another was—Which had the most right to complain, the Negroes or the Indians. Another—which was the strongest, wind or water." (9)

"When Abe was about seventeen, somethin' happened that

druv him nigh crazy," Dennis tells us. "Thar was a feller come over from England—Britisher, I reckon. . . . So when this furrin feller spoke in Congress about that Garden o' Eden he was goin' to fence in on the Wabash, we soon heerd about it. Boats brung news every week. An' one day arly in the winter, a big keel-boat come down from Pittsburgh over the Ohio. They called it 'The Boatload o' Knowledge.' It had such a passel o' books an' machines an' men o' l'arnin' on it. Then little rowboats an' rafts crossed over from Kaintucky an' ox teams an' pack-hosses went through Gentryville and struck across kentry. . . .

"Abe'd tell you in a minute. . . . Thar wasn't sca'cely anything else talked about fur a spell. I reckon some folks thought it was New Jerusalem an' nobody'd have to work. Anyway, thar was a lot o' worthless cusses lit out fur that settlemint. Abe'd a broke his back to go an' it nigh about broke his heart when he couldn't.

" 'Denny, thar's a school an' thousands o' books thar an' fellers that know everything in creation,' he'd say, his eyes as big 'n hungry as a hoot-owl's. The schoolin' only cost a hundred dollars a year an' he could 'a worked out his board but Abe might jist as well 'a wished fur a hundred moons to shine at night. . . .

"An' thar it was—only about sixty miles west of us an' Abe couldn't go! The place petered out after awhile, as it was sartin to do with all them ornery fellers in it livin' off the workers. But I reckon it lasted long enough fur Abe to 'a l'arned what he wanted to know.

"Well, I reckon Abe put it out o' his mind after awhile. If he couldn't git a thing he wanted he knowed how to do without it an' mebbe he looked at it diffrunt afterwards. But things'd ben easier fur him if he could 'a gone to that school." *(10)*

The settlement on the Wabash River was called New Harmony. It was founded in 1824 by a wealthy British businessman named Robert Owen who caused a stir when he announced the purchase of a tract of land in Indiana to form an experimental community.

"I am come to this country to introduce an entire new state of society," he proclaimed, "to change it from the ignorant, selfish system to an enlightened social system which shall unite all interests into one and remove all cause for contest between individuals." *(11)*

Some years earlier, Owen had created a model town in Scotland and he hoped to establish similar communities all over the world. He believed that a community was happiest when every member worked for the benefit of all. His high ideals attracted over a thousand settlers to the new Indiana town, including some of the leading scholars and intellectuals in America. New Harmony also drew its share of misfits, profiteers and shady dealers. Some of the colonists worked for the benefit of all and some didn't, prompting endless quarrelling that finally destroyed New Harmony after only three years.

In retrospect, Abe Lincoln never missed the unsuccessful educational experiment. And in a place where "books wasn't as plenty as wildcats" and where there was "absolutely nothing to excite ambition for education," a guiding angel found Abe and noticed his peculiar ambitions. Offering gentle encouragement and unfailing support she pushed him along in the direction he wanted to go, doing her level best to clear away any obstacles in his path. Abe Lincoln's best educational benefactor was his step-mother.

"She didn't have no eddication herself but she knowed what l'arnin' could do fur folks," said Dennis. "She wasn't thar very long before she found out how Abe hankered after books. . . . *(12)* Aunt Sairy'd never let the children pester him. She always said Abe was goin' to be a great man some day. An' she wasn't goin' to have him hendered." *(13)*

Said Mrs. Lincoln: "When Abe was reading, my husband took particular care not to disturb him—would let him read on and on till Abe quit of his own accord. . . . *(14)* He would ask my opinion of what he had read and often explained things to me in his plain and simple language. . . . *(15)*

"Abe read all the books he could lay his hands on and when he came across a passage that struck him he would write it down on boards if he had no paper and keep it there till he did get paper. Then he would rewrite it, look at it, repeat it. . . . *(16)* Frequently he had no paper to write his pieces down on. Then he would put them with chalk on a board or plank, sometimes only making a few signs of what he intended to write. . . . *(17)* When the board would get too black he would shave it off with a drawing knife and go on again. *(18)*

"He had a copybook," revealed Mrs. Lincoln, "a kind of scrapbook in which he put down all things and then preserved them." *(19)* Ten badly torn pages have survived the years, providing the earliest samples of writing by his own hand.

PAGE 1:

"Abraham Lincoln
his hand and pen
he will be good
but god knows when."

"Time.
What an empty vaper tis
and days how swift they are
swift as an indian arrow fly
or like a shooting star.
The present moment just is here
then slides away in haste.
That we can never say they're ours
but only say they're past."

PAGE 2:

"Long Measure &C &C"
(These are exercises in computation in miles,
furlongs, poles, yards, feet and inches)

PAGE 3:

"Multiplication 1824"
(Multiplication problems—in large script in lower-
right hand corner: "Abraham Lincolns Book.")

PAGE 4:

"Long Division 1824"
(Division problems. The word 'long' has been torn away.)

At the bottom on the left: "Abraham Lincolns Book."

In the lower right-hand corner:

"Abraham Lincoln is my name
And with my pen I wrote the same
I wrote in both haste and speed
And left it here for fools to read."

PAGE 5:

"Compound Multiplication"

"What is Compound Multiplication."

"When several numbers of divers Denomination
are given to be multiplied by one Common
Multiplier this is called Compound Multiplication."

"Compound Division."

"When several numbers of Divers Denomination are given to be
divided by a common divisor this is called Compound Division."

At the bottom of the page:
"Abraham Lincoln His Book."

PAGE 6:

"Simple Interest"

"Case 1"

"A testator left his son besides providing for his education &c
$1500 to receive the amount thereof at 6 percent per annum
when he should arrive at the age of 21 years which his guardian
then found to be $2332.50 cents. How old was the Boy at his
fathers decease."

PAGE 7:

"Simple Interest"

(Problems and computation)

PAGE 8:

"Compound Interest"

(Problems and computation)

PAGE 9:

"Discount March 1st 1826"

(Problems and computation)

"The Single Rule of Three"

(Problems and computation) *(20)*

The most important service Mrs. Lincoln performed for her book-happy step-son was to persuade Tom Lincoln to allow Abe to set aside some of his chores in order to read. "I induced my husband to permit Abe to read and study at home as well as at school," she recalled. "At first he was not easily reconciled to it but finally he, too, seemed willing to encourage him to a certain extent. . . . *(21)* Mr. Lincoln never made Abe quit reading to do anything if he could avoid it. He would do it himself first." *(22)*

Tom Lincoln was a practical man. To his mind, all the education a man needed was what could help him in his daily life. He saw no sense in dwelling on fanciful things—history, poetry, science, philosophy. Years later, after Abe had left home and his odd reading behavior had intensified, Tom complained about his son's misspent energies: "I suppose Abe is still fooling hisself with eddication. . . . I tried to stop it but he has got that fool idea in his head and can't be got out. Now I hain't got no eddication but I get along far better than if I had." *(23)*

Yet Tom had an inkling that his son was blessed with an uncommon gift. "Old Tom couldn't read himself," remarked a family friend, "but he wuz proud that Abe could and many a time he'd brag about how smart Abe wuz to the folks around about." *(24)*

It was Abe's "peculiarsome" gift that set him apart from his neighbors. Abe was hungry. The more he learned about the world the greater his appetite grew. He wanted to know all about everything. It was a keen, unending hunger that could never be satisfied. Like a starving man, he looked everywhere for his nourishment.

"I can say this," observed Abe. "That among my earliest recollections I remember how when a mere child I used to get irritated when anybody talked to me in a way I could not understand. I don't think I ever got angry at anything else in my life. But that always disturbed my temper and has ever since.

"I can remember going to my little bedroom after hearing the neighbors talk . . . with my father and spending no small part of the night walking up and down and trying to make out what was the exact meaning of some of their—to me—dark sayings. I could not sleep though I often tried to when I got on such a hunt after an idea until I had caught it. And when I thought I had got it, I was not satisfied until I had repeated it over and over, until I had put it in language plain enough, as I thought, for any boy I knew to comprehend. This was a kind of passion with me and it has stuck by me. For I am never easy now when I am handling a thought till I have bounded it north and bounded it south and bounded it east and bounded it west." *(25)*

Listening. Questioning. Observing. Discussing. This was high school and college in the backwoods country when the nation was young. Said Dennis Hanks: "We learned by sight, scent and hearing. We heard all that was said and talked over and over the questions heard—wore them slick, greasy and threadbare." *(26)*

11.

"Chronicles of Reuben"

As Abraham Lincoln turned into his teens, romance was in the air. Dennis, now a man of twenty-two, was making sweet eyes at Abe's fourteen-year-old step-sister, Elizabeth Johnston. Abe watched them get married. But, the new Mr. and Mrs. Dennis Hanks didn't go too far. They set up home in a cabin about a mile away, so they were always coming around. Still, twelve-year-old Abe may have noticed that Dennis, now that he was a married man, just wasn't the same old rascal anymore.

During the summer of 1826, Abe was seventeen and he saw two weddings right in his own cabin. Close as he was to his mischievous step-sister Matilda, he could only have shared in her joy when she married Squire Hall. Then, on August 2, Abe saw the most important marriage of his young life. He watched his beloved sister Sarah exchange vows with Aaron Grigsby.

"I knew Abraham's own sister Sarah," offered John Hanks. "She was a short-built woman, eyes dark gray, hair dark brown. She was a good woman—kind, tender and good natured . . . a smart woman. That is my opinion." (1)

Sarah Lincoln Grigsby was nineteen years old when she married. "Sally Lincoln was older than Abe. Sally married Aaron Grigsby, my brother, in August 1826," recalled Nattie Grigsby. (2)

Abe's pal, Nattie, became her brother-in-law. He knew Sally well. "Sally was a quick-minded woman . . . extraordinary mind.

She was industrious, more so than Abraham. . . . Her good humored laugh, I can see now, is as fresh in my mind as if it were yesterday. She could, like her brother Abe, meet and greet a person with the very kindest greeting in the world. Make you easy at the touch and word." *(3)*

Like many youngsters growing up in frontier communities, Aaron and Sarah knew each other since they were children. The Lincolns and the Grigsbys were members of the Little Pigeon Creek Church and the children played together whenever the congregation gathered.

Sarah Lincoln grew to be a fine, hard-working young lady. She took a job working for the Crawfords and one time, her boyfriend Aaron came to call on her. The Crawford's young son Samuel sneaked a peak at the young lovers and caught them smooching. "One day I ran in, calling out 'Mother! Mother! Aaron Grigsby is sparking Sally Lincoln! I saw him kiss her!" he revealed years later. "Mother scolded me and told me I must stop watching Sally or I wouldn't get to the wedding." *(4)*

The marriage of his only sister was an exciting time for Abe. They were close. She had held his little hand as they had trudged through forest pathways together on their way to school. Sarah always looked out for Abe the way a mother would, especially when their own mother died. They shared their grief and their joys together. Every year, their birthday celebration was a happy event for both of them since they celebrated their birthdays within two days of each other.

Legend has it that Abraham composed a song in honor of the new bride and groom. It was a light-hearted and humorous way of reminding Aaron Grigsby to take proper care of his new wife. "This song was sung at Abraham's sister's wedding," wrote Elizabeth Crawford. "I do not know (whether) A. Lincoln composed this song or not. The first that I ever heard of it was the Lincoln family sung it. I rather think that A.L. composed it himself, but I am not certain. I know that he was in the habit of making songs and singing them." *(5)*

ADAM AND EVE'S WEDDING SONG

When Adam was created, he dwelt in Eden's shade,
As Moses has recorded; and soon an Eve was made.
Ten thousand times ten thousand
Of creatures swarmed around
Before a bride was formed,
And yet no mate was found.

The Lord then was not willing
The man should be alone
But caused a sleep upon him
And took from him a bone.

And closed the flesh in that place
And then he took the same
And of it made a woman
And brought her to the man.

Then Adam, he rejoiced
To see his loving bride,
A part of his own body,
The product of his side.

This woman was not taken
From Adam's feet we see,
So he must not abuse her
The meaning seems to be.

This woman was not taken
From Adam's head, we know,
To show she must not rule him,
'Tis evidently so.

This woman, she was taken
From under Adam's arm,
So she must be protected
From injuries and harm. (6)

Now that the boys and girls of his age were beginning to notice each other, there were plenty of social gatherings where they could meet. Abe went right along with the rest of the boys. "Always attended house raisings, log rolling, corn shucking and workings of all kinds," said Nattie Grigsby. (7)

Abe was impossible to miss in any crowd. He towered over the

80

other boys. His great strength and athletic prowess gave him special status among his peers. But it was his warmth, his wit and sense of fun that drew people around him. "When he appeared in company, the boys would gather and cluster around him to hear him talk," said Grigsby. "He made fun and cracked his jokes making all happy. But the jokes and fun were at no man's expense. He wounded no man's feelings. . . . He naturally assumed the leadership of the boys." (8)

"He was so odd, original and humorous and witty that all the people in town would gather around him," remarked Dennis. "He would keep them there till midnight or longer, telling stories, cracking jokes. . . . I would get tired, want to go home— cuss Abe most heartily." (9)

Yet, Abe was not popular with the girls of his age. He certainly was not good-looking. What a sight! Kate Roby went to school with Abe, and they became great friends. She gave a careful account of his appearance: "His skin was shriveled and yellow. His shoes, when he had any, were low. He wore buckskin breeches, linsey-woolsey shirt and a cap made from the skin of a squirrel or coon. His breeches were baggy and lacked by several inches meeting the tops of his shoes, thereby exposing his shin-bone, sharp, blue and narrow." (10)

"All the young girls of my age made fun of Abe," one of the local ladies remembered. (11) Another explained that she stayed away from him because of "his awkwardness and large feet." (12)

Abe was good natured, and he didn't seem to mind. Said his step-brother John Johnston, "Abe didn't take much truck with girls." (13)

Kate Roby agreed. "Abe did not go much with the girls . . . didn't like girls much. Too frivolous." (14)

His friend, David Turnham, remembered that "he did not seem to seek the company of the girls and when with them was rather backward." (15)

Abe usually laughed off his shyness with women. "A woman is the only thing I am afraid of that I know can't hurt me." (16)

In his young days, Abraham Lincoln's relationships with women were mostly in his dreams. The image of a special woman—he called it his first love—played on his mind. His adolescent fancy wove a great dramatic tale which he never forgot. Years later, he confided his daydream to a Springfield journalist:

"Did you ever write out a story in your mind? I did when I was a little codger."

Then Abe went on to explain: "One day, a wagon with a lady and two girls and a man broke down near us, and while they were fixing up, they cooked in our kitchen. The woman had books and read us stories, and they were the first I ever heard.

"I took a great fancy to one of the girls and when they were gone I thought of her a great deal. One day when I was sitting out in the sun by the house, I wrote out a story in my mind. I thought I took my father's horse and followed the wagon and finally found it, and they were surprised to see me. I talked with the girl and persuaded her to elope with me. And that night I put her on my horse and we started off across the prairie.

"After several hours we came to a camp. And when we rode up we found it was the one we had left a few hours before—and we went. The next night, we tried again and the same thing happened. The horse came back to the same place. And then we concluded that we ought not to elope. I stayed until I had persuaded her father to give her to me.

"I always meant to write that story out and publish it, and I began once. But I concluded it was not much of a story. But I think that was the beginning of love with me." (17)

There were more weddings. On April 16, 1829, two of the Grigsby boys, Reuben Jr. and Charles took brides. The entire frontier community came to the Grigsby place to frolic at the grand reception for the two brides and two grooms.

Everyone was there but the Lincolns. By this time, the Lincoln family and the Grigsbys were at odds. First, there was the wild fracas between William Grigsby and John Johnston, which wound up with Abe battling half the boys in town. The two families seemed to unite when Abe's sister married Aaron Grigsby. But then, in the winter of 1828, when tragedy struck Sarah down, Abe could not forgive the Grigsbys.

After Lincoln's death, Billy Herndon hunted down some of the old-timers still around Gentryville, Indiana, and discovered that they remembered the Grigsby wedding well. The occasion was infamous. That was how Herndon unearthed the curious story of Abe Lincoln's plan of revenge against the Grigsbys, the scandalous, riotous tale of "The Chronicles of Reuben."

"One of the Grigsby boys married Lincoln's sister. Lincoln thought that the Grigsbys mistreated her and the Lincolns and the Grigsbys fell out," explained Herndon.

"Two [other] Grigsby boys were subsequently married on the same night. . . . Old Man Grigsby, for the two boys, held an infair, as was the custom at the time, at his house. The neighbors were invited except Abraham, and all went along as merry as a Christmas bell.

"Abraham got the ears of some of his chums who were in the house and at the infair. Abraham was not invited and so he felt huffy and insulted. He therefore told the boys inside this: 'Let's have some fun.' 'Well,' said the boys inside.

"It was arranged between the insiders and outsiders that the two married couples should be put to bed . . . all changed around and in the wrong places." (18)

"After the infair was ended," added Joseph Richardson, who recalled the incident for Herndon, "the two women were put to bed. The candles were blown out upstairs. The gentlemen, the two husbands, were invited and shown to bed. Charles Grigsby got into bed with, by accident as it were, Reuben Grigsby's wife, and Reuben got into bed with Charles' wife." (19)

Herndon went on: "Both husbands got in the wrong bed by direction made between Abraham and the invited insiders. . . .

"Soon, however, a scream and a rattling of boards aloft were heard and all was confusion worse confounded. A candle was lit and things found out and explained to the satisfaction of the women and men.

"Probably," Herndon guessed, "the women knew the voices of their loved ones and by that means the terrible mistake was found out. But who caused it and what for were not found out for some time. Here is Abraham, who was joyous and revenged that night—the good saint at one of his jokes." (20)

That wasn't the end of Abe's prank. A short narrative, written in the reverent style of the Old Testament, and a crude little poem turned up by the roadside near the Grigsby home. It was called "The Chronicles of Reuben." "Chronicles" was a biting satire of the Grigsby wedding, poking barbs at the entire

Grigsby clan and at some of the neighbors, especially Josiah Crawford, who shortly before the wedding made Abe work for three days to pay for his damaged book. (See page 00) The grand climax of the narrative was a hilarious account of the husband-wife mix-up.

"Lincoln was by nature witty, and here was his chance," said Richardson. "So he got up a witty poem called the 'Book of Chronicles,' in which the infair, the mistake in partners, Crawford and his blue nose came in each for his share. . . . This called the attention of the people to Abe intellectually.

"Abe dropped the poem in the road carelessly—lost it, as it were. It was found by one of the Grigsby boys." *(21)*

"Chronicles" was an immediate hit throughout the countryside. The Grigsby's misadventure was on people's lips everywhere. There were folks who committed the entire text to memory and repeated it over and over with gusto. Some remembered it as long as they lived.

"This poem is remembered here in Indiana in scraps better than the Bible, better than Wake's hymns," Richardson claimed. *(22)*

Samuel Crawford remembered what happened when he read it. "I took the 'Reuben's Chronicles' to Gentryville and read them in public. R. D. Grigsby, being present, got very mad over it." *(23)*

Betsy Grigsby was one of the unlucky brides. She left her own version of the affair. "We formed a procession, my husband (Reuben Jr.) and me, Charles and his wife in front. The messenger, Josiah Crawford, led the way down the long lane blowing all the time on his tin horn. Old Man Reuben Grigsby met and welcomed us. . . .

"There was a big crowd and we did not finish eating until after dark. . . . Yes, they have a joke on us. They said my man got into the wrong room and Charles got into my room but it wasn't so. Lincoln just wrote that for mischief. Natty Grigsby told us it was all written down, all put on record. Abe and my man often laughed about that." *(24)*

"Lincoln did write what is called the 'Book of Chronicles,' a satire on the Grigsbys and Josiah Crawford," Nat Grigsby admitted to Herndon several months after Lincoln died. "The satire was good, sharp, cutting and showed the genius of the boy. It hurt us then, but it's all over now. There is now no family in the broad land who, after this, loved Lincoln so well and who now look upon him as so great a man. We all voted for him. . . . I was for Lincoln and Hamlin first, last and always." (25)

Hot on his search for Lincoln's roots, Billy Herndon visited the Crawford home with Nattie Grigsby on September 16, 1865. He spoke to Mrs. Crawford, now old and blind, who told him sadly that her husband Josiah had died only that spring. The old woman remembered the "Chronicles" but was too embarrassed to recite it. "The poem is smutty and I can't tell it to you," she said. "Will tell it to my daughter-in-law. She will tell her husband and he shall send it to you." (26)

Several months later, Herndon received a copy of the "smutty" poem and the entire "Chronicles of Reuben" from Samuel Crawford. Nat Grigsby wrote to assure Herndon that these versions were accurate. "I think they are correctly written," said Grigsby. (27)

THE POEM

I will tell you a joke about Josiah and Mary.
It is neither a joke or a story.
For Reuben and Charles had married two girls
But Billy has married a boy.

The girls he had tried on every side
But none could he get to agree.
All was in vain, he went home again
And since that, he is married to Natty.

So Billy and Natty agreed very well.
And mamma's well pleased at the match.
The egg it is laid, but Natty's afraid
The shell is so soft that it never will hatch.

But Betsy, she said: "You cursed baldhead,
My suitor you can never be.
Besides, your low crotch proclaims you a botch
And that never can answer for me." (28)

CHRONICLES OF REUBEN

"Now there was a man whose name was Reuben, and the same was very great in substance, in horses and cattle and swine and a very great household. It came to pass when the sons of Reuben grew up that they were desirous of taking to themselves wives, and being too well known as to honor in their own country, they took a journey into a far country and there procured for themselves wives.

"It came to pass also that when they were about to make the return home they sent a messenger before them to bear the tidings to their parents. These, inquiring of the messengers what time their sons would come, made a great feast and called all their kinsmen and neighbors in and made great preparations.

"When the time drew nigh, they sent out two men to meet the grooms and their brides with a trumpet to welcome them and accompany them. When they came near unto the house of Reuben, the father, the messenger came on before them and gave a shout, and the whole multitude ran out with shouts of joy and music playing on all kinds of instruments. Some were playing on harps, some on viols, and some blowing on ram's horns. Some were also casting dust and ashes towards heaven, and chief among them was Josiah, blowing his bugle and making sound so great the neighboring hills and valleys echoed with the resounding acclamation. When they had played and their harps had sounded till the grooms and brides approached the gates, Reuben, the father, met them and welcomed them to his house.

"The wedding feast now being ready, they were all invited to sit down to eat, placing the bridegrooms and their wives at each end of the table. Waiters were then appointed to serve and wait on the guests. When all had eaten and were full and merry, they all went out again and played and sung till night, and when they had made an end of feasting and rejoicing, the multitude dispersed, each going to his own home.

"The family then took seats with their waiters to converse while preparations were being made in an upper chamber for the brides and grooms to be conveyed to their beds. This being done, the waiters took the two brides upstairs, placing one in a room at the right hand of the stairs and the other on the left.

The waiters then came down and Nancy, the mother, then gave directions to the waiters of the bridegrooms, and they took them upstairs and placed them in the wrong rooms. The waiters then all came downstairs. But the mother, being fearful of a mistake, made enquiry of the waiters and learning the true facts, took the light and sprang upstairs.

"It came to pass that she ran to one of the rooms and exclaimed, 'O, Lord, Reuben, you are in bed with the wrong wife!' The young men, alarmed at this, ran out with such violence against each other they came near knocking each other down. The tumult gave evidence to those below that the mistake was certain. At last, they all came down and had a long conversation about who made the mistake, but it could not be decided. So endeth the chapter." (29)

12.

"Why Dost Thou Tear More Blest Ones Hence . . ."

Abraham was in love with words. Since he was a young boy learning the ABC's from his mother, shaping letters and words on slats of wood with a piece of charcoal from the fireplace, Abe used words as playthings. When he discovered that sounds rhyme, he revelled at the silly ways he could put them together.

He wrote a mock epitaph for a local Kickapoo Indian named Johnny Kongapod, which for all its clever turn of words, contained a grain of his true religious belief.

> "Here lies poor Johnny Kongapod.
> Have mercy on him gracious God,
> As he would do if he was God
> And you were Johnny Kongapod." *(1)*

Abe dashed off a little verse in Joseph Richardson's copybook—clever lines, but also a good piece of advise.

> "Good boys who to their books apply
> Will all be great men by and by." *(2)*

He loved nature. He loved ideas. "There was more in Abe's head than wit and fun," observed a more serious-minded friend. *(3)*

The mind of the young man was opening. He began to observe the world beyond the surface of things, searching for deeper causes. "He dwelt altogether in the land of thought," wrote Herndon. "His deep meditation and abstraction easily induced the belief among his horny-handed companions that he was lazy." (4)

Joseph Richardson noticed that he "was witty and sad and thoughtful by turns." (5)

In Abe's 1824 copybook, Herndon discovered an interesting verse that opened a window to the subtle and mystical questions turning in his mind. In these lines, the young Lincoln peers beyond everyday matters to muse on the fleeting and insubstantial nature of a moment in time.

"On another page were found, in his own hand, a few lines which it is also said he composed," said Herndon. "Nothing indicates that they were borrowed and I have always, therefore, believed that they were original with him. Although a little irregular in meter, the sentiment would, I think, do credit to an older head." (6)

> Time, what an empty vapor 'tis,
> And days, how swift they are;
> Swift as an Indian arrow—
> Fly on like a shooting star.
> The present moment just is here,
> Then slides away in haste;
> That we can never say they're ours,
> But only say they're past. (7)

His mind explored the arena of thoughts, feelings and memories. What was the "mid-way world" where "things decayed and loved ones lost" rise in "dreamy shadows" of "liquid light"? Years later, the day he returned home to Indiana after fifteen years away, childhood memories rushed in torrents of images. There were pleasant memories—"woods, fields and scenes of play," friends from "young childhood grown strong, manhood gray." Yet there was sadness, pain, horror—thoughts of those "lost and absent." The fields became "tombs" with "every spot a grave." Strange, he felt, to walk upon "the very spot where grew the bread that formed my bones."

Abraham explained how the poem came to him during the Presidential campaign of 1844. "In the fall of 1844, thinking I might aid some to carry the State of Indiana for Mr. Clay, I went into the neighborhood in that state in which I was raised, where my mother and only sister were buried, and from which I had been absent about fifteen years.

"That part of the country is, within itself, as unpoetical as any spot of the earth. But still, seeing it and its objects and inhabitants aroused feelings in me which were certainly poetry—though whether my expression of those feelings is poetry is quite another question." *(8)*

> My childhood's home I see again,
>   And sadden with the view;
> And still, as memory crowds my brain,
>   There's pleasure in it too.
>
> O Memory! Thou midway world
>   'Twixt earth and paradise,
> Where things decayed and loved ones lost
>   In dreamy shadows rise,
>
> And, freed from all that's earthly vile,
>   Seem hallowed, pure and bright,
> Like scenes in some enchanted isle
>   All bathed in liquid light.
>
> As dusky mountains please the eye
>   When twilight chases day;
> As bugle-notes that, passing by,
>   In distance die away;
>
> As leaving some grand waterfall,
>   We, lingering list its roar—
> So memory will hallow all
>   We've known, but know no more.
>
> Near twenty years have passed away
>   Since here I bid farewell
> To woods and fields and scenes of play
>   And playmates loved so well.
>
> Where many were but few remain
>   Of old familiar things;
> But seeing them to mind again
>   The lost and absent brings.

The friends I left that parting day,
How changed, as time has sped!
Young childhood grown, strong manhood gray,
And half of all are dead.

I hear the loved survivors tell
How nought from death could save,
Till every sound appears a knell,
And every spot a grave.

I range the fields with pensive tread,
And pace the hollow rooms,
And feel companion of the dead;
I'm living in the tombs.

And now away to seek some scene
Less painful than the last—
With less of horror mingled in
The present and the past.

The very spot where grew the bread
That formed my bones, I see.
How strange, old field, on thee to tread,
And feel I'm part of thee! (9)

Sometimes pain deepens the mind. When the wounds heal and an earnest search for understanding begins, the mind has already lengthened its reach. It looks back into the soul, deep into the uncharted territory of unfathomable life. There is some profound questioning. Why??? Answers come only from the deep.

Abraham knew the pain of dying. As a small boy, he saw the tiny blue body of his newborn brother taken from life. A few years later, he watched as life left his mother, as she laid there still, cold, empty.

Now, another great tragedy etched its mark onto Abraham's soul. His sister was married less than a year when she became pregnant. Tom and Sarah Lincoln looked forward to their new grandchild. And Abe was about to become an uncle. They had "a very bright future before them," Nancy Grigsby, Aaron's niece, later said. "And Sally was much thought of and loved by all her husband's people." (10)

On January 20, 1828, Sally went into labor. The baby was

coming. Before the night was over, both mother and baby were dead.

"I remember the night she died," recalled Mrs. J. W. Lamar, one of the neighbors. "My mother was there at the time. She had a strong voice and I heard her calling father. . . . He went after a doctor but it was too late. They let her lay too long." *(11)*

That night, Abe was doing a job for Old Man Grigsby at the Grigsby home. He "was out in our little smoke house at our house doing a little carpenter work," one of the Grigsbys remembered, "when Aaron, Sarah's husband, came running up from his house a quarter of a mile away and said that Sarah had just died. We went out and told Abe. I will never forget that scene. He sat down in the door of the smoke house and buried his face in his hands. The tears slowly trickled from between his bony fingers and his gaunt frame shook with sobs. We turned away." *(12)*

"This was a hard blow to Abe, who always thought her death was due to neglect," one of his friends said. "From then on he was alone in the world, you might say." *(13)*

The Little Pigeon Creek Baptist Church had just opened a new cemetery near the meetinghouse. Sarah Lincoln Grigsby was laid into the ground there, her stillborn baby in her arms. They were one of the first to be buried in the new churchyard cemetery. A slab of sandstone carved with her initials marked the grave.

Abraham pondered long over the mysteries of life and death. One episode was unaccountably perplexing. When he was sixteen, he saw one of his friends and school mates suddenly, frighteningly, go berserk. The scene turned in his mind, a haunting presence, dangling unexplained for years afterward.

The boy, Matthew Gentry, grew up as a "fortune-favored child," into the wealthiest family in the community. Abe knew him as a "bright lad." One day, without warning, his "reason fled." He became a "mad-man," a "howling crazyman," begging, swearing, weeping, praying. In his frenzy he struggled with his father, tried to kill his mother, and maimed himself. Some neighbors gathered and finally bound his arms and legs as he glared with "burning eyeballs" and "maniac laughter."

Some fifteen years later, when Abe returned to Gentryville,

he was shocked to see the same young man, now grown old, still locked in "mental night." Sharply detailed observations flowed into words, picturing a man in a most wretched condition. So, a poem was born.

"The subject of the present one is an insane man," explained Abe. "His name is Matthew Gentry. He is three years older than I and when we were boys we went to school together. He was rather a bright lad and the son of the rich man of our very poor neighborhood.

"At the age of nineteen, he unaccountably became furiously mad, from which condition he gradually settled down into harmless insanity. When . . . I visited my old home in the fall of 1844, I found him still lingering in this wretched condition. In my poetizing mood I could not forget the impressions his case made upon me." (14)

He ended the verses with a question, a plea to the "awe inspiring prince"—Death itself—a prayer for understanding of the laws of life and death. Abraham had tasted life and seen too much of death. He seemed to have a sense that this all powerful force of nature's night would be back to claim those in the world he loved most. Brother. Mother. Sister. All devoured by death. In a few years, a beautiful young woman whom he cared about— some say they nearly married—would be taken away. Later, two of his sons would die while they were children. And, after taking charge of a torn nation he would see a generation of young men damned and destroyed. Finally, before he was yet old, death would find him as well.

So the poet addressed his question, seeking some inkling, some light to be shed, some reasonable answer. Why, he yearned to know, would death take so many of God's good and gentle people while letting a howling madman pass? "Why dost thou tear more blest ones hence, and leave him ling'ring here?"

But here's an object more of dread
  Than ought the grave contains—
A human form with reason fled,
  While wretched life remains.

Poor Matthew! Once of genius bright,
  A fortune-favored child—

Now locked for aye in mental night,
    A haggard mad-man wild.

Poor Matthew! I have ne'er forgot,
    When first, with maddened will,
Yourself you maimed, your father fought,
    And mother strove to kill.

When terror spread, and neighbors ran,
    Your dang'rous strength to bind;
And soon a howling crazyman
    Your limbs were fast confined.

How then you strove and shrieked aloud,
    Your bones and sinews bared;
And fiendish on the gazing crowd,
    With burning eyeballs glared—

And begged and swore and wept and prayed,
    With maniac laughter joined;
How fearful were those signs displayed
    By pangs that killed thy mind!

And when at length, tho' drear and long,
    Time soothed thy fiercer woes,
How plaintively thy mournful song
    Upon the still night rose.

I've heard it oft, as if I dreamed,
    Far distant, sweet and lone,
The funeral dirge, it ever seemed
    Of reason dead and gone.

To drink its strains, I've stole away,
    All stealthily and still,
Ere yet the rising God of day
    Had streaked the Eastern hill.

Air held his breath; trees, with the spell,
    Seemed sorrowing angels round,
Whose swelling tears in dew-drops fell
    Upon the listening ground.

But this is past, and nought remains
    That raised thee o'er the brute.

Thy piercing shrieks and soothing strains
  Are like, forever mute.

Now fare thee well—more thou the cause
  Than subject now of woe.
All mental pangs, by time's kind laws
  Hast lost the power to know.

O Death! Thou awe-inspiring prince,
  That keepest the world in fear;
Why dost thou tear more blest ones hence,
  And leave him ling'ring here? *(15)*

13.

"I Can See The Quivering and Shining of That Half-Dollar Yet"

The great Ohio River flowing into Mother Mississippi formed a natural highway for travelers moving through the innards of New America. Beginning at Pittsburgh, the Western Waters connected cities, villages and hamlets, large and small, for almost the length of the nation from north to south.

The great waters touched eleven states—Pennsylvania, West Virginia, Ohio, Kentucky, Indiana, Illinois, Tennessee, Missouri, Mississippi, Arkansas and Louisiana before flowing into the Gulf of Mexico at New Orleans.

Newfangled, smoke-belching steamboats made the over-water connection to the West possible. The first steamboat cruised the Ohio River in 1811. Three years later there was a second steamboat. By 1826, 160 new steamboats had been launched. Still, steamboat travel was risky business. More than half of those steamboats built between 1811 and 1826 were no longer running due to accident damage or mechanical failure. Many sat at the bottom of the river.

One of the most famous river disasters occurred on the Ohio River, not far from Little Pigeon Creek. In May of 1825, Revolutionary War hero Marquis de Lafayette cruised upriver on a triumphal tour of the United States. His steamer hit a snag during a storm and went down, pouring all aboard into the river. No one drowned and the Marquis paddled a lifeboat safely to the Kentucky shore. There is a story that one Kentuckian opened his home to Lafayette and by the next morning the whole town showed up at the house to greet him.

The river swallowed many good men. If swirling currents didn't get you, the river gangs did. Bandits like Mike Fink, who lived on the river and claimed they were "half horse and half alligator," preyed on passenger ships and cargo boats to loot them bare.

Ambitious traders and travelers knew the dangers of the river and went anyway. A parade of steamboats passed each other on the three-week voyage from Pittsburgh to New Orleans. Flat-boats loaded with fruits and vegetables, meats, grains, furniture, plows, wagons and livestock crossed paths. Houseboats and arks carried whole families over the waterway. The disenchanted set sail for new waters. New settlers waded ashore. Merchandise from the north, south, east and west passed along the water highway, Main Street, United States.

In 1826 Abe was seventeen and got a job working for James Taylor, whose farm ran along the banks of the Anderson Creek near where it joined the Ohio. Abe plowed, set up fences and did odd jobs around the fields. He also became a skilled hog butcher. He learned how to handle the club so it could kill instantly with a blow right between the eyes of a cow or a hog. Then he would drench the carcass in barrels of scalding water to make the job of skinning the animal easier. After carving out the insides, he would slice the meat into quarters for his customers.

Taylor owned the ferry that connected the settlements on both sides of Anderson Creek. One of Abe's jobs was to operate the ferry to carry passengers, cargo and livestock about a hundred feet across the creek. For his labor as a farm boy and ferryman, Abe was paid six dollars a month. When he did butchering, his wage was increased by thirty-one cents.

Many people had business on the other side of the creek so Abe was constantly busy. When foot passengers came to the ferry without any cargo, Abe would leave the regular ferry, a large flatboat, tied up and scull in a small rowboat. The price of a round trip was 6¼ cents.

One ferry passenger remembered the tall boatman. "I can see now, how with one sweep of the oars, he could send his boat from shore to shore at low water." *(1)* Another remarked about "his gentle manner to the children." *(2)*

At that time, Abe lived at the Taylor farmhouse, sharing a room with the owner's son. Green Taylor described how the two spirited young men got along. "It was during the season that Abe was operating the ferry across Anderson River for my father that we were told to go to the crib and husk corn. Abe taunted me about a certain girl in Troy that I did not like and kept it up until I tore the husk off a big ear of corn and threw it at him. It struck him just above the eye. . . . This blow left a scar that Lincoln carried to his grave." *(3)*

When he had some spare time, Abe worked on the banks of the Ohio River, cooking up a scheme to make some extra money. Dennis Hanks, Squire Hall (Matilda's husband) and Abe got the idea to cut piles of wood and leave them stacked up at the shore. Passing steamboats often sent crewmen ashore to cut wood for fuel. When they did, the boys gladly sold their stock of cut wood. For each wood pile they charged twenty-five cents.

By the time he was eighteen, Abe learned enough about the ways of the river to go into the ferry business for himself. Wielding an ax, a saw and a carving knife, Abe designed and built his own boat. He cut down trees, planed them into planks and pegged the pieces together so that the boat would float. It was his own boat, fashioned from the forest.

He set the craft into the Ohio River at Bates Landing, about a mile and a half from the mouth of Anderson Creek. Customers came. He ferried passengers out to waiting steamships and he picked up passengers from the steamships and brought them to shore.

Once, when he was President, he reminisced about his days as a ferryman. "Seward," he asked his Secretary of State, "did you ever hear how I earned my first dollar?

"Well," said Abe, "I was about eighteen years of age. . . . I was contemplating my new boat and wondering whether I could make it stronger or improve it. . . . Two men with trunks came down to the shore in carriages and looking at the different boats, singled out mine and asked, 'Who owns this?'

"I answered modestly, 'I do.'

" 'Will you,' said one of them, 'take us and our trunks out to the steamer?'

" 'Certainly,' said I.

"I was very glad to have the chance of earning something, and supposed that each of them would give me a couple of bits.

"The trunks were put in my boat, the passengers seated themselves on them and I sculled them out to the steamer. They got on board and I lifted the trunks and put them on the deck. The steamer was about to put on steam again when I called out, 'You have forgotten to pay me.' Each of them took from his pocket a silver half-dollar and threw it on the bottom of my boat. I could scarcely believe my eyes as I picked up the money.

"You may think it was a very little thing," said Abe, "and in these days, it seems to me like a trifle, but it was a most important incident in my life. I could scarcely credit that I—the poor boy—had earned a dollar in less than a day; that by honest work I had earned a dollar." (4)

There was more to the story. Abe confided the fateful epilogue to Leonard Swett, fellow lawyer and Abe's friend from his Illinois circuit riding days. Swett recalls, "Afterwards, playing upon a flatboat which was fastened so as to reach out into the stream, he dropped his half dollar from the farthest end of the boat. . . ."

"I can see the quivering and shining of that half-dollar yet . . .," moaned Abe. "In the quick current it went down the stream and sunk from my sight forever." (5)

One day, someone called to him from the Kentucky shore. Abe rowed out to find him. No one was there. He stepped out of the boat to have a look around when two men jumped out of the bushes, grabbed hold of him and threatened to "duck" him in the river. They gave him a warning—he had no right operating a ferry on the river and he'd better stop.

The two men were the Dill brothers. They had an exclusive

license granted by the state of Kentucky to operate a ferry across the Ohio River. They were out to make sure that nobody interfered with their business.

There was no river "ducking." One look at the giant ferryman's muscular arms probably persuaded the Dill brothers to settle their dispute peaceably. They insisted that Abe come with them so that they could tell their case to the judge.

The three men marched a few hundred yards to the home of Squire Samuel Pate, the local Justice of the Peace. A warrant was sworn by John T. Dill for the arrest of one Abraham Lincoln of the state of Indiana. The case of "The Commonwealth of Kentucky versus Abraham Lincoln" began.

Abe was charged with violating "An Act Respecting the Establishment of Ferries." This was a statute of Kentucky law based on the original act that admitted Kentucky to the Union, and granted to Kentucky jurisdiction over the Ohio River. The Kentucky law stated that "if any person whatsoever shall, for reward, set any person over any river or creek whereupon public ferries are appointed, he or she so offending shall forfeit and pay five pounds current money for every such offence." (6)

Squire Pate gavelled the trial into session and the plaintiffs introduced their evidence. The defendant, they claimed, had transported passengers from the Indiana shore to steamboats on the Ohio River without a license to operate a ferry on that river. The only party with a license to carry passengers across the Ohio River from the Kentucky shore to the Indiana shore was John T. Dill.

The defendant admitted the facts as alleged. But he contended that he did not violate the statute and did not infringe on the rights of the authorized ferry operator.

He told the judge that he had not intended to violate the law. He was not claiming the right to "set any person over any river or creek," only the right to set them part way across. The Dill's ferry, which was based on the Kentucky shore, could not always be on the Indiana side when a steamer was approaching, he reasoned. It seemed fair that passengers who came to the Indiana shore to meet the steamer should have the right to hire a boat to carry them out to the steamer.

Squire Pate announced his ruling. Since there was no evidence that indicated that the defendant had "set any person over any river or creek," the case was dismissed.

The judge was impressed by the young man's sincerity, poise, and ability to use reason. After the Dills left, the Squire invited Abe to sit with him on his porch. They had a long talk about law and business. Squire Pate advised Abe to find out about the law, especially where it involved his business. He said that many difficulties arise because people do not inform themselves of the laws and statutes. Every man should know something about the law, the Squire told him.

They shook hands and left as friends. This was not the last time Squire Pate would see Abe. Whenever the court was in session, Abe rowed across the river and sat at the back of the courtroom, observing the law at work, listening to statements of witnesses, following arguments of lawyers, seeing how Squire Pate directed the whole show.

Abraham Lincoln's first encounter with the law inspired him. He wanted to learn more. Soon afterward, he found a copy of the Revised Statutes of Indiana in a friend's library. He devoured the pages with the same appetite he had earlier showed for *Aesop's Fables* and *Pilgrim's Progress*. It became his first course at law school.

14.

"River Man"

In the fall of 1828, James Gentry, the main shopkeeper in Gentryville, needed a hired hand. He was looking for a skilled, reliable boatman to take his supplies of pork, flour, bacon, produce and livestock down the Mississippi River to New Orleans to trade for profit.

He knew he could trust Abe Lincoln. His honesty was beyond question. He showed that he could handle the tricky currents, snags and sand bars on the river. Gentry was certain that this raw-boned giant could manhandle any bushwackers or river pirates who had ideas of looting the boat.

In pioneer days, most business was done by barter. You could take soap, cloth, pots and pans, or any item from the shelf of the local store in return for some of your farm produce. Storekeepers always kept large supplies of produce on hand, which they could sell at many of the settlements along the Mississippi.

James Gentry was a successful businessman. "I know," he once said, "when I buy an article in Louisville for a dollar and sell it in Gentryville for two dollars, I double my money every time." *(1)*

For his latest venture to New Orleans, Gentry hired a crew of two. He sent his son Allen to look after his business. Abe was in charge of the boat. For devising, engineering and constructing a flatboat, loading the cargo, seeing the cargo safely a thousand miles down river, negotiating business deals and returning with a handsome profit, Abe was paid eight dollars a month.

For two years now, Abe had been watching steamers and

flatboats rolling up and down the great waterway. He heard the talk of passengers and crewmen about life on the river. He became very interested in his father's stories about his journey to New Orleans twenty-two years before. Now he questioned his father closely—how could he steer the flatboat through strong winds and tugging currents? How could he shift directions quickly to avoid fallen trees and sand bars? And how about the fabled city of New Orleans—was it really like they say? Tom Lincoln reminded his son that back in 1806 there was no such thing as a steamboat to bring flatboat crews home in comfort. In those days they had to walk or ride horseback.

Abe and Allen got to work near the water's edge, cutting down giant oaks and poplars and hewing them into planks. They began to assemble the hull, bottom-side up. When it was ready, they hitched a team of oxen to the end of a rope to turn the hull over. The boat was about 65-feet long and 18-feet wide. It had a cabin for shelter and two pairs of long oars at the bow and stern.

While the boat was under construction, Abe lived at the home of Alfred Grass near the river bank. He was at work on the boat all day and would come home tired. Still he kept his evenings free for his favorite pastime. One of the family remembered how Abe "would sit in the evening near the table with the rest of the family until the tallow dip (candles) had burned out. Then he would lie down on his back with his head toward the open fireplace so as to get the light upon the pages of the book, and there he would often read until after midnight. . . . He would bake the top of his head or wear himself out for want of rest, but he was always up in the morning ready for work." (2)

The flatboat was finished in December but the crew was not yet ready to leave. A hitch developed in their plans. Mrs. Allen Gentry, the former Kate Roby, Abe's school friend, was due to have a baby. It was an event no father would want to miss. So they waited. Then on December 18, 1828, the second James Gentry was born. Two weeks later the boys were off to New Orleans.

They poled and paddled by day through clear and still waters and windblown whitecaps. At night they pulled ashore and when they spotted other craft approaching they waved a lantern or a piece of burning firewood.

Along the Ohio they passed by "Cave-in-Rock," a huge cavern on the Illinois shore with its infamous sign: Wilson's Liquor Vault and House of Entertainment. Inside, a few years later, explorers would find 60 human skeletons, boatmen and travelers, all lured and robbed by the Wilson gang.

One river traveler, a member of the British Parliament, happened to make the journey downriver a few weeks before Abraham and Allen. He wrote his impressions in a diary describing the same scenes the boys would see: "During the whole day we had no view save the interminable forest and dull ragged banks on both sides. . . . Very few settlements have yet been attempted and these generally on high bluffs. . . . We passed only one today where I observed something like the appearance of a village. . . .

"We saw several flocks of wild turkeys on the shore. One of our party killed a bird from the boat with his rifle. Most of the Americans in this part of the country are excellent shots. . . .

"The number of steamboats here is almost incredible. Went on board several that were lying below us. The largest, called the "Washington," is built like a three story house and with every accommodation that could be found in a good hotel." Flatboats, he said, were "built something like an immense coffin."

When the Englishman's boat crossed the Ohio into the Mississippi, he noted that "you soon discover the difference in the character of the two rivers. The Ohio moving slow and placid whilst the Mississippi sweeps along with a fierce and tempestuous current." (3)

Every day the nineteen-year-old boatman learned more about the tricks of this vast "Father of Waters." He learned to handle the bends and sweeps of the river with a quick, sure tug on the oars. He could steer a steady course through sudden violent rainstorms and blasts of shifting winds.

Yet the river had its feints and illusions. Abe had to keep his wits about him. From far downriver he would hear a growing roar and rumble. Dangerous white rapids? Or was it the river current beating against a downed tree trunk? Out of the dark morning mists he'd see a huge black form slowly coming at him. A steamer wildly off course, its captain asleep? Or maybe the dim light and drizzly air were playing tricks on his eyes, seeming to propel a perfectly still island?

When they reached Baton Rouge, about 150 miles above New Orleans, the boys tied their boat for the night near the plantation of Madame Duchesne and expected to stay a few days. Here was a ripe market and the boys hoped to do brisk business. This was the Louisiana "sugar coast," rows of prosperous sugar plantations side by side along the shore. "The nature of part of the cargo load . . . made it necessary . . . to linger and trade along the Sugar Coast," Abe said. (4)

Here, while they slept, the mortal dangers of the river were silently creeping up on them. Here might have ended the life of a future President. "One night," relates Abe, "[We] were attacked by seven negroes with intent to kill and rob." (5)

The raiders were eyeing the merchandise, ready to kill the witnesses and send the boat to the bottom. Seven of them could not overpower the two furious boatmen. Abe grabbed a crab-tree club. His long arms swinging in giant sweeps, the club mauled flesh and crushed bone. The attackers kept their distance. When they decided they'd had enough they jumped off the boat and lit out for the woods. The boatmen followed to make sure they weren't coming back.

"[We] were hurt some in the melee," said Abe, "but succeeded in driving the negroes from the boat, and then cut cable, weighed anchor, and left." (6)

As the boat pulled away, Abe dabbed at his bloody face with a bandana. The gash healed, said Leonard Swett, "making a scar which he wore always, and which he showed me at the time of telling this story." (7)

In a few days the boys were paddling their flatboat into the harbor of the exotic city of New Orleans. Abe had never seen such a large city. Nothing in any Kentucky or Indiana village could prepare him for the experience in New Orleans.

The English scribe who visited New Orleans a few weeks before Allen and Abe arrived saw a city that was "built like an old French provincial town—the same narrow streets, old fashioned houses and lamps suspended by a chain across the road. . . ."

He saw "bogs, swamps, morasses in every direction. . . . Mosquitoes are, of course, abundant. Even now they swarm in mirriads [myriads] as bad as in the worst places in the West Indies.

"I should suppose that New Orleans . . . is not famous for its morality or religious feeling. Those who come here on account of trade think only of making money as fast as they can and trouble themselves very little about other matters." (8)

Miles and miles of water-going craft of all sorts lay at anchor outside the city—steamers, flatboats, arks, rafts, schooners and sloops from all over the world. These ships would soon be off for such faraway places as Hamburg, Gibraltar, Bremen, Nantz, Havana, Vera Cruz, New York and Philadelphia.

There were sailors and deckhands from many nations jabbering to each other in strange tongues Abe could not understand. He heard conversations in French, Dutch, Creole, Swedish, Italian, Spanish and Russian. He heard, for the first time, a sort of English spoken with a curious twang ("Ow, blimey mates!") when he met British sailors. A mix of languages flew past his ear like the chattering of animals at dawn.

He passed saloons by the dozen, where beautiful women sipping French wine or Jamaica Rum whispered and laughed with the sailors. He saw the posters around town advertising a public showing of an Egyptian mummy and sarcophagus over three thousand years old.

Gangs of slaves passed, handcuffed by the hundreds, headed for work in the cotton fields. "We stood and watched the slaves sold in New Orleans and Abraham was very angry," said Allen Gentry. (9)

The boys remained for a few days until they sold the rest of their cargo and their boat. Then they booked passage on a steamer heading north. This was Abe's first trip aboard a Mississippi steamship. On the way up the Mississippi and on to the Ohio they passed dozens of steamers on their way to or from New Orleans. The steamships had names like "DeWitt Clinton," "Isabella," "Patriot," "Lady Washington," "Montezuma," "Amazon," "Crusader," "Daniel Boone" and "Lady of the Lake."

Abe passed his twentieth birthday away from home. By spring of 1829 he was back home in Indiana working on his father's farm and hiring out to neighbors, felling trees, splitting rails, plowing fields, grinding meal, or feeding livestock. Whatever Abe had left of the $24 he earned on his three-month trip to New Orleans he turned over to his father. This was the law and the custom for a boy under twenty-one years of age. Said Dennis: "Tom owned Abe's time." (10)

Abe was changed now. Gentryville no longer satisfied him. He had a taste of the great world beyond his small frontier village. The "Great Rivers" called to him. He longed to be a steamboat captain piloting his craft up and down the "Father of Waters." "He was all fur bein' a river man fur a while," remarked Dennis. (11)

A neighbor, William Wood, knew about the steamboat business and recalled the day in 1829 when Abe suddenly appeared at his door. "Abe came to my house one day and stood round about timid and shy. I knew he wanted something. I said to him—'Abe, what is your care?'

"Abe replied—'I want you to go to the river and give me some recommendation to some boat.'

"I remarked—'Abe, your age is against you. You are not twenty-one yet.'

" 'I know that, but I want a good start,' said Abe."

Wood knew that Abe was capable and probably could handle a boat as well as any man. But he could not go against the custom. Explained Wood: "I concluded not to go for the boy's good." (12)

15.

"Snowbirds"

Fall 1829. Abe was looking ahead to February 12, 1830. On that date he would be twenty-one years old. He would be, in the eyes of the community, his own man.

He had been waiting anxiously for the time when he could leave home and begin to find his way in the world. Before he left he wanted to make sure his parents could manage without him. He decided to leave them a little going away present. The log cabin they called home in Indiana was now twelve years old, weathered and needing repair. Abe began to build a new and better cabin for his parents.

"Saw him cutting down a large tree one day," says William Wood. "I asked him what he was going to do with it. He said he was going to saw it into planks for his father's new house." (1)

Then suddenly the plans changed. "The house was not completed," Wood said. (2)

Abe sold some of the lumber to Josiah Crawford and what was left he used to fashion wagon wheels, axles and a carriage. The entire household of Lincolns, Johnstons, Hankses, Halls, their wives, children and grandchildren, were moving to Illinois.

"I reckon it was John Hanks 'at got restless fust an' lit out fur Illinois an' wrote fur us all to come an' he'd get land fur us," said Dennis. (3)

"I moved from Kentucky to Illinois in the fall of 1828 . . .," John Hanks explained. "I wrote to Thomas Lincoln what kind of a country it was." (4)

The Indians called it "Sangamo"—"land of plenty to eat."

Said Herndon: "The final syllable of this name was then pro-
nounced to rhyme with 'raw.' " *(5)*

Dennis was easy to persuade. The milk sickness was back in
the territory. In one week Dennis lost four milk-cows and eleven
calves. He had to be taken to bed with the sickness and nearly
died. "I'm goin' to git out o' here and hunt a country where the
milk-sick is not," resolved Dennis. "It's like to ruin me. . . . *(6)*
This was reason enough, ain't it, for leaving?" *(7)*

Dennis visited his cousin John in Illinois and was greatly
impressed. He decided to move his family there and had no
trouble selling the idea to his brother-in-law Squire Hall. So
their wives, Elizabeth Johnston Hanks and Matilda Johnston
Hall began packing their belongings. When Sally Lincoln got
wind of this she "could not think of parting with them," *(8)*
according to Dennis. Finally, said Dennis, "the proposition . . .
met with the general consent of the Lincoln family." *(9)*

Tom Lincoln prepared his family for a move once more. The
Lincoln farm on Little Pigeon Creek did not prove to be a wise
investment. After buying his eighty acres at $2 an acre and
tending the land for fourteen years, Tom had to sell it for a loss.
Charles Grigsby paid him $125 for the farm.

They joked about how moving was in Tom's blood. "Tom was
always ready to move . . . always lookin' fur the land o' Canaan,"
said Dennis. *(10)* They said that the family had moved so often
that the chickens could tell the signs of the next move and
would walk up to Tom and lay belly-up with their feet in the air
waiting to be tied and loaded on the wagon.

Since the church played such an important role in the lives of
settlers on the frontier, families often requested letters of dismission from their home church. This would show their new
neighbors that they were good citizens and God-fearing people.
On December 12, 1829, the records of the Little Pigeon Church
noted that "The church granted Brother Tho. Lincoln and wife
a letter of Dismission." *(11)*

A few weeks later, on January 10, 1830, another entry
appeared in the church records. "Sister Nancy Grigsby informed
the church that she is not satisfied with Br. and Sister Lincoln.
The church agreed and called back their letters until satisfaction
could be obtained." *(12)*

Bad feelings remained between the Grigsbys and the Lincolns. Nancy Grigsby was still smarting from the "Chronicles of Reuben" prank some months earlier when Abe turned two of her boys into laughingstocks on their wedding night; still angry over the wild brawl instigated by Abe himself when he interfered in a fair fight between her son William and Abe's step-brother John Johnston; still brooding over the Lincoln family's bitterness at the untimely death of Sarah Lincoln Grigsby, the wife of Reuben Grigsby was not about to let the Lincolns leave Indiana without a smudge on their good name.

Whatever objection Mrs. Grigsby raised was not taken seriously. An addition to the January 10 note states: "The parties convened at Wm. Hoskins and agreed and settled the difficulty." (13)

Apparently, Mrs. Grigsby's objection did nothing to affect Tom Lincoln's good standing in the church. At the next meeting Mrs. Grigsby was complaining again. The record shows that: "Sister Grigsby laid in a charge against Sister Elizabeth Crawford for falsehood." (14) A committee of five men was appointed to settle the case. It was ordered that "the decision of the above committee shall be the decision of the church." (15) One of the men appointed to judge the fairness of Mrs. Grigsby's charge was Brother Thomas Lincoln.

By the middle of February the Lincolns were ready to go. The family of four that endured their first Indiana winter in an open-faced hunter's hut fourteen years earlier was no longer. Only Abe and his father were left of the original Lincolns. Now there were three families. "There was thirteen in the three families," recounted Dennis. "Thos. Lincoln, wife, Abe. J.D. Johnston, Squire Hall, wife (Matilda Johnston Hall), son. Dennis F. Hanks, wife (Elizabeth Johnston Hanks), 3 daughters, one son. (16)

"Piled everything into ox-wagons an' we all went— Linkhorns, an' Hankses an' Johnstons, all hangin' together," said Dennis. "I reckon we was like one o' them tribes o' Israel that you kain't break up nohow." (17)

Abe had just passed his twenty-first birthday. He was, by law and custom, a man. He had every right to strike out on his own. But he would not desert his father, now past fifty, at a time when the hardship and struggle of making a new home out of wilderness land was about to begin all over again.

Abe decided to celebrate his coming of age by trying a new business venture. James Gentry's son told how Abe spent his last evening in Indiana at his father's store: "He and Lincoln spent considerable time on that last night making selection of notions." (18) Abe picked up thirty dollars worth of pins, needles, thread, buttons, tinware and assorted household items. He planned to peddle his stock along the route to earn a few extra dollars. Now, at twenty-one, he was entitled to keep every penny earned.

Before leaving there was a silent vigil by the graveside of Nancy Hanks Lincoln, now twelve years in the ground. The family also paid a last visit to Abe's sister Sarah in the church-yard cemetery just as they had stopped at the grave of baby Thomas Lincoln fourteen years before in Kentucky.

"March 1, 1830," he wrote in his autobiographical sketch, "Abraham, having just completed his twenty-first year [actually, he just celebrated his twenty-first birthday], his father and family with the families of the two daughters and sons-in-law of his stepmother left the old homestead in Indiana and came to Illinois. Their mode of conveyance was wagons drawn by ox-teams and Abraham drove one of the teams." (19)

Dennis's young daughter later recalled that they made the trip with "three covered wagons, two drawn by oxen and one by horses, and two saddle horses." (20)

Whenever a family left their village for good, it was traditional for all their friends and neighbors to gather round them as they pulled away to wish them well. "I well remember the day when the Lincolns started for Illinois," said James Gentry. "Nearly all the neighbors was there to see them leave." (21)

"I helped to hitch the two yoke of oxen to the wagon and went with them half a mile," remembered Redmond Grigsby. (22)

One of James Gentry's sons later planted a cedar tree at the Lincoln home in memory of his friend Abraham.

Years later, his boyhood friend David Turnham recalled him fondly: "I was well and intimately acquainted with Mr. Lincoln from March 1819 until he left for Illinois, having lived in one mile of him all that time. Went to school with him, hunted game with him, worked on the river filling up a flat boat with him where the surrounding influence was very bad. I believe I knew as much of Abraham Lincoln until he left Indiana as any other man living and I never knew anything dishonorable of him." (23)

Bellowing "Haw!" or "Git up!" the men whipped the animals into action and the wagons pulled away. "It took us two weeks to git thar," said Dennis, "raftin' over the Wabash, cuttin' our way through the woods, fordin' rivers, pryin' wagons an' steers out o' sloughs with fence rails, an' makin' camp.

"Abe cracked a joke every time he cracked a whip an' he found a way out o' every tight place while the rest of us was standin' 'round scratchin' our fool heads." (24)

"Mr. Lincoln once described this journey to me," said Billy Herndon. "He said the ground had not yet yielded up the frosts of winter; that during the day the roads would thaw out on the surface and at night freeze over again, thus making travelling, especially with oxen, painfully slow and tiresome.

"There were, of course, no bridges and the party were consequently driven to ford the streams unless by a circuitous route they could avoid them. In the early part of the day (they) were also frozen slightly and the oxen would break through a square yard of thin ice at every step.

"Among other things which the party brought with them was a pet dog which trotted along after the wagon. One day the little fellow fell behind and failed to catch up till after they had crossed the stream. Missing him, they looked back and there, on the opposite bank he stood, whining and jumping about in great distress. The water was running over the broken edges of the ice and the poor animal was afraid to cross. It would not pay to turn the oxen and wagon back and ford the stream again in order to recover a dog and so the majority, in their anxiety to move forward, decided to go on without him."

"I could not endure the idea of abandoning even a dog," said Abe. "Pulling off shoes and socks, I waded across the stream and triumphantly returned with the shivering animal under my arm. His frantic leaps of joy and other evidences of a dog's gratitude amply repaid me for all the exposure I had undergone." (25)

112

Meanwhile, Abe was doing some brisk business. According to the son of Captain William Jones, a clerk at Gentry's store, Abe was filling his pockets with silver: "When the Lincolns reached their new home near Decatur, Illinois, Abraham wrote back to my father stating that he had doubled his money on his purchases by selling them along the road." (26)

Travelling salesmen were not always welcome, Abe discovered. One day, he carried his pack of needles and knickknacks to the door of a farmhouse. He heard wailing and whimpering inside and when he peeked in he saw an assortment of youngsters, boys and girls from seventeen months to seventeen years. Every one was howling like wolves in a pack. Their mother, red-haired and red-faced, waved a whip as she eyed the stranger at her doorway.

Abe got the impression that there wouldn't be much use in asking the woman if she wanted some needles, thread or pots and pans.

The woman demanded to know what he was doing there.

"Nothing, madam," he answered. "I merely dropped in as I came along to see how things were going."

"Well, you needn't wait," barked the woman. "There's trouble here, and lots of it too. But I kin manage my own affairs without the help of outsiders. This is jest a family row. But I'll teach these brats their places ef I have to lick the hide off every one of 'em. I don't do much talkin' but I run this house so I don't want no one sneakin' round tryin' to find out how I do it, either." (27)

They finally crossed into Illinois. "Reached the county of Macon and stopped there some time within the same month of March," said Abe. (28)

They passed through the town of Decatur, near where John Hanks lived. Years later, as a prominent lawyer, Abraham visited Decatur. One of his colleagues remembered when they walked past the courthouse together: "Lincoln walked out a few feet in front and after shifting his position two or three times said as he looked up at the building, partly to himself and partly to me—'Here is the exact spot where I stood by our wagon when we moved from Indiana twenty-six years ago. This isn't six feet from the exact spot.'

"I asked him if he, at that time, had expected to be a lawyer and practice law in that courthouse, to which he replied: 'No, I didn't know I had sense enough to be a lawyer then.' " (29)

They spent the night at John Hanks' place, four miles outside Decatur. The next morning, Hanks led them to the spot he had chosen for them, "ten miles west of Decatur and about a hundred steps from . . . the Sangamon River and on the north side of it on a kind of bluff," he said. (30)

"It was a purty kentry up on the Sangamon," observed Dennis. (31)

"Here [we] built a log cabin . . . ," said Abe, "Made sufficient rails to fence ten acres of ground. Fenced and broke the ground and raised a crop of sown corn upon it the same year." (32)

"The house—the logs of it I cut myself in 1829 . . . ," said John Hanks. "Gave them to old man Lincoln." (33)

Said Dennis: "Abe helped put up a cabin fur Tom on the Sangamon." (34)

They barely got settled in their new home when nature reminded them that she was to be reckoned with. "In the autumn," said Abe, "all hands were greatly afflicted with ague and fever." (35)

"We had fever'n ager turrible!" agreed Dennis. (36)

"They were greatly discouraged," admitted Abe, "so much so that they determined on leaving the county. They remained, however, through the succeeding winter." (37)

This was "the winter of the very celebrated 'deep snow' of Illinois," Abe said. (38) It was Christmas week. Snows blasted blankets of white two-and-a-half feet deep. The blizzard raged for two days. When it stopped, the white cover was frozen solid. Then another storm buried the prairie until the snow was four feet deep.

Temperatures fell suddenly by forty degrees. If you were caught outside your clothing might have frozen to your skin. The feet of geese and chickens stuck fast to the ice. Cows, hogs and horses froze or starved. Men on horseback caught on the prairie during the storm killed their mounts, disemboweled them and crawled inside the carcasses to keep warm. Those who made it to a town were stuck to their saddles and had to be taken down attached and carried indoors to thaw out.

Homes and villages were cut off from each other for weeks.

Travel was impossible. Families with no reserve stocks of meat or corn starved to death in their cabins. Those with no wood to burn froze.

By February, the Lincolns were running out of food. Abe made a desperate run to the nearest neighbor, the Warnicks, three miles away. When he reached their house, his feet were nearly frozen. Mrs. Warnick packed his feet in snow to take out the frostbite then rubbed them in grease. He was laid up for days.

Spring came. The snow cover melted and the prairie swelled with rivers of water and mud. The Illinois settlers who survived the ordeal always referred to the winter of 1830-31 as the year of the "deep snow." They called themselves "Snowbirds." (39) They were happy to be alive.

16.

"I Found Him No Green Horn"

As the deep snow began to melt, a refreshing spring breeze blew in from the Sangamon River. He was windy: a fast-talking, hard-drinking hustler, a maker of schemes, a chaser of dreams. His name was Denton Offut and he was well known in Sangamon County for his trading operations up and down the Sangamon River. In his nimble fingers, Abe's life was about to take a new turn.

"He was certainly an odd character," says Herndon. *(1)* His cronies maintained that he was "a clear-headed, brisk man of affairs." Others knew better. "Wild, noisy, reckless," they called him. They said he was "rattlebrained, unsteady and improvident." *(2)* One of his acquaintances described him as a "wild harum-scarum kind of a man." *(3)*

Denton Offut was now in Decatur, brewing up a new scheme. He had recently acquired a large stock of goods that he could unload for a handsome profit down in New Orleans. He needed some hired help to get it there and came to town looking for John Hanks.

"Offut came to my house in February 1831," said Hanks. "Wanted to hire me to run a flatboat for him, saying that he had heard that I was quite a flatboat man in Kentucky. He wanted me to go badly." *(4)*

Hanks knew a good business deal when he saw one. If he was going to make the trip he'd need an experienced and reliable crew. "I went and saw Abe and John Johnston . . . ," he said.

"Introduced Offut to them. We made an engagement with Offut at 50 cents per day and $60 to make the trip to New Orleans." *(5)*

Added Abe: "[We] were to join him—Offut—at Springfield, Illinois so soon as the snow should go off. When it did go off, which was about the first of March 1831, the county was so flooded as to make traveling by land impracticable. . . . Purchased a large canoe and came down the Sangamon River in it. This is the time and the manner of Abraham's first entrance into Sangamon County." *(6)*

"Abe and I came down the Sangamon River in a canoe in March 1831," recalled John Hanks. "Landed at what is now called . . . Jamestown, five miles east of Springfield. . . . We left our canoe . . . walked afoot to Springfield and found Offut. He was at a tavern. Probably Elliot's. It was Elliot's." *(7)*

Andrew Elliot kept the Buckhorn Inn, the finest tavern in Springfield. A painted figure of a buck's head swung freely above the front door. Inside, the boys found Offut cheerfully sipping Mr. Elliot's fine spirits.

Offut had promised that a boat would be waiting for them when they came to town. "Learned from him that he had failed in getting a boat," said Abe. *(8)*

The boys were undaunted. They could build their own boat and told Offut so. He agreed to hire them to build a flatboat at twelve dollars a month.

John Hanks described how the boys went to work on Offut's new enterprise: "Abe, Johnston and myself went down to the mouth of Spring Creek . . . five miles north of Springfield . . . and there cut the timbers to make the boat. . . . We then rafted the logs down to the Sangamon River, to what is called Sangamontown, seven miles northwest of Springfield.

"When we got to Sangamontown we made a shanty shed. Abe was elected cook. We sawed our lumber at Kirkpatrick's Mill. . . . We finished making and launching the boat in about four weeks." *(9)*

Sangamontown was a small flourishing frontier settlement on the Sangamon River. Newcomers were watched closely. The three men who appeared on the river bank to work on a boat did not escape scrutiny. One villager, Caleb Carman, stopped to talk to the men and was impressed by the tall one. "When I first saw him I thought him a green horn, though after half hour's conversation with him I found him no green horn." *(10)*

Abe called himself "chief cook and bottle-washer." *(11)* His appearance was so striking that he attracted everyone's attention. John Roll, who helped them work on their raft, observed that: "He was a tall, gaunt young man, dressed in a suit of blue homespun jeans, consisting of a round-about jacket, waistcoat and breeches which came to within about four inches of his feet. The latter were encased in rawhide boots, into the tops of which—most of the time—his pantaloons were stuffed. He wore a soft felt hat which had at one time been black, but now, as its owner dryly remarked, 'was sunburned until it was a combine of colors.' " *(12)*

When evening came the men of the town gathered near the mill to "shoot the breeze," tell their stories, joke, whittle and talk. Abe quickly won over the entire village with his tales and yarns. Some of the men would peel a log and use it for a bench so that they could sit and listen to Abe's stories. "Whenever he'd end up in his unexpected way, the boys on the log would whoop and roll off," said John Roll. *(13)*

Someone noticed the effect from the men repeatedly falling off the log. It was polished shiny like a mirror. The men blamed Abe for this and christened their seat "Abe's log."

"Abe was full of jokes during all this time," remarked John Hanks. "Kept us all alive." *(14)*

"I saw Abe at a show one night at Sangamontown," remembered Caleb Carman. "The showman cooked eggs in Abe's hat. Abe, when the man called for his hat, said—'The reason why I didn't give you my hat before was out of respect to your eggs, not care for my hat.' *(15)*

"It caused a great laugh," said Carman. "But Lincoln turned the joke very well, as he always did on any occasion." *(16)*

The boat was ready in April. A few days before the boys were set to leave some of the men found themselves in a dangerous predicament. Abe was called on to make a daring rescue. John Roll was there and witnessed the excitement:

"It was the spring following the winter of the deep snow. Walter Carman, John Seamon and myself, and at times others of

the Carman boys, had helped Abe in building the boat. . . .
When we had finished we went to work to make a dugout or
canoe to be used as a small boat with the flat. We found a
suitable log about an eighth of a mile up the river and with our
axes went to work under Lincoln's direction.

"The river was very high, fairly booming. After the dugout
was ready to launch we took it to the edge of the water and made
ready to let her go. Walter Carman and John Seamon jumped in
as the boat struck water, each one anxious to be the first to get a
ride. As they shot out from the shore they found they were
unable to make any headway against the strong current. Carman
had the paddle and Seamon was in the stern of the boat.

"Lincoln shouted to them to 'head up stream' and 'work back
to shore' but they found themselves powerless against the
stream. At last they began to pull for the wreck of an old
flatboat, the first ever built on the Sangamon, which had sunk
and gone to pieces leaving one of the stanchions sticking above
the water. Just as they reached it, Seamon made a grab and
caught hold of the stanchion when the canoe capsized, leaving
Seamon clinging to the old timber and throwing Carman into
the stream. It carried him down with the speed of a mill-race.
Lincoln raised his voice above the roar of the flood and yelled to
Carman to swim for an old tree which stood almost in the
channel. . . .

"Carman, being a good swimmer, succeeded in catching a
branch and pulled himself up out of the water, which was very
cold and had almost chilled him to death. There he sat shivering
and chattering in the tree.

"Lincoln, seeing Carman safe, called out to Seamon to let go
the stanchion and swim for the tree. With some hesitation he
obeyed . . . while Lincoln cheered and directed him from the
bank. As Seamon neared the tree he made one grab for a branch
and missing it, went under the water. Another desperate lunge
was successful and he climbed up beside Carman. Things were
pretty exciting now, for there were two men in the tree and the
boat was gone.

"It was a cold, raw April day and there was great danger of the
men becoming benumbed and falling back into the water.
Lincoln called out to them to keep their spirits up and he would

save them. The village had been alarmed by this time and many people had come down to the bank.

"Lincoln procured a rope and tied it to a log. He called all hands to come and help roll the log into the water and after this had been done, he, with the assistance of several others, towed it some distance up the stream. A daring young fellow by the name of Jim Dorrell then took his seat on the end of the log and it was pushed out into the current with the expectation that it would be carried down stream against the tree where Seamon and Carman were.

"The log was well directed and went straight to the tree. But Jim, in his impatience to help his friends, fell a victim to his good intentions. Making a frantic grab at a branch, he raised himself off the log which was swept from under him by the raging water and he soon joined the other two victims upon their forlorn perch.

"The excitement on shore increased and almost the whole population of the village gathered on the river bank. Lincoln had the log pulled up the stream and securing another piece of rope called to the men in the tree to catch it if they could when he should reach the tree. He then straddled the log himself and gave the word to push out into the stream.

"When he dashed into the tree he threw the rope over the stump of a broken limb and let it play until it broke the speed of the log and gradually drew it back to the tree, holding it there until the three now nearly frozen men had climbed down and seated themselves astride. He then gave orders to the people on the shore to hold fast to the end of the rope which was tied to the log and leaving his rope in the tree he turned the log adrift. The force of the current, acting against the taut rope, swung the log around against the bank and all on board were saved.

"The excited people, who had watched the dangerous experiment with alternate hope and fear, now broke into cheers for Abe Lincoln and praises for his brave act. The adventure made quite a hero of him along the Sangamon and the people never tired telling of the exploit." (17)

17.

"I'll Hit It Hard"

"It was in connection with this boat that occurred the ludicrous incident of sewing up the hogs eyes," Abe recalled. "Offut bought thirty-odd large fat live hogs but found difficulty in driving them from where he purchased them to the boat and thereupon conceived the whim that he could sew up their eyes and drive them where he pleased." *(1)*

"We caught them," related John Hanks, "Abe holding their heads and I their tails while Offut sewed up their eyes." *(2)*

"It proved to be no benefit," offered Coleman Smoot, "for the hogs scattered in every direction causing much trouble." *(3)*

"We tried to drive them aboard but could not," Hanks complained. "They would run back past us." *(4)*

Said Abe, "In their blind condition, they could not be driven out of the lot." *(5)*

"At last," Hanks said, "becoming tired, we carried them to the boat." *(6)*

Finally the boys were ready to go. The Ark, packed tight with barrels of meat, produce and dozens of squealing hogs, merged into the downriver currents of the Sangamon River bound for New Orleans. Their adventures were just beginning.

"We landed at the New Salem mill about April 19th and got fast (stuck) on Rutledge's mill dam . . .," said John Hanks. "On the dam part of a day and one night." *(7)*

Their one-thousand-mile journey had barely begun and already their boat was stranded. For twenty-four hours the bow hung helplessly in the air over the dam's edge. The cargo was slowly slipping astern, dangerously unbalancing the boat. Crowds of New Salem residents gathered atop the bluff overlooking the river to watch the befuddled boatmen. They called to the boys, shouting their advice and encouragement. Denton Offut stood on the shore, watching his financial empire slowly going under.

Ingoring the catcalls and comments from the shore, the tall boatman went to work to save his plunging craft. "We will have to get the boat to the shore and unload it or it will sink," he barked to his mates. (8)

"We unloaded the boat," said Hanks. "That is, we transferred the goods from our boat to a borrowed one. We then rolled the barrels forward. Lincoln bored a hole in the end over the dam. The water which had leaked in ran out and we slid over." (9)

The New Salem crowd greatly appreciated this show of resourcefulness by the tall boatman. They gave him a rousing cheer. Offut was beside himself with glee. He swore to the amused New Salemers that he would be back. He promised them a steamboat, the first ever to navigate the Sangamon. It troubled his spirit of ingenuity not the slightest to think that the Sangamon River ran dangerously low in summer and froze in winter.

"Offut said he intended to build it with rollers underneath so that when it came to a sand bar it would roll right over and runners underneath for to run on the ice," explained Coleman Smoot. "Offut seemed to think that with Lincoln as pilot . . . there was no such thing as fail." (10)

"By thunder!" Offut bellowed, "She would have to go!" (11)

"We then proceeded," said John Hanks, "Offut, John Johnston, Abe Lincoln and myself down the Sangamon River. . . . We kept our victuals and, in fact, slept down in the boat at one end. Went down by a kind of ladder through a scatter hole. . . . Rushed through Beardstown in a hurry—people came out and laughed at us. Passed Alton, Cairo and stopped at Memphis, Vicksburg, Natchez.

"I can say we soon—say in May—landed in New Orleans," Hanks said. (12) They tied their flatboat beside thousands of others and stepped out, walking nearly a mile over boats at anchor until they reached the shore.

The boys lingered in New Orleans for a month, drinking in the city like world travelers. "For the first time," wrote Herndon, "Lincoln beheld the true horrors of human slavery." (13)

Everywhere were signs of trading and dealing in human flesh. Advertisements and posters offered to "pay the highest prices in cash for good and likely Negroes." (14)

One trading company sent out this notice: "We have now on hand and intend to keep throughout the entire year a large and well-selected stock of Negroes, consisting of field hands, house servants, mechanics, cooks, seamstresses, washers, ironers, etc., which we can sell and will sell as low or lower than any other house here or in New Orleans. Persons wishing to purchase would do well to call on us before making purchases elsewhere as our fresh and regular arrivals will keep us supplied with a good and general assortment. Our terms are liberal. Give us a call." (15)

One businessman announced: "I will at all times pay the highest cash prices for Negroes of every description and will also attend to the sale of Negroes on commission, having a jail and yard fitted up expressly for boarding them." (16)

Another proclaimed that: "The undersigned would respectfully state to the public that he has forty-five Negroes now on hand, having this day received a lot of twenty-five direct from Virginia—two or three good cooks, a carriage driver, a good house boy, a fiddler, a fine seamstress, and a likely lot of field men and women—all of whom he will sell at a small profit." (17)

There were buyers: "Wanted—I want to purchase twenty-five likely Negroes between the ages of 18 and 25 years, male and female, for which I will pay the highest prices in cash." (18)

And more sellers: "For sale—several likely girls from 10 to 18 years old, a woman 24, a very valuable woman 25, with three very likely children." (19)

"We saw Negroes chained, maltreated, whipped and scourged," related Hanks. "Lincoln saw it. His heart bled. Said nothing much. Was silent from feelings. Was sad. Looked bad. Felt bad. Was thoughtful and abstracted. I can say knowingly that it was on this trip that he formed his opinions of slavery. . . . I have heard him say often and often. . . . It ran its iron in him then and there—May 1831." *(20)*

"One morning," wrote Herndon, "in their rambles over the city, the trio passed a slave auction. A vigorous and comely mulatto girl was being sold. She underwent a thorough examination at the hands of the bidders. They pinched her flesh and made her trot up and down the room like a horse to show how she moved and in order, as the auctioneer said, that 'bidders might satisfy themselves' whether the article they were offering to buy was sound or not. The whole thing was so revolting that Lincoln moved away from the scene with a deep feeling of 'unconquerable hate.' Bidding his companions follow him he said: 'By God, boys! Let's get away from this. If ever I get a chance to hit that thing (meaning slavery), I'll hit it hard.'

"This incident was furnished me in 1865 by John Hanks," noted Herndon. "I have also heard Mr. Lincoln refer to it himself." *(21)*

Years later, Lincoln wrote about a steamboat journey he took as a young man. It haunted him, preyed on his conscience. It forced him to come face to face with the American horror that was slavery. "There were on board ten or a dozen slaves shackled together with iron," he said. "That sight was a continued torment to me." *(22)*

Slavery, the harrowing cancer that would bring a nation to war with itself, would finally be destroyed—years later—after four years of anguished bloodletting. The war would be nearly over when President Lincoln would condense a lifelong revulsion toward the buying and selling of human flesh into one simple, sharp-edged sentence. "Whenever I hear anyone arguing for slavery," he would later say bitterly, "I feel a strong impulse to see it tried on him personally." *(23)*

When the boys had enough of New Orleans they headed for home. "Offut, Johnston, Abe and myself left New Orleans in June 1831," Hanks recalled. "We came to St. Louis on the steamboat together, walked to Edwardsville, twenty-five miles east of St. Louis—Abe, Johnston and myself. Offut stayed behind in St. Louis. Abe and Johnston went to Coles County and I to Springfield, Sangamon County. Thomas Lincoln had moved to Coles County in 1831, in, say, June." *(24)*

Abe went home again to help his father with yet another move. He didn't remain long, probably just over a month. While he was there, he heard a loud, good-natured challenge. The undisputed champion wrestler in the county was a giant named Dan Needham. The champ had been hearing all about the new tall boy over at Goose Nest. "I can fling him three best out of four any day," he boasted. *(25)*

There was a house-raising at Wabash Point and a big crowd was there. Abe and Big Dan eyed each other and a war of nerves was on. The two giants stood face to face, each six feet four, each a mountain of muscle. "Abe," said Tom Lincoln, "rassle 'im." *(26)*

They set up a ring and the crowd egged them on. Four times Needham went down. The last time, Big Dan lost his head and came at Abe fists flying. Abe calmed him down with his friendly manner and finally Needham offered Abe his hand. "Well I'll be damned," he said. *(27)*

If Abe could beat all comers with his fists and brawn, he showed he could win with words as well. He was in Decatur with John Hanks one day. It was election time and one of the candidates was there making a speech. "It was a bad one," Hanks remembered. "I said Abe could beat it. I turned down a box or keg and Abe made his speech. The other man was a candidate. Abe wasn't. Abe beat him to death.

"The man, after the speech was through, took Abe aside and asked him where he had learned so much. . . . Abe explained, stating his manner and method of reading and what he had read. The man encouraged Lincoln to persevere." *(28)*

Abe was now twenty-two years old. He was the wrestling champion of Coles County, Illinois. He had conquered the Mississippi and been down to New Orleans twice. He was a farm hand, a butcher, a boatman, a carpenter, a merchant and a clever speech maker. He was his own man. Abraham Lincoln was ready to take on the world.

"It must 'a ben about that time 'at Abe left home fur good," said Dennis Hanks. *(29)*

So Abe said his goodbyes to his father, his step-mother, his step-sisters and cousin Dennis and to all his little nieces and nephews. Many years would pass before he would see them again. He collected his belongings, which didn't amount to much, and wrapped them in a bandanna tied to the end of a stick. Slinging the bundle over his shoulder, Abe headed down the road to make his mark on history.

18.

"Floating Piece of Driftwood"

"Abraham stopped indefinitely and for the first time, as it were, by himself, at New Salem . . .," Abe wrote in his third-person autobiography. "This was in July 1831." (1)

New Salem, Illinois—population 100—was one of many villages that sprang up along the Sangamon River. It was about the same size as another small hamlet growing to the north called Chicago.

For a thousand years, shaggy buffalo, wild horses and Indians roamed the high bluffs overlooking the river where the village of New Salem appeared. "To reach it . . .," said Herndon, "the traveler must ascend a bluff a hundred feet above the general level of the surrounding county. . . . Skirting the base of the bluff is the Sangamon River, which, coming around a sudden bend from the south-east, strikes the rocky hill and is turned abruptly north. Here is an old mill driven by water-power and reaching across the river is the mill-dam on which Offut's vessel hung stranded in April 1831. As the river rolled . . . over the dam . . . the roar of water, like low, continuous, distant thunder, could be distinctly heard through the village day and night." (2)

New Salem began as a commercial enterprise that involved the entire community. "My father moved to and laid out the town of New Salem in the summer of 1829," said R. B. Rutledge. (3) James Rutledge and John Cameron bought the high land on the bluff and the rights to the river below. Here they built a mill-dam. A thousand wagon loads of gravel and stones were laid into the river and packed solid. "At times," recalled R. B. Rutledge, "when it was necessary to construct a dam to afford the proper water power, word would be sent through the neighborhood and the people would come ten and fifteen miles en masse and assist gratuitously in the work. . . . This is . . . an illustration of the generosity and nobleness of the settlers. . . .

"The mill was a saw and grist mill . . . the first one built on the Sangamon River. . . . Supplied a large section of country with its meal, flour and lumber.

"At that period, New Salem was a small village of not more than ten or fifteen families who lived in log cabins and who were as social and familiar as persons are who find themselves thus isolated from the great world outside." (4)

Farmers came from fifty miles around to have their grain mashed into flour and to buy salt, sugar, coffee, hardware and cloth at Rutledge's store. The stage coach, called the "mud wagon" by the settlers, came once a week carrying mail to the New Salem Post Office. At the peak of its prosperity, New Salem had two mills, two doctors, a school, a church, a saloon, a blacksmith, and four stores.

Many settlers could trace their roots back to Kentucky and Virginia. More distant roots were sprinkled into the population: Yankees from New England, Easterners from New York, some Pennsylvania Dutch and recent immigrants from Britain, Germany and France.

They worked hard and they played hard. Every Saturday, farm hands from around the countryside came riding into town. It was their day off and they were looking for a good time. They drank, wrestled and fought. There were horse races and foot races.

One of their favorite sports was gander pulling. A tough old goose was hung by his feet from the limb of a tree. His long slender neck was greased till it was too slippery to hold. Then the boys paid ten cents for a chance to get the gander. On horseback they would charge toward the struggling goose at full gallop then lunge out to grab the unfortunate bird by the neck. The rider who managed to pull its head clean off won the goose and the money.

On the frontier, disputes were settled with fists. Once, two men lost their heads and let angry words fly. They agreed to work out their differences on the other side of the river. The whole town watched them paddle across where they stripped and fought like wolves. When they didn't come back their friends grew concerned and sent a search party over. They found the two men down, exhausted and bleeding. They made them shake hands and brought them home. One man nursed his wounds for a year before he died.

There was another New Salem, where quiet, hard-working families strove to live decent and God-fearing lives. "Many . . . citizens never had to contend with its barbaric customs," said one resident. "Only those who trained in that school were subject to its conditions." (5)

There were barbecues, dances, house-raisings, wolf hunts and camp meetings. At quilting bees each guest would "take his or her needle as the case may be for any man can quilt as well as the woman." (6)

One popular pastime was shooting for beef. Someone would spread the word that there would be a beef shooting. Men gathered with their rifles at the appointed hour and wrote their names on a list alongside the number of shots they planned to take. The fee was twenty-five cents a shot. A board with a painted cross at the center served as the target. Judges graded the shots and the five best shooters won a part of the beef. The best shot got the hide. The next best had his choice of hindquarters and the third took the other hindquarters. The fourth took his choice of forequarters and the fifth got the remaining forequarter. The sixth won all the lead shot into the target.

The respectable folks in town tried to keep the forces for good in the community in balance. The church kept growing. One Sunday fifty men, women and children took their baptism in the Sangamon River. Dr. John Allen, a Presbyterian elder who organized the first Sunday School in the village, founded a spirited Temperance Society, which met regularly to try to find ways to discourage the general use of liquor. Members were required to make a lifelong pledge to drink no intoxicating liquors.

Whiskey was everywhere on the frontier. Good and decent folks who worked hard during the day looked for good times when their work was done. Wherever people gathered, laughed, sang, danced, at weddings, sporting events, meetings of all kinds, the whiskey would flow to help them have a good time.

Even church members would not give up their spirits. When Mentor Graham, New Salem's only schoolmaster, joined Dr. Allen's Temperance Society, the church trustees showed their displeasure by voting to suspend him. Then, to make sure their gesture would not be taken to mean an unqualified support of intoxication, they suspended another member of the congregation who had gone blind drunk.

One church member, puzzled by these actions, brought a bottle of whiskey to the next meeting. "Brethering," he announced, waving his whiskey bottle. "You have turned one member out because he would not drink and another because he got drunk. And now I wants to ask a question." He held the bottle over his head. "How much of this here critter does a man have to drink to remain in full felloership in this church?" (7)

New Salem began as a typical pioneer community on the edge of the frontier. "In the days of land offices and stage coaches it was a sprightly village with a busy market," Herndon wrote. "It had its day of glory." (8)

A dozen years after Rutledge and Cameron built their dam its promise of booming prosperity never materialized. The people all disappeared; New Salem became a deserted village. Abe was long gone by then. "With the departure of Lincoln from its midst, it went into rapid decline. (9) . . . Not a building, scarcely a stone is left to mark the place where it once stood," (10) Herndon said fifty years later. By then, New Salem had become a cow pasture.

When Abe arrived in New Salem it was alive and busy. He came there looking for Denton Offut, ready to begin a new career as a businessman, merchant and clerk.

"During this boat enterprise acquaintance with Offut, who was previously an entire stranger, he conceived a liking for

Abraham," Abe explained in his autobiography. "Believing he could turn him to account, he [Offut] contracted with him to act as clerk for him on his return from New Orleans, in charge of a store and mill at New Salem." (11)

When Abraham Lincoln ambled down the main street of New Salem, he saw some men gathered outside a cabin and he walked over. They immediately recognized him as the quick-thinking boatman who saved his craft from tipping over the mill several months before. When they asked him how things were going he told them he was just like a "floating piece of driftwood." (12)

It was Election Day in the state of Illinois. The men were voting. The clerk spotted the tall stranger and asked if he wanted to vote. So, for the first time in his life, Abe voted. According to the election returns dated August 1, 1831, Abraham Lincoln voted for a Congressman, two Justices of the Peace and two Constables. (13)

Serving as clerk for the election was the town schoolmaster, Mentor Graham. He remembered Abraham Lincoln's first appearance in New Salem. "The first time I saw him was an election day. We were deficient a clerk for the polls. Mr. Lincoln . . . was asked by some of us if he could write."

"Yes, a little," replied Abe.

"Will you act as clerk of elections today?" Graham asked.

Said Abe: "I will try and do the best I can if you request."

"He was then sworn in," said Graham, "and acted as clerk of the August election." (14)

He was hired on the spot. The custom in those days was to vote by word of mouth. Each voter stood in turn before the election judge to say which candidates he wanted to vote for. The judge would announce the voter's name and his candidates and the names would be duly recorded by the clerks. All of New Salem voted. That was how Abe got to know the names and faces of almost all the men in town on his first day there.

"Rapidly made acquaintances and friends," he observed. (15)

The folks at New Salem were drawn to this tall giant in the same way Gentryville was—by his dose of pleasant spirits and his knack for making people laugh. As that first afternoon wore on, the new clerk began to use the long moments between ballots for telling stories, delighting the crowd of voters and hangers-on.

Billy Herndon's cousin J. R. Herndon was one of those New Salem residents who happened to be standing around the election table. "In the afternoon, as things were dragging a little, Lincoln—the new man—began to spin out a stock of Indiana yarns," he remembered. "One that amused me more than any other he called the Lizard Story."

"The meeting house," Lincoln began, "was in the woods and quite a distance from any other house. It was only used once a month. The preacher, an old line Baptist, was dressed in coarse linen pantaloons and shirt of the same material. The pants, manufactured after the old fashion, with baggy legs and a flap in front, were made to attach to his frame without the aid of suspenders. A single button held his shirt in position and that was at the collar.

"He rose up in the pulpit and with a loud voice announced his text thus: 'I am the Christ whom I shall represent today.' About this time, a little blue lizard ran up his roomy pantaloons. The old preacher, not wishing to interrupt the steady flow of his sermon, slapped away on his legs expecting to arrest the intruder. But his efforts were unavailing and the little fellow kept on ascending higher and higher.

"Continuing the sermon, the preacher slyly loosened the central button which graced the waist-band of his pantaloons and with a kick, off came that easy-fitting garment. But meanwhile, Mr. Lizard had passed the equatorial line of waist-band and was calmly exploring that part of the preacher's anatomy which lay underneath the back of his shirt.

"Things were now growing interesting but the sermon was still grinding on. The next movement on the preacher's part was for the collar button and with one sweep of his arm off came the tow linen shirt.

"The congregation sat for an instant as if dazed. At length, one old lady in the rear of the room rose up and glancing at the excited object in the pulpit shouted at the top of her voice: 'If you represent Christ then I'm done with the Bible!' " (16)

19.

"The Best Feller That Ever Broke Into This Settlement"

"You ask, first: 'When did you first become acquainted with Lincoln?' " wrote R. B. Rutledge in a reply to Herndon. " 'Where was it and what was he doing?' I answer: In the year 1831 in the town of New Salem, Illinois. He was at that time a clerk in the store of Denton Offut, having just returned with Offut from New Orleans, with whom he had gone on a flatboat as a hand. . . . At that time he boarded with John Cameron, a partner of my father in laying out the town of New Salem." (1)

Sometime during the summer of 1831 two men driving an ox-team unloaded a thousand dollars worth of merchandise in front of a little log house at the edge of the bluff just overlooking the mill. Offut's long-awaited goods had arrived and soon the store was open for business. "Lincoln was placed in charge," said Herndon. (2)

His nose for fast deals always twitching, Offut added still another venture to his ever-growing business empire. Explained Herndon, "In keeping with his widely known spirit of enterprise Offut rented the Rutledge and Cameron mill which stood at the foot of the hill and thus added another iron to keep company with the half-dozen already in the fire. As a further test of his business ability Lincoln was placed in charge of this also." (3)

Ever the shrewd operator, Offut hired eighteen-year-old Bill Greene, son of the well-respected Squire Bowling Greene, as

Lincoln's assistant. Young Bill knew well all the citizens in town and could tell the head clerk whose money was good and whose wasn't. "Between the two," said Herndon, "a lifelong friendship sprang up." (4)

"Mr. Lincoln and I clerked together for Offut about 18 months," recalled Billy Greene. "Slept in the same cot. . . . When one turned over the other had to do likewise." (5)

Once, a small-time gambler got the best of Bill on a crooked deal and he (Bill) came back to the store hopping mad. Abe calmed him down with an idea on how he could get even. He told Bill to make a bet with this lowlife that he (Abe) could hoist a whiskey barrel off the floor, hold it over his head and take a drink from the bunghole. Bill found the gambler and bet him the best fur hat in the store. They watched as Abe lifted the barrel off the floor and, squatting down, held it between his knees as his mouth found the bunghole. He sucked in a mouthful of whiskey, then let the barrel down slowly, got up, and spat the whiskey on the floor. Bill won his bet.

Everyone was impressed by the way Abe could find quick solutions to almost any problem. No one was more impressed then Denton Offut. "Offut relied in no slight degree on the business capacity of his clerk," Herndon noted. "In his effusive way he praised him beyond reason." (6)

"He knows more than any man in the United States," boomed Offut. "Some day he will be President. . . . He can outrun, outlift, outwrestle and throw down any man in Sangamon County." (7)

The town liked Offut's new man, but they remained skeptical. Remarked one resident, "Honors such as Offut accorded to Abe were to be won before they were worn at New Salem." (8)

Talk of the clerk at Offut's reached a wooded settlement four miles out of town. It was called Clary's Grove after John Clary, the first settler to build a cabin in that part of the woods. Now there were about twenty-five farmers in that little hamlet.

Everybody in the county knew about the "Clary's Grove Boys." Led by Bill Clary, brother of the original pioneer, and Jack Armstrong, the toughest fighter in the county, they stirred up all the "rowdyism or revelry in a circuit of twenty miles," remembered one New Salemite. (9)

"The boys . . . were a terror to the entire region," observed Billy Herndon. *(10)* They descended on New Salem every Saturday to meet the farm boys from the other villages and raise a little hell. They would cut the girth of a man's saddle—the strap around the horse's belly—and roll with laughter when the unsuspecting rider tried to mount and fell flat, pulling the saddle on top of him. They might sneak stones under the saddle so that when the owner sat atop his horse the stones pressed hard into the horse's backbone sending the animal into fits of frenzy that would throw even the toughest riders. Sometimes they would clean a horse up by trimming the animal's mane and tail.

Billy Herndon had family in New Salem and knew many of the boys personally. He swears that they were not such a bad set of men. "They were friendly and good natured," he said. "They could trench a pond, dig a bog, build a house; they could pray and fight, make a village or create a state. They would do almost anything for sport or fun, love or necessity. Though rude and rough . . . sparkling in pure deviltry for deviltry's sake, yet place before them a poor man who needed their aid, a lame or sick man, a defenseless woman, a widow or an orphaned child, they melted into sympathy and charity at once. . . . There never was under the sun a more generous parcel of rowdies." *(11)*

The Clary's Grove Boys made it their business to size up any new man in the community and find out what he was made of. "A stranger's introduction was likely to be the most unpleasant part of his acquaintance with them," said Herndon. *(12)*

They were "roughs and bullies," said Jimmy Short, "who were in the habit of winning all the money of strangers at cards and then whipping them." *(13)*

Lincoln was the new man in town when Offut's boasting reached the ears of Bill Clary, who owned a saloon about thirty steps from Offut's store. They passed heated words in the street. Offut was claiming for all to hear that his clerk Lincoln could outwrestle anybody. Is that so—went Clary—could he throw Jack Armstrong?

There could only be one way to settle the matter. Each one put up ten dollars on his man and word spread that the big fight was on—the new man, Lincoln, versus Jack Armstrong, a bear of a man who had never been thrown.

"Armstrong was a man in the prime of life," recalled R. B. Rutledge, "square-built, muscular and strong as an ox . . . and the best fighter in Sangamon." *(14)*

"Armstrong was a regular bully," added Jimmy Short. "Very stout and tricky in wrestling." *(15)*

"Jack Armstrong was a powerful twister," said one New Salem man. *(16)*

"As strong as two men," offered another. *(17)*

"Lincoln was a scientific wrestler," said Jimmy Short, whose main science was to avoid getting hurt. Lincoln was a reluctant warrior. *(18)*

"We tried to get Lincoln to tussle and scuffle with Armstrong," said one man. "L. refused, saying—'I never tussled and scuffled and will not.' " *(19)*

"I don't like this wooling and pulling," said Abe. *(20)*

"At last," said a New Salemite, "we got them to wrestle." *(21)*

"The match took place in front of Offut's store," recalled R. B. Rutledge. "All the men of the village and quite a number from the surrounding country were assembled." *(22)*

"We bet knives and whiskey," a man said. *(23)*

"The contest began," said R. B. Rutledge, "and Jack soon found so worthy an antagonist." *(24)*

"They wrestled for a long time without either being able to throw the other," said Jimmy Short, "until Armstrong broke holds and caught L. by the leg." *(25)*

"Partly threw him," said J. M. Rutledge. "I did not think it fairly done." *(26)*

"Would have brought him to the ground had not Mr. Lincoln seized him by the throat and thrust him at arm's length from him," *(27)* said R. B. Rutledge.

"L. at last picked up Armstrong," an eyewitness said. "Swung him around." *(28)*

The Clary's Grove Boys were shocked to see their champion treated so rudely. They swarmed around Abe, spitting threats and taunts, looking to give him a whipping. Abe braced himself against a wall and told the gang to come on. He was ready.

"I noticed Lincoln standing with his back against a storehouse near by where they wrestled, and a crowd of men standing around him," remembered J. M. Rutledge. "There was like to be a fight." *(29)*

Suddenly Jack Armstrong was pushing his way through the crowd, offering his hand to Abe. He told everyone that Lincoln won fair and square. Said Jack: "He's the best feller that ever broke into this settlement." *(30)*

So began a warm friendship between Lincoln and the Armstrong family. Hannah Armstrong, Jack's wife, recalled how they accepted Abe into their home. "Abraham would come to our house; drink milk and mush, corn bread, butter; bring the children candy. Would rock the cradle of my baby. . . . He would nurse babies, do anything to accommodate anybody. . . . I fixed his pants, made his shirts. . . .

"Jack Armstrong and Lincoln never had a word. They did wrestle—no foul play—all in good humor. Commenced in fun and ended in sport." *(31)*

"After this wrestling match Jack Armstrong and his crowd became the warmest friends and staunchest supporters of Mr. Lincoln," said Rutledge. *(32)* He was one of them. True, his habits were more civilized. He didn't drink whiskey, play cards, cuss, or tussle. The roughest language he used was an occasional "By Jing!" *(33)* But the boys respected him anyway. He was the man who had saved the flatboat when it had stuck on the dam. He had told the hilarious lizard story. He could outrun all the footracers in Sangamon County. He was strong and tough and he could throw them all. And he was smarter than any of them.

Time after time they marveled at his great power. "Trials of strength were very common among the pioneers," said Rutledge. "Lifting weights, as heavy timbers piled one upon another, was a favorite pastime and no workman in the neighborhood could at all cope with Mr. Lincoln in this direction." *(34)*

After some playful grappling with Lincoln, Rowan Herndon swore that Abe was "by far the stoutest man that I ever took hold of. I was a mere child in his hands and I considered myself as good a man as there was in the country." *(35)*

The Clary's Grove Boys made Abe their leader. "Managed . . . to obtain complete control over them," declared one of the two physicians in New Salem. *(36)*

Years later, after Jack had passed on, Hannah wrote to Abe, then a prominent Springfield attorney. Her boy, the same boy Abe rocked in his cradle, was on trial for murder. She wanted Abe to be his lawyer.

"In reference to the trial of my son, I wrote to Lincoln first," she remembered. "Went to see Lincoln at Springfield. Saw him in his office. He promised to come down to defend my son. . . . After the trial was over, L. came down to where I was. . . . I asked him what he charged me. Told him I was poor. He said: 'Why Hannah, I shan't charge you a cent, never. Anything I can do for you I will do for you willingly and freely without charges.' " (37)

This was the celebrated case where Lincoln waited until the last possible moment to present to the jury an almanac that showed that there was no moonlight on the night the star witness was supposed to have seen the crime. When the jury realized the witness was lying, the Armstrong boy was acquitted.

"In all matters of dispute about horse racing or any of the popular pastimes of the day, Mr. Lincoln's judgement was final to all . . . ," Rutledge reported. "People relied implicitly upon his honesty, integrity and impartiality." (38)

When a fight broke out, Abe could walk between the grapplers and send them home laughing. R. B. Rutledge recalled an incident that showed Abe's influence on the rough, brawling crowd. "Two neighbors had a law suit. The defeated (Clark) declared that although he was beaten in the suit he could whip his opponent. This was a formal challenge and was at once carried to the ears of the victor (Wilcox) and as promptly accepted.

"The time, place and seconds were chosen . . . Mr. Lincoln being Clark's and John Brewer (was) Wilcox's second. The parties met, stripped themselves all but their breeches, went in, and Mr. Lincoln's principal was beautifully whipped. . . .

"After the conflict, the seconds conducted their respective principals to the river, washed off the blood and assisted them to dress. During this performance, the second of the party opposed to Mr. Lincoln remarked: 'Well, Abe. My man has whipped yours and I can whip you!'

"Now this challenge came from a man who was very small in

size. Mr. Lincoln agreed to fight provided he would chalk out his size on Mr. Lincoln's person and every blow struck outside of that mark should be counted foul. After this sally there was the best possible humor and all parties were as orderly as if they had been engaged in the most harmless amusement." (39)

Abe never went looking for a fight but if a nasty fellow needed a good thrashing Abe took his stand. A stranger came into the store one day with a chip on his shoulder, spewing foul language into the ears of the ladies. No decent man would allow such profane language in the presence of women. When Abe asked him to stop, the man became belligerent and boasted that he could do whatever he wanted to and nobody could stop him. Then he aimed a string of hot words at Abe.

The clerk walked slowly to the abusive stranger, saying, "Well, if you must be whipped I suppose I might as well whip you as any other man." (40) They went outside the store, and Abe proceeded to throw the man down in the dirt. He rubbed smartweed in the man's face until he cried for mercy.

20.

"I Am Young and Unknown"

Storekeepers were citizens of great importance to the folks in small country hamlets like New Salem. They gathered regularly before the storekeeper to pick up life's necessities and to pass along a cheerful word. Storekeepers always knew what was happening in the world. Newspapers from far-off cities passed through their hands. Everyone's latest happenings were related to the storekeeper, and he was always willing to share the news.

Stores filled up on rainy days and on Saturday afternoons when farm work was light. Here they gathered to discuss, debate, and dissect an encyclopedia full of topics. The storekeeper had a special place at these proceedings. He was the master of ceremonies, the moderator, the referee. Hotly disputed facts or theories were laid before him. His pronouncements and opinions counted. Folks could repeat the words of a storekeeper because he would know what he was talking about.

Throughout the summer and fall of 1831, Offut's storekeeper reveled in his new career. For the first time he could earn some money without breaking his back. When the ladies wanted a dozen yards of calico, he would measure and cut. When some men asked for whiskey, he would tip the barrel and pour it out. His long arms reached over shelves for pots, pans, buttons, hides, furs, and tools of all kinds. He counted Offut's money and kept his books.

Once, he closed the store for the evening to count the day's earnings and realized that he had taken six cents too much from a customer. He knew just who it was, so he walked three miles to her home to return the money.

140

On another evening, he sold a half pound of tea just before the store closed. When he opened up the next morning, he found that he had left the weight on the scale. He realized that he had accidentally used a four-ounce weight to measure eight ounces of tea. Immediately, he weighed the remainder of the tea, locked up the shop, and ran off to deliver it.

Stories like that passed among the New Salem folk. They mentioned Lincoln's name with admiring smiles and affectionate laughter. They began calling him "Honest Abe." He was beginning to make a name for himself—boatman, storekeeper, wrestler, humbler of ruffians.

Abe's greatest notoriety came as an entertainer. "He was known as a storyteller before he was heard of either as a lawyer or politician," related Herndon. "He loved a story, however extravagant or vulgar, if it had a good point. . . . If it was merely a ribald recital and had no sting in the end, if it exposed no weakness or pointed no moral, he had no use for it. . . . As a mimic he was unequalled and with his characteristic gestures he built up a reputation for storytelling—although fully as many of his narratives were borrowed as original." (1)

"His laugh was striking," said one of the New Salem crowd. (2)

"He seemed to see the bright side of every picture," said another. (3)

He had crowds rolling to his funny ballads. "Listen to one," says Herndon, " 'How St. Patrick Came to be Born on the 17th of March.' Who composed it or where Lincoln obtained it I have never been able to learn. Ellis (A. Y. Ellis, a great friend of Abe's, who clerked with him at the store) says he often inflicted it on the crowds who collected in his store on winter evenings." Here it is:

The first factional fight in old Ireland, they say,
Was all on account of Saint Patrick's birthday.
It was somewhere about midnight, without any doubt,
And certain it is, it made a great rout.

On the eighth day of March, as some people say,
St. Patrick at midnight he first saw the day;

While others assert 'twas the ninth he was born—
'Twas all a mistake—between midnight and morn.

Some blamed the baby, some blamed the clock.
Some blamed the doctor, some the crowing cock.
With all these close questions sure no one could know,
Whether the babe was too fast or the clock was too slow.

Some fought for the eighth, for the ninth some would die;
He who wouldn't see right would have a black eye.
At length these two factions so positive grew,
They each had a birthday, and Pat, he had two.

Till Father Mulcahay who showed them their sins,
He said none could have two birthdays but as twins.
"Now boys, don't be fighting for the eight or the nine;
Don't quarrel so always—now why not combine?"

Combine eight with nine. It is the mark.
Let that be the birthday. Amen! said the clerk.
So all got blind drunk, which completed their bliss,
And they've kept up the practice from that day to this. *(4)*

Customers flocked in, stayed for a round of stories and laughs, then went on their way. The store would be crowded for a time, then empty. When the cold weather came and people stayed home, there were many hours when the storekeeper was alone.

"Silence found him," Sandburg said. "He met silence. In the making of him as he was, the element of silence was immense." *(5)*

Alone, within himself, he noticed familiar stirrings rise up in the silence. He was hungry, wondering, wanting to know. He could remember that hunger as a boy, alone, laying in his loft at night, replaying the words of grown-up conversations. "I could not sleep . . . ," he would say, ". . . trying to make out what was the exact meaning of some of their—to me—dark sayings." *(6)*

Something was missing in his life, and he began to look for it. He mentioned to a friend that he wanted to "get hold of something that was knotty." *(7)*

Said Herndon, "Lincoln had long before realized the deficiencies of his education. Resolved—now that the conditions were favorable—to atone for early neglect by a course of study." *(8)*

He wanted to make his mark in the world. But who would listen to half-formed notions? "Nothing was more apparent to him than his limited knowledge of language and the proper way of expressing his idea," said Herndon. *(9)*

He visited Mentor Graham one day, and they talked about his education and ambition. "I had a notion of studying grammar," Abe told him. *(10)*

"I replied to him this," Graham said later. "If you ever expect to go before the public in any capacity, I think it is the best thing you can do." *(11)*

"If I had a grammar I would commence now," said Abe. *(12)*

"There was none in the village," Graham remembered, "and I said to him I knew of a grammar at one Vaners, about six miles away, which I thought he could get. . . . He got up and went on foot to Vaners and got the book. He soon came back and told me he had it. . . . The book was Kirkham's grammar, an old volume." *(13)*

"He, at once, applied himself to the book," said Herndon. "Sometimes he would stretch out at full length on the counter, his head propped up on a stack of calico prints, studying it. Or he would steal away to the shade of some inviting tree and there spend hours at a time in a determined effort to fix in his mind the arbitrary rule that 'adverbs qualify verbs, adjectives, and other adverbs.' " *(14)*

"He could be seen usually when in pursuit of his ordinary avocations with his book under his arm," remembered R. B. Rutledge. "At a moment of leisure, he would open it, study, close it, and recite to himself." *(15)*

When afternoons dragged at the store he would call his assistant clerk Billy Greene, hand over the book, and say—here, ask me some questions. Some thirty years later, when Bill Greene visited his old friend at the White House, Lincoln introduced him to the Secretary of State as the man who taught him grammar. Later, an embarrassed Greene turned to the President. "Abe," he said, "What did you mean by telling Mr. Seward that I taught you grammar? Lord knows I don't know any grammar myself, much less could I teach you."

Abe replied, "Bill, don't you recollect when we stayed in Offut's store at New Salem and you would hold the book and see if I could give the correct definitions and answers to the questions?"

"Yes," said Billy, "but that was not teaching you grammar."

"Well," responded the President, "that was all the teaching of grammar I ever had." *(16)*

During the winter, the storekeeper began appearing regularly at meetings of the New Salem Debating Society. R. B. Rutledge described his first speech before the club. "As he rose to speak, his tall form towered above the little assembly. Both hands were thrust down deep in the pockets of his pantaloons.

"A perceptible smile at once lit up the faces of the audience, for all anticipated the relation of some humorous story. But he opened up the discussion in splendid style to the infinite astonishment of his friends. As he warmed with his subject, his hands would forsake his pockets and would enforce his ideas by awkward gestures, but would very soon seek their resting place. He pursued the question with reason and argument so pithy and forcible that all were amazed." *(17)*

James Rutledge was impressed. As founder of New Salem and President of the Debating Society he was well respected for his fine wit and wide knowledge. Here was a man who owned a library of nearly thirty books. R. B. Rutledge recalled his father's reaction to the storekeeper's maiden speech. "The President, at his fireside after the meeting, remarked to his wife that there was more in Abe's head than wit and fun; that he was already a fine speaker. All he lacked was culture. . . .

"From that time," he continued, "Mr. Rutledge took a deeper interest in him. Soon after, Mr. Rutledge urged him to announce himself as a candidate for the legislature. This he—at first—declined to do, [saying] that it was impossible to be elected. It was suggested that a canvass of the county would bring him prominently before the people and in time would do him good." *(18)*

In 1832, politics was on everyone's mind. President Andrew Jackson was campaigning for re-election and Henry Clay was his main rival. At saloons, at stores, at mills, or wherever men gathered to shoot the breeze, you were either a Jackson man or a Clay man. When they weren't discussing national issues they spoke about the problems of their country or their state. It was the height of achievement for any man to win election to government.

To become a candidate, all a person had to do was to make a public announcement discussing issues of importance and have an enthusiastic group of followers to print posters and distribute leaflets. Lincoln's friends recognized his talent and began pushing him to run. "Encouraged by his great popularity among his immediate neighbors," wrote Lincoln in his autobiography, "he . . . ran for the legislature." *(19)*

Lincoln and his friends worked with great care to write his first public announcement. James Rutledge and Mentor Graham helped him compose it. "I corrected, at his request, some of the grammatical errors in his first address to the voters of Sangamon County," recalled John McNeil, *(20)* who would always consider himself as Lincoln's friend despite the whispers around town that Abe was in love with his bride-to-be, the beautiful Miss Ann Rutledge.

On March 9, 1832, printed handbills were distributed around the county announcing that Abraham Lincoln was a candidate for the Illinois State Legislature.

"To the people of Sangamon County—," read the notice, "Having become a candidate for the honorable office of one of your Representatives in the next General Assembly of this state, in accordance with an established custom and the principles of true Republicanism, it becomes my duty to make known to you, the people whom I propose to represent, my sentiments with regard to local affairs."

The candidate came out for improving the system of transportation in Sangamon County. "No other improvement that reason can justify us in hoping for can equal in utility the railroad. It is a never-failing source of communication between places of business remotely situated from each other."

Yet the cost! "There is always a heart-appalling shock accompanying the account of its cost . . . $290,000. . . . The improvement of the Sangamon River is an object much better suited to our infant resources."

He reminded the voters that when it came to the Sangamon River, he was the man who knew what he was talking about. "From my peculiar circumstances, it is probable that for the last twelve months I have given as particular attention to the stage of the water in this river as any other person in the country." He recounted his experience in building and operating vessels along the river. "I think I may say, without the fear of being contradicted, that its navigation may be rendered completely practicable."

The candidate spoke strongly in favor of education. "Upon the subject of education . . . I can only say that I view it as the most important subject which we as a people can be engaged in. That every man may receive at least a moderate education and thereby be enabled to read the histories of his own and other countries, by which he may duly appreciate the value of our free institutions, appears to be an object of vital importance . . . to say nothing of the advantages and satisfaction to be derived from all being able to read the Scriptures."

The candidate maintained that he would be independent but open minded. "I have spoken as I have thought," he declared. "I may be wrong. . . . But holding it a sound maxim that it is better to be only sometimes right than at all times to be wrong, so soon as I discover my opinions to be erroneous, I shall be ready to renounce them."

The address concluded on a personal note: "Every man is said to have his peculiar ambition. . . . I have no other so great as that of being truly esteemed of my fellow-men, by rendering myself worthy of their esteem. . . . I am young and unknown to many of you. I was born and have ever remained in the most humble walks of life. I have no wealthy or popular relations or friends to recommend me. My case is thrown exclusively upon the independent voters of this county. If elected, they will have conferred a favor upon me for which I shall be unremitting in my labors to compensate. But if the good people, in their wisdom, shall see fit to keep me in the background, I have been too familiar with disappointments to be very much chagrined.

Your friend and fellow citizen,

A. Lincoln." (21)*

---

*This handbill was published in the Sangamo Journal, March 15, 1832.

21.

"They Surely Thought It Was a Dream"

April 1832. New Salem was buzzing with the news. All the towns and settlements along the Sangamon River were stirred to a frenzy. A steamer was coming, the first ever to brave the narrow Sangamon River. Successful passage of a steamship along the Illinois waterway would open up the entire region for commerce from all over the young nation.

Captain Vincent Bogue hired the steamboat Talisman in Cincinnati and announced his intention to carry merchandise up the Illinois River to Beardstown where it would turn up the Sangamon River and finally pull in at Springfield. Up and down the Sangamon, business began to boom. Newspapers ran advertisements for merchandise from the east. Posters promised cheap goods, easy travel, new opportunities. Landlords along the riverbank subdivided their real estate into lots that went up for sale. New towns were planned. The whole countryside glowed with optimism, awaiting a new era of prosperity.

Captain Bogue himself sent word from Cincinnati to the towns upriver—make the way passable for the giant steamer. Clear out the rocks. Cut down overhanging limbs. Sweep up stray logs and driftwood. The Sangamon, a raw, wild, virgin stream, would be tamed.

A small army of men armed with long handled axes met the

boat at Beardstown and went to work, hacking away at the woods along the riverbank. Among them was a man from New Salem, the candidate for the state legislature, the young store-keeper who boosted the promise of steamship travel along the Sangamon. The candidate was Abraham Lincoln.

The Talisman puffed and smoked upriver, chugging past waving, cheering crowds. Billy Herndon, then fourteen, was there. He remembered: "I and other boys on horseback followed the boat along the river's bank as far as Bogue's Mill where she tied up. There we went aboard and, lost in boyish wonder, feasted our eyes on the splendor of her interior decorations. . . .

"I remember the occasion well for two reasons," said Herndon. "It was my first sight of a steamboat and also the first time I ever saw Mr. Lincoln." (1)

Bogue's Mill, the end of the journey for the Talisman, was about five miles from Springfield. The whole town turned out at the Springfield courthouse for a grand reception and dance in honor of the captain and the crew. Homespun poets celebrated the gala event in song:

> O, Captain Bogue, he gave the load,
> And Captain Bogue, he showed the road;
> And we came up with a right good will,
> And tied our boat up to his mill.
>
> Now we are up the Sangamo,
> And here we'll all have a grand hurra,
> So fill your glasses to the brim,
> Of whiskey, brandy, wine and gin.
>
> Illinois suckers, young and raw,
> We're strung along the Sangamo,
> To see a boat come up by steam,
> They surely thought it was a dream. (2)

—*Sangamo Journal*, April 5, 1832

The Talisman tied up at Bogue's mill for a week. Experienced boatmen were saying that the return trip would not be a simple matter. Passage upriver was greatly aided by swift spring currents, swollen by the run-off of melting snow. The water was receding now and unless they headed back downstream quickly, the river might become too shallow for the steamer to pass. Captain Bogue hired two Illinois boatmen to pilot the steamer downriver, two men who knew the tricky currents and snags of the Sangamon better than anyone. He hired Rowan Herndon and Abraham Lincoln.

The two navigators took the huge vessel down the Sangamon slowly. They averaged four miles a day. The river was so shallow that the bottom was constantly scraping. The ship was always threatening to run aground. When they reached New Salem, the steamer could not pass the mill dam owned by Cameron and Rutledge, the same dam that caught Lincoln and his flatboat the year before.

Captain Bogue wanted the dam dismantled so that his boat could go through. Cameron and Rutledge protested vehemently. While the debate raged back and forth, the crowd onshore and passengers and crew lent their voices to the ruckus. The boat went nowhere.

The poets sang:

> And when we came to Salem dam
> Up we went against it jam!
> We tried to cross with all our might,
> But found we couldn't and staid all night. (3)

—*Sangamo Journal*

A cooler head pointed to a law stating that no one had the right to dam up or in any way to obstruct a navigable stream. Since Bogue and his men had just demonstrated that the Sangamon was navigable, they claimed the right to remove the dam. Cameron and Rutledge looked on disconsolately as the crew began to dismember the dam. Finally, the Talisman was ready to push on to Cincinnati. "When we struck the dam she hung," recalled the pilot, Rowan Herndon. "We then backed off and threw the anchor over. We tore away part of the dam and raising steam, ran her over on the first trial." (4)

Herndon and Lincoln piloted the vessel as far as Beardstown where they each pocketed a salary of forty dollars for their efforts. The Talisman went on to Cincinnati and oblivion. "As soon as she was over, the company that chartered her was done with her," said Rowan Herndon. (5) Captain Bogue realized that his expedition on the Sangamon only proved the difficulty of steamboat travel on the river and he swore he would never do it again. The Talisman was the first and last steamboat carried by the waters of the Sangamon. A few months later, the Talisman met its fiery end while docked at the wharf in St. Louis.

Meanwhile, Abe's promising career as a merchant was in danger of coming to an abrupt end. "In less than a year, Offut's business was failing," recalled Abe. (6) Offut could no longer put off his creditors who were demanding money for their merchandise. One day, some men appeared at the store waving some legal papers and took possession of all the stock.

According to Lincoln, Offut just "petered out." (7) New Salem was not surprised when his business failed and just as happy when he left town. "He talked too much with his mouth," remarked one New Salem resident. (8) And that summed up the career of Denton Offut.

However, a wild character like Offut could not be down for long. In 1873 Herndon received a letter from a Baltimore physician. "I fished up from memory that some twenty-five years ago one Denton Offut appeared in Baltimore, hailing from Kentucky, advertising himself in the city papers as a veterinary surgeon and horse tamer, professing to have a secret to whisper in the horse's ear . . . by which the most . . . vicious horse could be quieted and controlled. For this secret he charged five dollars, binding the recipient by oath not to divulge it. I know several persons, young fancy horsemen, who paid for the trick.

"Offut advertised himself not only through the press but by his strange attire. He appeared in the streets on horseback and on foot, in plain citizens' dress of black but with a broad sash across his right shoulder of various colored ribbons, crossed on his left hip under a large rosette of the same material, the whole rendering his appearance most ludicrously conspicuous." (9)

In 1860, the same year that his former clerk was elected President of the United States, Denton Offut published a book. It was titled: *The Educated Horse: Instructions for Educating Horses and Other Animals to Obey a Word, Sign, or Signal and to Work or Ride, Also Showing How Children May Be Taught to be Quiet and Obedient by Kindness and Without Punishment.* (10)

Lincoln did hear from Offut again. When he was a prominent

attorney in Springfield, a former New Salem resident told him how he bumped into Offut in a small town in Mississippi. He watched Offut's exhibition of animal obedience and training. After the show he approached Offut and they spoke about old times. Offut was especially interested in his protégé Lincoln and seemed pleased to hear that he was now a famous man.

"Mr. Offut gave me a message to deliver to you . . .," said the New Salem man.

"Tell it to me," said Lincoln. "Tell it just as Offut said it."

"He told me to say to you—'Tell Lincoln to get out of his rascally business of politics and law and do something honest, like taming horses.' "

Lincoln rolled with delight. "That's Offut," he cackled. "That's just like Offut." *(11)*

22.

"Captain Abraham Lincoln's Company of the First Regiment of the Brigade of Volunteers"

It was a quiet April morning when a mud-soaked rider came whooping and galloping through the streets of New Salem. He was calling for fighting men. He passed around a bundle of handbills signed by the Governor of Illinois. Black Hawk had crossed the Mississippi into white man's land. Terrified settlers appealed to the Governor for help and he promptly signed a proclamation calling for volunteers to sign up for a thirty-day campaign to drive the Indians back across the Mississippi.

Every able bodied male between eighteen and forty-five was required to join the Army Reserve. It was the law. The men met to practice military drills twice a year. The penalty for missing these drills was one dollar. "As a dollar was hard to raise," said one old timer, "everybody drilled." *(1)*

Lincoln was a member of the Sangamon County Militia. When the call came for volunteers, he stepped forward. He was out of work now with Offut's store closed. Since he was a candidate for the state legislature, a thirty-day stint as an Indian fighter would show the voters that he wasn't shy about serving the community in time of need. Said one comrade, Lincoln "volunteered to serve his country with the balance of the patriotic boys to defend the frontier settlers . . . from the savage's tomahawk and scalping knife." (2)

For hundreds of years the peaceful Sac tribe planted corn, hunted, fished and buried their dead at the mouth of the Rock River in northwestern Illinois. When white settlers moved in they leveled the forest, building their cabins, forts and roads, and chased away the wild game animals. The Sacs were forced to move farther and farther north and west to hunt for food. Soon, they found themselves encroaching on Sioux territory, fending off war parties by Sioux braves.

In 1804, Sac tribesmen sold the rights to their ancient homeland to the United States Government. The key stipulation in the treaty was a promise that the Indians could return there to hunt, fish and raise corn until such time as the land was officially surveyed and properly deeded.

For nearly thirty years, the Sac nation and the American pioneers lived along the river in uneasy suspicion. Anger and violence flared up on both sides. During the War of 1812, when Britain made an ill-fated effort to recapture the lost American colonies, Black Hawk enlisted the Sacs on the side of Britain hoping an American defeat would bring the return of their homeland. This made the settlers ever more distrustful. They called Black Hawk and his tribe "that British Band."

Black Hawk was chief of the Sac tribe for forty years. His great-grandson would give twentieth-century America one of its finest athletes, the legendary full-blooded Sac Indian named Jim Thorpe. Black Hawk was born in the ancient village of the Sacs three miles from the picturesque spot where the Rock River flows into the Mississippi. He became a brave at fifteen when he took his first scalp. From then on he could wear paint and feathers and carry a red tomahawk.

The old chief ached seeing his homeland desecrated. White settlers lived there now. His people longed to see the graves of their departed loved ones. Black Hawk's daughter was buried there. Spring was coming and the tribe needed to grow their corn.

Black Hawk never recognized the authority of those tribesmen who signed away their land. "My reason teaches me that land cannot be sold," he wrote. "The Great Spirit gave it to his children to live upon and cultivate, as far as is necessary, for their subsistence; and so long as they occupy and cultivate it they have the right to the soil. But if they voluntarily leave it, then any other people have a right to settle upon it. Nothing can be sold but such things as can be carried away." (3)

He did not trust the white settlers or their government. He believed that his tribe had been tricked out of their land. "The white people brought whiskey to our village," he explained. "They made our people drunk and cheated them out of the horses, guns and traps. I visited all the whites and begged them not to sell my people whiskey. One of them continued the practice openly. I took a party of my young men, went to his house, broke in the head of the barrel and poured out the whiskey. I did this for fear some of the whites might get killed by my people when they were drunk." (4)

In 1831, Black Hawk gathered his finest young braves and crossed the Mississippi to drive the white settlers out. He was met by a large force of U.S. Army troops. General Atkinson persuaded Black Hawk to return west of the Mississippi. In exchange for 60,000 bushels of corn for his people, Black Hawk promised never to cross the river again. The Sacs moved on. "I touched the goose quill to the treaty and was determined to live in peace," he said. (5)

But the Sac homeland was never far from his mind. That winter, Black Hawk believed that his Indian neighbors, the Ottawas, Chippewas, Winnebagoes, Pottawottomies and the Fox would join a renewed effort against their common enemy. He had hopes that the British would send guns, ammunition and provisions in the spring. The Great Spirit and the Voices of the Fathers seemed to be commanding the noble Sac chief to move, once and for all, to drive the settlers from Indian land. Never was there such a powerful alliance of great warriors to do battle against the white man.

At sunup on April 6, 1832, Black Hawk painted his face and tied a string of eagle feathers around his head. Leading five hundred warriors, he crossed the Mississippi and traveled 35 miles beyond the village of his birth, burning farms, leaving cabins in ruins, murdering whole families and taking as many white scalps as he could. When General Atkinson sent an emmisary to warn Black Hawk to turn back, the proud warrior would only reply, "We come to plant corn." (6)

News of the Indian massacres traveled fast. Settlers fled their homes all over the northwest part of Illinois and took refuge in forts under the protection of the U.S. Army. General Atkinson sent word to the Governor that he needed reinforcements. On April 16th, Governor Reynolds dispatched a corps of riders to spread the word throughout the state. Volunteers were ordered to assemble at Beardstown, forty miles from New Salem, on April 22.

New Salem answered the call almost to a man. Lincoln left to sign up for the war alongside the Clary's Grove Boys. The Sangamon County Militia gathered at Richland the day before all troops were due at Beardstown. Here, they camped for the night and held an election for Captain.

Lincoln later told Leonard Swett, a lawyer friend, about how he came to be chosen as Captain. "A line of two was formed by the company," explained Swett, "with the parties who intended to be candidates for officers standing in front. The candidate for captain then made a speech to the men, telling them what a gallant man he was, in what wars he had fought, bled and died and how he was ready again, for the glory of his country, to lead them. . . . When the speechmaking was ended, they commanded those who would vote for this man or that to form a line behind their favorite. . . . Then they counted back and the fellow who had the longest tail to his kite was the real captain." (7)

Billy Greene related that Lincoln's opponent for the position was Bill Kirkpatrick, who owned a saw-mill outside New Salem. Lincoln and Kirkpatrick were feuding over two dollars that Lincoln claimed Kirkpatrick owed him. The mill owner had once hired Abe to move some heavy logs. He told Abe he would buy him a cant hook to help move the logs. Forget the cant hook, Abe told him. He would move the logs himself, without the cant hook, if Kirkpatrick would give him the two dollars the tool would cost. Kirkpatrick agreed. But on pay day, Lincoln was short two dollars.

When Lincoln saw Kirkpatrick step forward as a candidate for captain, he saw a way to make a little mischief. He leaned over to Greene and said, "Bill, I believe I can make Kirkpatrick pay me that two dollars he owes me on the cant hook. I'll run against him for captain." *(8)*

The boys from Clary's Grove huddled with Abe and made a pact among themselves. "We'll fix Kirkpatrick," they told each other. *(9)*

"The boys seized Lincoln," continued Swett, "and pushed him out of the line and began to form behind him, and cried—'Form behind Abe!' In a moment of irresolution, he marched ahead and when they counted back he had two more than the other captain." *(10)*

"I was elected Captain of the volunteers," said Abe, "a success which gave me more pleasure than any I have had since." *(11)*

"I cannot tell you," Abe told Swett, "how much the idea of being captain of that company pleased me." *(12)*

Now he was Captain Lincoln "of the First Regiment of the Brigade of Mounted Volunteers commanded by Brigadier General Samuel Whiteside." One of his first acts as Captain was to appoint Jack Armstrong as his first Sergeant. Bill Kirkpatrick became the quartermaster.

The volunteers were a special breed of soldier. There were no uniforms. No two men looked alike. They wore homemade buckskin breeches and coon skin caps. Everyone had a flintlock rifle and a powder horn. Every man carried his own blanket.

"They were a hard looking set of men, unkempt and unshaved," wrote one newspaper reporter. *(13)* Hardy and weathered, the men could wrestle wildcats, outlast bears and face down the fiercest Indian warrior who ever swung a tomahawk. But they had no use for military discipline. They liked Captain Lincoln and respected him. But no one could tell them how to fight. Said Herndon, "I heard Mr. Lincoln say once . . . that to the first order given one of them, he received the response—'Go to the devil, sir!' " *(14)*

Military tactics and precision drilling were something new to the Captain, who led his men with something less than iron discipline. "I remember his narrating his first experience in drilling his company," reported a newspaperman. "He was marching with a front of over twenty men across a field when he desired to pass through a gateway into the next enclosure."

"I could not for the life of me," said the Captain, "remember the proper word of command for getting my company endwise so that it could get through the gate. So as we came near the gate I shouted—'This company is dismissed for two minutes when it will fall in again on the other side of the gate!' " *(15)*

The new Captain was unfamiliar with military rules and regulations. There was a general standing order that no firearm should be discharged within fifty yards of camp. Someone heard a pistol shot and when the officers asked questions, they found that the culprit was Captain Lincoln. His sword was taken away and he was arrested and spent the night in the brig.

One night, a soldier of the Sangamon County Company broke into the officers' quarters and removed their supply of whiskey. The next morning, some of the men could not be roused out of bed for the march and the soldiers who did wobbled and fell. An inquiry could not determine the guilty parties. It was ordered that the Captain take full responsibility for the drunkenness of his men. Again, Captain Lincoln was arrested but since he was needed in the field he was made to carry a wooden sword for two days. "And this," said one of his men, "although he was entirely blameless in the matter." *(16)*

The Captain's troubles with the military authorities only increased Lincoln's popularity with the men. They knew he would stand up for them. When his volunteers complained he took their grievances to the top brass. Bill Greene remembers how Captain Lincoln challenged a regular army officer on behalf of his men. "Sir," he scolded, "you forget that we are not under the rules and regulations of the War Department at Washington. We are only volunteers under the orders and regulations of Illinois. Keep in your own sphere and there will be no difficulty. But resistance will hereafter be made to unjust orders. My men must be equal in all particulars—in rations, arms, camps—to the regular army." *(17)*

The men learned that Captain Lincoln was a man who meant what he said and who always put honor first. When an old Indian strayed into camp he was quickly surrounded. The men were about to kill him. "Our boys thought he was a spy," said Bill Clary. *(18)*

Trembling with fear, the old warrior produced a safe-conduct pass. It was, said Billy Greene, "written by General Lewis Cass stating that the Indian was a good and true man." *(19)*

This was not good enough. "The letter is a forgery," one voice claimed. *(20)*

"Make an example of him," bellowed another. *(21)*

"The Indian is a damned spy," a man roared. *(22)*

"We came to fight Indians," said another. *(23)*

Suddenly, Clary saw Lincoln as he "jumped between our men and the Indian." *(24)*

The Captain told them firmly, "Men, this must not be done. He must not be shot and killed by us." *(25)*

When somebody muttered that he was a coward, Lincoln's face hardened. Billy Greene remembered that he threw back a quick challenge to the mob. "If any man thinks I am a coward," growled Lincoln, "let him test it." *(26)*

There was a standoff. When the men realized that their Captain would not back down they let the old Indian pass.

No one wanted to cross this man Lincoln. He had a reputation in Illinois as the wrestler who threw Armstrong and Needham. The Clary's Grove Boys were saying that no man in the army could beat him.

This perked the ears of a Union County giant named Lorenzo Thompson. He knew all about Lincoln's reputation and was out to show that it wasn't so. Friends of Thompson and Lincoln arranged a championship match and the betting was on. Hats, knives, whiskey, blankets, tomahawks, saddles, horses, silver, the men would stake anything on their wrestler.

When the match began the two giants circled each other warily, tossing quick paws and feints, feeling each other out. During a lull in the match, Lincoln turned to the men in his corner and said, "Boys, this is the most powerful man I ever had hold of." *(27)*

The match was for the best two out of three falls. Thompson was a monster and for a while Lincoln held him off. Then Thompson got the crotch hoist on him and threw Lincoln on his back. Round one—Thompson.

The second grapple was even tougher. Lincoln knew that he was in for the fight of his life. Thompson got to him and sent him tumbling down. But Lincoln grabbed hold and Thompson fell beside him. The Clary's Grove Boys then swarmed into the ring to protect their man, calling the match a "dog-fall" because of Thompson's foul tactics. Thompson's men stood them off in the middle of the ring and for a moment it looked like a rumble.

Lincoln got up. "Boys," he said to his friends, "Give up your bets. If this man hasn't thrown me fairly, he could." (28)

So his friends paid their bets and went away but they always claimed it was "a dog-fall wrestle" and that Lincoln could still throw any man in the army. Afterwards, Lincoln told his friends about this man Thompson: "I never had been thrown in a wrestling match until the man from that company did it. He could have thrown a grizzly bear." (29)

23.

"Charges Upon the Wild Onions . . . Bloody Struggles with the Mosquitoes"

On April 27th, a force of sixteen hundred men set out from Beardstown to find Black Hawk and his "British Band" of warriors. They trudged through swamps, forded frigid streams, slept in mud and dined in the rain. They marched to Yellow Banks on the Mississippi and reached Dixon on the Rock River by May 12. Here they found the first battle of the war. It became known notoriously as Stillman's Defeat.

On the night of May 14th, Major Isaiah Stillman led a detachment of 340 men to scout the area for signs of Black Hawk. They set up camp about twelve miles from Dixon. Indian lookouts held them under observation the whole time and reported the news to Black Hawk. The old warrior, realizing now that there would be no aid from other Indian tribes and no supplies from the British, decided to end hostilities and bring his people back across the Mississippi. He sent a party of three braves to the army camp waving a white flag to ask for a peace conference with General Atkinson. Five more braves watched their comrades from a distant hill.

Meanwhile, Stillman's men busied themselves by drinking the company's stock of whiskey. When they saw three Indians approaching they quickly remembered that they were supposed to be fighting Indians. They jumped them, pummeled them wildly and left them for dead. They spotted the other five braves "spying" in the distance and started after them, managing to kill two.

Three surviving braves reached Black Hawk with the brutal story of how his emissaries of peace were murdered. The old warrior flew into a rage and raised a war whoop. He took all the braves he had with him, numbering about forty, and charged after the whites, too angry to consider that he was outnumbered eight to one.

Black Hawk led a furious charge on Stillman's Rangers and, to his surprise, the white men put up no resistance. When the Indians stormed the camp whooping and yelping, the white men dropped everything and took off in wild panic, not even stopping to mount their horses. Stillman's men ran into the woods, across the prairie, over hills, through rivers and swamps until, one by one, they straggled into the main garrison at Dixon. The first of the men to show up breathlessly reported that their camp had been stampeded by an overwhelming force of two-thousand savages and that everyone had been massacred but him. As the day wore on, more and more of the bedraggled men appeared until by nightfall, all but eleven men were accounted for.

Black Hawk, now more convinced than ever that the white man could not be trusted, was on the warpath in earnest. Telltale signs of Indian wrath were left behind at every stop— homes deserted or left in smoldering ashes, surrounded by corpses of cattle and hogs, scalps of whole families dangling from tree limbs to taunt arriving army troops.

The Indians roamed the land at will. No army could find them. They were masters at warfare by ambush, setting out false trails, appearing here then there, striking suddenly like a thunderclap, then vanishing. They were an army of phantoms. The volunteer soldiers seethed in frustration. Tired, hungry, angered at the slow progress of the campaign, they were ready to go home. One company under the command of Colonel Zachary Taylor (soon to become President of the United States), refused

161

to cross the Rock River into Indian territory, claiming that they had only signed up to protect the state and should not be required to leave its borders.

Colonel Taylor listened patiently to their complaints, then cooly showed them the backbone of a soldier. "I feel that all gentlemen here are my equals," he assured the rebellious crowd. "In reality, I am persuaded that many of them will, in a few years, be my superiors and perhaps in the capacity of members of the Congress. . . . I expect to obey them as interpreters of the will of the people. And the best proof that I will obey them is now to observe the orders of those whom the people have already put in the place of authority. . . . In plain English, Gentlemen and fellow citizens, the word has been passed on to me from Washington to follow Black Hawk and to take you with me as soldiers. I mean to do both." (1)

He informed his reluctant warriors that the flatboats were in front of them, ready to carry them over the river to follow the trail of Black Hawk. Behind them, a wall of Uncle Sam's infantry stood, rifles ready, waiting for the order to escort every last one of them aboard. The mutineers grumbled that fighting Indians was better than fighting the U.S. Army so they headed for the boats.

Captain Lincoln and his men kept marching, twenty-five miles one day, twenty miles another day. Tired from walking, hungry for a decent meal, exhausted from missing sleep and edgy for combat, the men cursed the army, and talked about going home. Sick of camp food, the men outraged local farmers by raiding their livestock, which they ate broiled, fried or toasted. "Some of the settlers complained that they made war upon the pigs and chickens," reported a news correspondent. (2)

Even Captain Lincoln complained about the camp food. "It is much like eating saddlebags," he said. (3)

On May 21, the men discovered the remains of three families that were murdered and scalped. Fifteen mutilated bodies were stewn around their homes. Neighbors told the army that two teenaged girls were missing from the carnage and probably kidnapped by the Indians. News like that rattled the men and filled them with a sense of doom.

Nighttime. The army set up camp near the Fox River. The

men set up their tents or slept fitfully in the open air. Suddenly, shouting, cursing, grabbing hats and guns. The horses were running wild, trampling half-asleep bodies, tumbling tents. A groggy bugle blared. Bewildered men formed a desperate battle line, ready to fire on the unseen enemy. There was no enemy. The horses had been spooked by some unnamed fear and broke into a furious, snorting gallop. The men spent the rest of the night gathering the horses and grumbling about lost sleep.

By this time, the military high command had seen enough of the Illinois fighting man. "The more I see of the militia the less confidence I have of their effecting anything of importance," reported Colonel Taylor to his superiors. (4) Governor Reynolds called a conference of captains and asked for a vote. Stay and fight the enemy or go home. Captain Lincoln cast his vote along with the others. When they counted the votes, it was a tie. The Illinois Militia had voted itself into paralysis.

This monumental show of ineptitude so enraged General Whiteside that he swore he would lead these men only to their discharge papers. Four days later, Captain Lincoln's company was officially disbanded.

Most of the men went home. Lincoln and a few others rejoined the army for another twenty days. "I was out of work," he explained, "and there being no danger of more fighting, I could do nothing better than enlist again." (5) On May 29th he was sworn into service as a private by Lieutenant Robert Anderson, who thirty years later would surrender Fort Sumter to the Confederate Army in the first battle of the Civil War.

Private Lincoln then re-enlisted for another thirty-day tour in the Independent Spy Corps of Captain Jacob Early, a Springfield physician and Methodist preacher who had served as a private with Lincoln in the Sangamon Militia. On June 25th, Captain Early's Spy Corps discovered the grisly remains of a skirmish with Black Hawk at Kellogg's Grove. A small detail of white scouts had made camp for the night. Silent moccasins crept up on the men—the execution was swift.

"I remember just how those men looked," said Lincoln, "as we rode up the little hill where their camp was. The red light of the morning sun was streaming upon them as they lay heads toward us on the ground. And every man had a round red spot on the top of his head about as big as a dollar, where the redskins had taken his scalp. It was frightful, but it was grotesque. And the red sunlight seemed to paint everything all over. I remember," he added, "that one man had buckskin breeches on." (6)

The Spy Corps marched into Wisconsin, through settlements named Turtle Village, Lake Koshkonong, White Water and Burnt Village. They slept on their muskets at night, performing scout duty for General Atkinson and the regular U.S. Army by day.

In the beginning of July, with provisions running out, they found the Wisconsin swamps and jungles impassable, even on foot. On July 10th, Early's Spy Corps returned to White Water on the Rock River to be honorably discharged and sent home with "the special thanks of Brigadier General H. Atkinson, Commander in Chief of the Army of the Illinois frontier." (7)

By now, Black Hawk's braves were going hungry and war weary. Sioux and Winnebago Indians, wise in the ancient ways of forest warfare, took their pay from the white man's army to help them thwart Black Hawk's tricks. On August 1st at Bad Axe most of Black Hawk's warriors were massacred. Black Hawk slipped away; but Sioux and Winnebago scouts trailed him and finally delivered him to the white man.

For a time, Black Hawk remained in the custody of one Lieutenant Jefferson Davis, who would become Lincoln's mortal enemy as the first President of the Confederate States of America. Black Hawk remembered Lieutenant Davis in his autobiography, calling him a "good and brave young chief with whose conduct I was much pleased." (8)

The elderly chief, now finally at peace in the white world, was brought to Washington to meet President Andrew Jackson. Both men were nearing seventy. Both were veterans of brutal military campaigns. Both had killed men and cheated death themselves.

The two old chieftains faced each other. Black Hawk finally said: "I am a man—and you are another. I took up the hatchet to avenge injuries which could no longer be borne. Had I borne them longer my people would have said, 'Black Hawk is a squaw. He is too old to be a chief. He is no Sac.' This caused me to raise the war-whoop. I say no more of it. All is known to you." (9)

Abe Lincoln's military career was over. He had fought an Indian war without harming a single Indian. He had marched with his Illinois brothers hundreds of miles into the rugged bowels of American wild country. He had smelled rotting corpses and laid bodies in the ground. Lying awake at night with his hands on his musket, his eyes may have scanned the glowing, star sprinkled heavens searching for answers—why do men go to war?

He grew close to the men of Illinois. All types of men became his friends. Many hours he spent talking with a lawyer from Springfield, Major John Stuart, who advised him that anyone studying law should begin by reading *Blackstone's Commentaries on the Laws of England.*

Years later, Lincoln could find nothing heroic in his military service. When General Lewis Cass became the Democratic candidate for President in 1848 (the same General Cass who signed the old Indian's safe conduct pass) he made a valiant saga of his own exploits during the Black Hawk War.

This made Lincoln laugh. "Did you know I am a military hero?" he crowed with evident sarcasm. "Yes sir. In the days of the Black Hawk War. I fought, bled, and came away.

"Speaking of General Cass' career reminds me of my own. . . . It is quite certain I did not break my sword, for I had none to break. But I bent a musket pretty badly on one occasion. If Cass broke his sword, the idea is, he broke it in desperation. I bent the musket by accident.

"If General Cass went in advance of me in picking huckleberries, I guess I surpassed him in charges upon the wild onions. If he saw any live fighting Indians, it was more than I did. But I had a good deal of bloody struggles with the mosquitoes, and although I never fainted from loss of blood, I can truly say I was often hungry. . . . I protest they shall not make fun of me, as they have of General Cass, by attempting to write me into a military hero." *(10)*

24.

"The Only Time I Ever Have Been Beaten"

When Lincoln returned to New Salem, Election Day was less than a week away. He soon discovered that his three months away from the campaign had been no handicap. "He became very popular whilst in the army," said Rowan Herndon. *(1)*

The voting public had not yet heard a stump speech from candidate Lincoln. His first campaign stop took him to Pappsville, where a crowd of Illinois farmers were looking over the hogs, bulls and steers up for auction. "There was a large gathering there on account of a sale of goods," related James Herndon, Rowan's brother. "He was the only candidate there and was called on to make a speech." *(2)*

The candidate climbed into the bed of a wagon where he could see the whole crowd. His campaign debut was about to begin with the traditional stump greeting, something like "Gentlemen and Fellow Citizens." But before he could speak his attention was drawn to some of the gentlemen and fellow citizens in the crowd who were pounding and mauling each other's heads. A band of thugs knocked a man down. From the speaker's platform he could see that it was his good friend Rowan Herndon.

Years later, Rowan Herndon described the fracas. "It was on that day that I whipped Jessy Dodson, and his friends attempted to show foul play. . . . I think he (Lincoln) was about to commence speaking when the fight commenced." *(3)*

The candidate leaped off the rostrum and waded through the crowd. When he reached the brawlers the disagreement was quickly settled. "He pitched them out like they were boys and told them his friend could whip the whole of them one at a time," said Rowan Herndon. "That ended the fuss." *(4)*

The crowd cheered the candidate as he marched back to the speaker's box to resume his speech. "Fellow Citizens," he began. "I presume you all know who I am—I am humble Abraham Lincoln. I have been solicited by many friends to become a candidate for the Legislature. My politics are short and sweet like the old woman's dance. I am in favor of a national bank. I am in favor of the internal improvement system and a high protective tariff. These are my sentiments and political principles. If elected, I shall be thankful. If not, it will be all the same." *(5)*

There were more speeches and rallies for the candidate. "I accompanied him on one of his electioneering trips to Island Grove," relates A. Y. Ellis. "He made a speech which pleased his party friends very well, indeed. . . . He told several anecdotes and applied them, as I thought, very well. He also told the boys several stories which drew them after him. I remember them, but modesty and my veneration for his memory forbid me to relate them." *(6)*

"I well remember how he was dressed," Ellis went on. "He wore flax and tow linen pantaloons—I thought about five inches too short in the legs—and frequently he had but one suspender, no vest or coat. He wore a calico shirt, such as he had in the Black Hawk War, coarse brogans, tan color, blue yarn socks and straw hat, old style, without a band." *(7)*

Stephen T. Logan, a Springfield lawyer who would later take Lincoln as his law partner, saw him for the first time during the '32 campaign. "He was a very tall and gawky and rough looking fellow then. His pantaloons didn't meet his shoes by six inches. But after he began speaking I became very much interested in him. He made a very sensible speech. . . .

"I knew nothing then about his avocation or calling at New Salem. The impression I had at the time was that he was sort of a loafer down there. . . . But one thing we very soon learned was that he was immensely popular, though we found that out more at the next election than then. . . . In the election of 1832 he made a very considerable impression upon me as well as upon other people." *(8)*

"I heard him speak frequently," said Rowan Herndon, "and he was a full match for any man that was on the track." *(9)*

Rowan Herndon reported one of the speeches he heard from the lips of candidate Lincoln. "Fellow Citizens," began Lincoln. "I have been told that some of my opponents have said it was a disgrace to have such a looking man as I am stuck up for the legislature. Now I thought this was a free country. That is the reason that I address you today. Had I known to the contrary I should not have consented to run.

"But I will say one thing," the candidate went on. "Let the shoe pinch who it may. When I have been a candidate before you some five or six times and have been beaten every time, I will consider it a disgrace and will be sure never to try it again."

Then he added defiantly, "I am bound to beat that man if I am beat myself." *(10)*

"And sure enough," said Rowan Herndon, "he was beat." *(11)*

When they counted the ballots Lincoln ran eighth in a field of thirteen candidates. The top four vote-getters were elected to the state legislature from Sangamon County, including John Stuart, the second leading candidate.

Lincoln's showing was astonishing for a political newcomer with no credentials to speak of and who barely campaigned. The town of New Salem turned out for Abe, giving him 277 out of 300 votes cast. Still, it was not enough. Lincoln had lost his first election. It was, said Lincoln, "the only time I ever have been beaten by the people." *(12)*

Lincoln was now at an important crossroad in his life. Later, he would write in his autobiography that "He was now without means and out of business, but was anxious to remain with his friends who had treated him with so much generosity, especially as he had nothing elsewhere to go to." *(13)*

He decided to stay in New Salem and make his fortune there. At the time, he was living with Rowan Herndon and his family. "He came to my house to board soon after his return from the army," his friend recalled. "During his stay at my house my family became much attached to him. He was always at home wherever he went. . . . He most always had one of my children around with him. . . . Very kind to the widows and orphans—chop their wood and read the news from all over the country once a week as we only had a weekly mail." *(14)*

It was here that young Billy Herndon first came to know his future law partner. Lincoln left a deep impression on the boy who would fifty years later become his biographer. "I had up to this time frequently seen Mr. Lincoln—had often, while visiting my cousins James and Rowan Herndon at New Salem, met him at their house. . . . There was something in his tall and angular frame, his ill-fitting garments, honest face, and lively humor that imprinted his individuality on my affection and regard. . . . He was my senior by nine years, and I looked up to him, naturally enough, as my superior in everything—a thing I continued to do till the end of his days." *(15)*

Comfortable in his surroundings, well respected in the community, Lincoln needed direction for his life. "He studied what he should do," he wrote of himself. "Thought of learning the blacksmith trade. Thought of trying to study law. Rather, thought he could not succeed at that without a better education." *(16)*

He wanted an occupation that would allow him time to read and study. "What he seemed to want," said Herndon, "was some lighter work, employment in a store or tavern where he could meet the village celebrities, exchange views with strangers, discuss politics, horse-races, cock-fights and narrate to listening loafers his striking and significant stories." *(17)*

In the fall of 1832 there were four stores in New Salem. Samuel Hill and John McNeil owned one. So did Reuben Radford. James Rutledge had a store and the Herndon Brothers ran another.

"But," said Herndon, "there seemed no favorable opening for him. Clerks in New Salem were not in demand just then." *(18)*

Soon, opportunity came knocking at the door of Abraham Lincoln, merchant and businessman. "My cousins, Rowan and James Herndon, were at that time operating a store," recalled Billy Herndon. "Tiring of their investment and the confinement it necessitated, James sold his interest to an idle, shiftless fellow named William Berry. Soon after, Rowan disposed of his to Lincoln. *(19)*

Said Rowan Herndon, "I sold him my stock of goods to Lincoln & Berry on credit." *(20)*

Men of business in new frontier towns did not deal much in money. Enterprises were bought and sold with promissory notes and IOU's, based on future earnings. That was how, in the spring of 1833, such an unlikely pair as Abraham Lincoln and William Berry found themselves in partnership, managing a business enterprise even though they were both paupers.

"I once asked Rowan Herndon what induced him to make such liberal terms in dealing with Lincoln, whom he had known for so short a time," said Billy Herndon.

"I believed he was thoroughly honest," answered Cousin Rowan, "and that impression was so strong in me I accepted his note in payment of the whole. He had no money, but I would have advanced him more had he asked for it." *(21)*

On March 6, 1833, the two businessmen signed a license granted by the Sangamon County Court to keep a tavern and sell liquor. So, Lincoln and Berry, according to Abe, "opened as merchants." *(22)*

25.

"The National Debt"

Prosperous business ventures need room to expand. The two merchants bought James Rutledge's entire stock of merchandise in exchange for a promissory note. Soon after the partners would also acquire the store of Reuben Radford, allowing Berry & Lincoln to claim ownership of three of New Salem's four stores.

The deal to close on the Radford property was a riotous frontier tale done in New Salem style, courtesy of the boys from Clary's Grove. Thomas Reep, one of the locals, recounted the unlikely details:

"Reuben Radford incurred the enmity of the Clary's Grove Boys, which resulted in Berry and Lincoln securing his stock of goods and moving into the store," began Reep. (1)

"The circumstances was as follows: Radford was a large man of great physical strength and announced his ability to look after his own rights and to protect them. He was told that such an attitude would cause the Clary's Grove Boys to try him out and they would surely lick him. If one couldn't then two or three together would.

"On the day in question, Radford, having occasion to go to the country, left his younger brother in charge of the store, admonishing him to be careful and directing him to sell the Clary's Grove Boys—in case any of them came in—but two drinks of liquor.

"Sure enough, the Clary's Grove Boys came and in peace got their two drinks of liquor. Being denied more, they shoved the protesting youth out of their way, stepped behind the counter and helped themselves. . . . They all got 'rip-roaring' drunk and turned things in the store topsy-turvy, broke the crockery and knocked out the windows, leaving chaos and ruin in their wake. Then they leaped on their horses and yelling like wild Indians, left the town for their homes.

"A bunch of them passed a short distance from where Radford was stopping in the country. Hearing their yells, he immediately feared the worst. Leaping on his horse, ran him all the way to New Salem where he dismounted from his panting and lathered steed and rushed into his store. Broken glass and crockery ware covered the floor and the contents seemed to be a total wreck.

"Stepping out, Radford declared that he would sell out to the first man who made him an offer.

"Just at that moment, William Greene, the erstwhile Offut clerk, came along, having been sent on horseback with some grist to the mill. Hearing Radford's words, he replied—'Sell out to me!'

"Radford replied—'I will. How much will you give?'

"Greene rode up to the side of the store and sticking his head through a broken window, surveyed the contents and offered Radford $400 for the stock, which Radford accepted.

"The news of the purchase traveled fast in New Salem and soon Lincoln came over to see his old friend and new competitor. Looking over the contents, he announced that they must take an inventory. Greene, not understanding the term and guessing that it might mean some sort of celebration along the line followed by the Clary's Grove Boys just before, replied—'Abe, I don't believe this store will stand another one just at this time.'

"Lincoln explained that by inventory he meant the listing of the goods and the setting opposite each item the value thereof. So they at once proceeded to make the inventory.

"Greene paid $23 cash and for the balance gave two notes each for $188.50 which was secured by a mortgage drawn and witnessed by Lincoln. . . .

"Before the inventory was completed, it was evident that the stock would run to nearly $900. Berry and Lincoln bought it from Greene, paying him $265 cash, principally in silver, assuming the payment of his notes for $377 to Radford and by turning over a horse, saddle and bridle owned by Berry. Berry and Lincoln then moved their stock into the new store building and bid fair to make considerable money, as competition had now been reduced to but one other store, that owned and operated by Hill. . . .

"The taking of the inventory and fixing of the papers covering the purchase from Radford and the sale to Berry and Lincoln kept young Greene till quite late that night and when he arrived home the family had retired. His father, however, was awake, waiting for him. . . .

" 'So, Billy,' the older Greene said, 'you are a merchant, are ye? You git along to bed now and in the morning I will thrash the merchant out you mighty quick.'

"Young Bill held his peace until he had stirred up the coals and lighted the room with fresh kindling. Then, reaching into his pockets, he began stacking up his silver on the floor with considerable jingle. . . .

" 'Pap,' said Billy, 'I was a merchant, but I've sold out and cleared this.'

"Whereupon Greene Sr. reached over and awaking his wife said—'Liz, git up and git Billy a fust rate supper. He's had a hard day of it.' " (2)

From such a promising beginning, the Berry-Lincoln enterprise went nowhere. They were an odd couple, neither with a nose for business. Berry was the son of the Reverend John Berry and had attended Illinois College with Billy Greene. But he picked up none of his father's moral, temperate ways, drinking hard, fighting mean and dealing cards with his cronies. "It always was a mystery to me," said friend George Spears, "why a man of Mr. Lincoln's integrity would enter into a partnership with such a character." (3)

Berry hung out in the back of the store drinking the stock of whiskey and pouring free rounds for his friends during intense bouts of poker. Lincoln was no more attentive to the customer's needs, but in a different way. He spent his time reading. Law, grammar, poetry and ancient history fed his mind while he was keeping store. He read Gibbons' *Decline and Fall of the Roman Empire* and Rollins' *Ancient History*. He read Robert Burns and Shakespeare. Customers would get an earful of the latest pages he'd been turning. One customer remembered how Lincoln would "refer to that great man Shakespeare. Also Lord Byron as being a great man. And Burns. . . . And Lord Nelson as being a great Admiral and Naval Commander. . . . George Washington was the greatest of all of them and was his great favorite." *(4)*

"As a salesman," says Herndon, "Lincoln was lamentably deficient. He was too prone to lead off into a discussion of politics or morality, leaving someone else to finish the trade which he had undertaken." *(5)*

Said one of his companions, "While clerking in the store . . . he would apply himself as opportunity offered to his studies. If it was but five minutes time, would open his book which he always kept at hand, study it, reciting to himself, then entertain the company present or wait on a customer without apparent annoyance from the interruption.

"Have frequently seen him reading while walking along the streets. Occasionally he would become absorbed with his book—would stop and stand for a few moments, then walk on. . . . If the company he was in was unappreciative or their conversation at all irksome, he would open his book and commune with it for a time until a happy thought suggested itself and then the book would again return to its . . . resting place under his arm." *(6)*

Lincoln continued to read anything he could get his hands on. "Lincoln was fond of short, spicy stories," said Herndon. *(7)* A. Y. Ellis, who clerked for him, gave him some popular novels like *Cousin Sally Dillard*, *Becky William's Courtship*, and *The Down-Easter and the Bull*.

"He never appeared to be a hard student," said R. B. Rutledge, "as he seemed to master his studies with little effort—until he commenced the study of law. In that he became wholly engrossed and began for the first time to avoid the society of men in order that he might have more time for study." *(8)*

The Law. The subject drew him. His friendly conversations with Squire Pate in Kentucky on the first day he presented himself in a court of law excited him. Reading the Statutes of

Indiana spurred him on. Long discussions with John Stuart encouraged him. If he ever became serious about studying law, Stuart told him to read Blackstone. Lincoln found a way to get Blackstone into his hands.

"One day," Lincoln remembered, "a man who was migrating to the West drove up in front of my store with a wagon which contained his family and household plunder. He asked me if I would buy an old barrel for which he had no room in his wagon and which he said contained nothing of special value. I did not want it, but to oblige him I bought it and paid him, I think, half a dollar for it. Without further examination, I put it away in the store and forgot all about it.

"Some time after, in overhauling things, I came upon the barrel, and emptying it upon the floor to see what it contained, I found at the bottom of the rubbish a complete edition of Blackstone's *Commentaries*. I began to read those famous works, and I had plenty of time. For during the long summer days, when the farmers were busy with their crops, my customers were few and far between. The more I read, the more intensely interested I became. Never in my whole life was my mind so thoroughly absorbed. I read until I devoured them." *(9)*

Russell Godby tells how he came upon Lincoln sitting barefoot against a pile of wood, sunken deeply into the pages of a book. "I asked him what he was reading," related Godby.

" 'I'm not reading,' he answered. 'I'm studying.' "

" 'Studying what?' I enquired."

" 'Law, sir' was the emphatic response."

Said Godby, "It was really too much for me as I looked at him sitting there proud as Cicero. 'Great God Almighty!' I exclaimed, and passed on." *(10)*

Meanwhile, the Berry and Lincoln enterprise continued to flounder. "While Lincoln at one end of the store was dispensing political information, Berry at the other end was disposing of the firm's liquors, being the best customer for that article of merchandise himself," said Herndon. "To put it more plainly—Lincoln's application to Shakespeare and Burns was only equalled by Berry's attention to spigot and barrel." *(11)*

"Of course," said Lincoln, "they did nothing but get deeper and deeper in debt." *(12)*

Finally the doors closed on Berry & Lincoln. Said Abe, "The store winked out." *(13)*

"They, like their predecessors, were ready to retire," said Herndon. "Two brothers named Trent coming along, they sold to them on liberal terms." *(14)*

By the time the Trent brothers' notes to Lincoln and Berry came due, they too had failed. "One morning in the late fall of 1834 the village awoke," recalled Thomas Reep. "Smoke spirals arose from the chimneys but none from the Trent Brothers' store. Its absence and the closed doors attracted the attention of the inhabitants. An examination was made and no one was seen about the building. Further investigation showed the families to have disappeared with their household goods during the night, leaving . . . their creditors to hold the bag." *(15)*

Lincoln and Berry set out on the enormous task of repaying their debts when, on January 10, 1835, Berry died, leaving the entire responsibility for the failed business on Lincoln's shoulders. He owed a sum close to $1100.

"That debt was the greatest obstacle I have ever met in my life," said Lincoln. "I had no way of speculating and could not earn money except by labor. And to earn by labor eleven hundred dollars, besides my living, seemed the work of a lifetime.

"There was, however, but one way," he went on. "I went to the creditors and told them that if they would let me alone, I would give them all I could earn over my living as fast as I could earn it." *(16)*

He joked about it and called it "The National Dept." *(17)* But fifteen years later, Lincoln was still saving part of his salary as a Representative in Washington to send to his creditors in New Salem. It was a backbreaking burden but he persisted until his debts were paid in full.

26.

"Oh! Why Should the Spirit of Mortal Be Proud?"

She was twenty, pretty and intelligent, with sandy hair and blue eyes, and she came from the most prominent family in New Salem. Her father was an educated man, owner of twenty-five or thirty books, founder of the New Salem Debating Society and the very first settler on the bluff that became New Salem.

In 1833, when twenty-four-year-old Abraham Lincoln came to board at the Rutledge Tavern, Ann Rutledge was engaged to be married. Her beau, New Salem storeowner John McNeil, an astute businessman, who encouraged Abe's political career, had gone back East and she was waiting loyally for him to return.

So begins one of the most familiar episodes in the life of young Lincoln. The details—unearthed by Herndon during his interviews with New Salem old-timers in the year after Lincoln's death—have been augmented, embellished, romanticized and mythologized until the story has become a folktale. Modern historians accept as fact that Lincoln knew Miss Rutledge and that they were close friends. However, if Lincoln did become miserably distraught at her death, as scholars concede, they contend this is no reason to make any unwarranted inferences about their relationship.

What was the relationship between Abraham Lincoln and Ann Rutledge? Was it a platonic friendship? Were they in love? We will never know.

But the residents of New Salem knew—or, at least, spoke

what they thought. Here they are, friends and neighbors who knew both Ann and Abraham, recalling the events as they had unfolded more than thirty years before. We'll hear from Ann's brothers and her cousin, who knew her well, from her teacher and her fiancé, the man who abandoned her and finally returned, to find her in the grave. We'll hear what they have to say—after all, they were there.

•   •   •

Billy Herndon: "The memory of Ann Rutledge was the saddest chapter in Mr. Lincoln's life." (1)

Jimmy Short: "Mr. L. boarded with the parents of Miss Ann Rutledge." (2)

R. B. Rutledge: "Boarded with my father during the years 1833 and 1834 as appears from papers still in the possession of my family." (3)

G. W. Miles: "Mrs. Bowling Greene says that Mr. Lincoln was a regular suitor of Miss Ann Rutledge for between two and three years." (4)

Rowan Herndon: "There was a Miss Rutledge. I have no doubt he would be married if she had of lived." (5)

Billy Greene: "He would have married her but she sickened and died." (6)

Billy Herndon: "I knew Miss Rutledge myself, as well as her father and other members of the family and have been personally acquainted with every one of the score or more of witnesses whom I at one time or another interviewed on this delicate subject." (7)

Mentor Graham: "I knew Miss Ann Rutledge. . . . Lincoln and her both were studying at my house. . . . She was about 20 years, eyes blue, large and expressive. Fair complexion. Sandy or light auburn hair. About 5 feet 4 inches. Face rather round—outlines beautiful. . . . Weight about 120-130. Hearty and religious. Amiable and kind." (8)

L. M. Greene: "She was amiable and of exquisite beauty and her intellect was quick, deep and philosophic as well as brilliant. She had a heart as gentle and kind as an angel and full of love and sympathy. Her sweet and angelic nature was noted by everyone who met her." (9)

R. B. Rutledge: "My sister Ann was born January 7, 1813 and died August 25, 1835. . . . In 1830, my sister being then but seventeen years of age, a stranger calling himself John McNeil came to New Salem." *(10)*

Billy Herndon: "Within three years he owned a farm and a half interest with Samuel Hill in the leading store. He had good capacity for business." *(11)*

R. B. Rutledge: "A friendship grew up between McNeil and Ann which ripened apace and resulted in an engagement to marry." *(12)*

Billy Herndon: "McNeil, having disposed of his interest in the store to Hill, determined to return to New York, his native state, for a visit. . . . Before leaving, he made to Ann a singular revelation. He told her the name McNeil was an assumed one—that his real name was McNamar." *(13)*

John McNamar: "I left behind me in New York my parents and brothers and sisters. They are poor and were in more or less need when I left them in 1829. I vowed that I would come West, make a fortune, and go back to help them." *(14)*

Billy Herndon: "He had accumulated up to this time, as near as we can learn, ten or possibly twelve thousand dollars." *(15)*

R. B. Rutledge: "It seems that his father had failed in business and his son, a very young man, had determined to make a fortune, pay off his father's debts and restore him to his former social and financial standing. With this view, he left his home clandestinely, and in order to avoid pursuit by his parents, changed his name." *(16)*

John McNamar: "I left here in '32 or '33 and came to the state of New York for the purpose of assisting my father's family. . . . Circumstances beyond my control detained me much longer away than I intended." *(17)*

R. B. Rutledge: "At all events, he was absent two or three years." *(18)*

Billy Herndon: "Meanwhile, a different view of the matter was taken by Miss Rutledge. Her friends encouraged the idea of cruel desertion. . . . Some contended that he had undoubtedly committed a crime in his earlier days and for years had rested secure from apprehension under the shadow of an assumed name, while others with equal assurance whispered in the unfortunate girl's ear the old story of a rival in her affections. . . . Ann began to lose faith." *(19)*

A. Y. Ellis: "She had a secret, too, and a sorrow—the unexplained and painful absence of McNamar." *(20)*

R. B. Rutledge: "In the meantime, Mr. Lincoln paid his addresses to Ann. Continued his visits and attentions regularly." *(21)*

Billy Herndon: "Lincoln began to court Miss Rutledge in dead earnest." *(22)*

Jimmy Short: "The Rutledges lived about a half a mile from me. Mr. L. came over to see me and them every day or two. I did not know of any engagement or tender passages between Mr. L. and Miss R. at the time. But after her death, which happened in '34 or '35, he seemed to be so much affected and grieved so hardly that I then supposed there must have been something of the kind." *(23)*

Mentor Graham: "Lincoln and she was engaged—Lincoln told me so. She intimated to me the same." *(24)*

R. B. Rutledge: "There is no kind of doubt as to the existence of this engagement. David Rutledge [another of her brothers] urged Ann to consummate it but she refused until such time as she could see McNamar, inform him of the change in her feelings, and seek an honorable release." *(25)*

Billy Herndon: "To one of her brothers she said—'As soon as his studies are completed we are to be married.' " *(26)*

R. B. Rutledge: "Mr. Lincoln courted Ann and engaged to marry her on the completion of the study of law. In this I am corroborated by James McRutledge, a cousin about her age and who was in her confidence. He says in a letter to me just received: 'Ann told me once in coming from a camp meeting on Rock Creek that engagements made too far ahead sometimes failed—that one had failed, meaning her engagement with McNamar, and gave me to understand that as soon as certain studies were completed she and Lincoln would be married.' I have no doubt but Ann had fully determined to break off the engagement with McNamar, but presume she had never notified him of the fact, as he did not return until after her death." *(27)*

John McNamar: "Mr. Lincoln was not to my knowledge paying particular attention to any of the young ladies of my acquaintance when I left for my home in New York. There was no rivalry between us on that score. On the contrary, I had every reason to believe him my warm personal friend. . . . I corrected at his request some of the grammatical errors in his first address to the voters of Sangamon County. . . . But by and by I was left so far behind in the race I did not deem my chances worthy of notice." *(28)*

R. B. Rutledge: "In August 1835 Ann sickened." *(29)*

Billy Herndon: "Late in the summer she took to her bed. A fever was burning in her head. Day by day she sank. . . . Her physician had forbidden visitors to enter her room, prescribing absolute quiet. But her brother relates that she kept enquiring for Lincoln so continuously, at times demanding to see him, that the family at last sent for him. On his arrival at her bedside the door was closed and he was left alone with her. What was said, what vows and revelations were made during this sad interview, were known only to him and the dying girl." *(30)*

John Rutledge: "I have heard mother say that Ann would frequently sing for Lincoln's benefit. She had a clear ringing voice. Early in her illness he called, and she sang a hymn for which he always expressed a great preference. It begins— 'Vain man, thy fond pursuits forbear.' You will find it in one of the standard hymn books. It was likewise the last thing she ever sung." *(31)*

Billy Herndon: "A few days afterward she became unconscious and remained so until her death." *(32)*

John Jones: "During her last illness he visited her sick chamber and on his return stopped at my house. It was very evident that he was much distressed and I was not surprised when it was rumored subsequently that his reason was in danger." *(33)*

R. B. Rutledge: "The effect upon Mr. Lincoln's mind was terrible. He became plunged in despair and many of his friends feared that reason would desert her throne." *(34)*

G. W. Miles: "Lincoln took her death very hard, so much so, that some thought his mind would become impaired." *(35)*

Billy Herndon: "To one friend he complained that the thought that the snows and rains fall upon her grave filled him with indescribable grief." (36)

G. W. Miles: "Bowling Greene went to Salem after Lincoln. Brought him to his house and kept him a week or two and succeeded in cheering him—Lincoln—up, though he was quite melancholy for months." (37)

Billy Herndon: "In the years that followed, Mr. Lincoln never forgot the kindness of Greene through those weeks of suffering and peril. In 1842, when the latter died and Lincoln was selected by the Masonic lodge to deliver the funeral oration, he broke down in the midst of his address. His voice was choked with deep emotion. He stood a few moments while his lips quivered in the effort to form the words of fervent praise he sought to utter and the tears ran down his yellow and shrivelled cheeks. Every heart was hushed at the spectacle. After repeated efforts, he found it impossible to speak and strode away, bitterly sobbing. . . .

"It was shortly after this that Dr. Jason Duncan placed in Lincoln's hands a poem called *Immortality*. The piece starts out with the line—'Oh! Why should the spirit of mortal be proud.' Lincoln's love for this poem has certainly made it immortal. He committed these lines to memory." (38)

A. Y. Ellis: "The time and the place he committed this to memory I never knew." (39)

Abraham Lincoln: "I am not the author. I would give all I am worth and go in debt to be able to write so fine a piece as I think that is." (40)

A. Y. Ellis: "Mr. Lincoln says he was shown the piece of poetry when he was a young man by a friend. I have the whole of it pasted in my scrap book." (41)

Oh, why should the spirit of mortal be proud?
Like a swift fleeting meteor, a fast-flying cloud,
A flash of the lightning, a break of the wave,
He passes from life to his rest in the grave.

The leaves of the oak and the willow shall fade,
Be scattered around and together be laid;
And the young and the old, the low and the high,
Shall molder to dust, and together shall lie.

The infant a mother attended and loved;
The mother that infant's affection who proved;
The husband, that mother and infant who blessed:
Each, all, are away to their dwelling of rest.

The maid on whose cheek, on whose brow, in whose eye,
Shone beauty and pleasure—her triumphs are by;
And the memory of those who loved her and praised,
Are alike from the minds of the living erased.

The hand of the king that the sceptre hath borne,
The brow of the priest that the mitre hath worn,
The eye of the sage, and the heart of the brave,
Are hidden and lost in the depths of the grave.

The peasant, whose lot was to sow and to reap,
The herdsman, who climbed with his goats up the steep,
The beggar, who wandered in search of his bread,
Have faded away like the grass that we tread.

The saint, who enjoyed the communion of Heaven,
The sinner, who dared to remain unforgiven,
The wise and the foolish, the guilty and just,
Have quietly mingled their bones in the dust.

So, the multitude goes—like the flower or the weed
That withers away to let others succeed;
So the multitude comes—even those we behold,
To repeat every tale that has often been told.

For we are the same that our fathers have been;
We see the same sights that our fathers have seen;
We drink the same stream, we feel the same sun,
And run the same course that our fathers have run.

The thoughts we are thinking, our fathers would think;
From the death we are shrinking, our fathers would shrink;
To the life we are clinging, they also would cling—
But it speeds from us all like a bird on the wing.

They loved—but the story we cannot unfold;
They scorned—but the heart of the haughty is cold;
They grieved—but no wail from their slumber will come;
They joyed—but the tongue of their gladness is dumb.

They died—aye, they died—we things that are now,
That walk on the turf that lies over their brow,
And make in their dwellings a transient abode,
Meet the things that they met on their pilgrimage road.

Yea, hope and despondency, pleasure and pain,
Are mingled together in sunshine and rain;
And the smile and tear, the song and the dirge,
Still follow each other, like surge upon surge.

'Tis the wink of an eye—'tis the draught of a breath,
From the blossom of health to the paleness of death,
From the gilded saloon to the bier and the shroud,
Oh, why should the spirit of mortal be proud? (42)

27.

"Did You Vote For Me?"

As Berry & Lincoln enterprises faltered, Abe felt the pinch of his empty pockets. "Lincoln was earning no money," said Herndon. *(1)*

"He had a running board bill to pay and nothing to pay it with," a friend added. *(2)*

He took odd jobs as a laborer, splitting rails and doing construction work and farm chores. Then came his first big break—an opportunity to serve in a government post. Said Abe, "Was appointed postmaster at New Salem." *(3)*

Lincoln was commissioned on May 7, 1833. He was chosen to replace Samuel Hill, his business rival, after the ladies of New Salem complained to postal authorities that Hill would make them wait for the mail while he served liquor to the men in his store. The Democratic administration of President Andrew Jackson allowed the post to go to Lincoln even though he was a Clay man; "the office being too insignificant to make . . . politics an objection," observed Abe. *(4)*

A lone horseback rider carried the mail into New Salem once a week. After 1834, a stagecoach en route to Springfield would make regular stops there.

Letter writers used no stamps or envelopes. They tried to squeeze all the message they could write on one page, writing sideways or diagonally across to save postage (out of respect for the fee-paying recipient). Then they folded the page and sealed it with wax. A fee was charged according to the number of pages

185

and the distance traveled. The person receiving the letter was expected to pay the postage. The postmaster calculated the charge, marking it on the upper right hand corner of the folded page. The rates for each page were 6¢ for 30 miles or less, 10¢ for up to 80 miles, 12½¢ for up to 150 miles, 18½¢ for 400 miles or less. Over 400 miles was 25¢ per page.

Once a week, Lincoln made the rounds of his customers. "Mr. Lincoln used to tell me that when he had a call to go to the country . . . he placed inside his hat all the letters belonging to people in the neighborhood and distributed them along the way," said Herndon. (5)

"He carried his office around in his hat," cracked one New Salemite. (6)

Everyone welcomed the mail, especially when the mailman was "Honest Abe." Folks would always ask him in and they would read the letter together and discuss what it said. If the customer was receiving a newspaper, Abe could tell him where to find all the interesting stories since he pored over every newspaper that came through his office.

As Postmaster, Lincoln received a modest salary and the privilege of mailing letters for free. This practice is called franking and postal regulations were quite strict on the matter. "If any person shall frank any letter or letters other than those written by himself or by his order on the business of the office, he shall, on conviction thereof, pay a fine of ten dollars." (7)

The Postmaster conducted his office in a genial manner, not allowing mere formalities to get in the way of service to his customers. One private letter, from Matthew Marsh to his brother George, illustrates Lincoln's freewheeling policy of administrative protocol. "The Postmaster is very careless about leaving his office open and unlocked during the day," complained Marsh. "Half the time I go in and get my papers without anyone being there, as was the case yesterday.

"The letter was only marked twenty-five," Marsh observed, "and even if he had been there and known it was double he would not have charged me any more. Luckily, he is a very clever fellow and a particular friend of mine. If he is there when I carry this to the office I will get him to frank it." (8)

Marsh's letter was folded and sealed. Sure enough, on the

outside of the letter in Lincoln's own hand was marked: "Free. A. Lincoln, P. M. New Salem, Ill. Sept. 22." (9)

Once Lincoln became miffed at one of his patrons who wanted a receipt for fees paid. "At your request," Lincoln wrote, "I send you a receipt from the postage on your paper. I am somewhat surprised at your request. I will however comply with it. The law requires newspaper postage to be paid in advance and now that I have waited a full year you choose to wound my feelings by insinuating that unless you get a receipt I will probably make you pay it again." (10)

Another government job beckoned for Lincoln. "Someone, probably a Democrat who voted for him in the preceding fall, recommended him to John Calhoun, then surveyor of the county, as suitable material for an assistant," said Herndon. (11)

The county surveyor's office was swamped with requests. Settlers flooding the prairie needed division lines to mark their farms. Speculators wanted their huge tracts of land parceled into lots. Towns needed to be laid. Miles of roads needed to be planned. Surveying was a skill in great demand on the frontier.

Lincoln took the job. "This procured bread and kept soul and body together," he said. (12)

Since Lincoln had little practical knowledge of the art of surveying and no acquaintance at all with its underlying mathematical principles, he could not go to work until these skills were thoroughly mastered. Calhoun lent him some books on surveying and told him to study hard until he felt that he knew enough to begin.

Lincoln paid a call on New Salem's school teacher, Mentor Graham. "Friend Graham has always been remarkable for his willingness to instruct the youth of the community," said Billy Greene. (13)

Said R. B. Rutledge of Lincoln, "Perhaps received more assistance from Mentor Graham than any other person." (14)

"In the month of July 1833, Mr. Lincoln came and lived with me and continued with me about six months," recalled Mentor Graham. "I was then teaching school. I taught him the rules of surveying. I do not think that Mr. Lincoln knew anything of arithmetic, especially geometry and trigonometry before he came to my house.

"I think," offered Graham, "I may say that he was my scholar and I was his teacher." *(15)*

The two went at the books with solemn resolution. Mentor Graham's daughter remembers how her father and Lincoln "frequently sat up till midnight engrossed in calculations." *(16)*

"It was here," said Graham, "that he commenced to study the English Grammar with me. . . . *(17)* He studied to see the subject matter clearly and to express it truly and strongly. I have known him to study for hours the best way of three to express an idea. *(18)*

"I have taught in my life four or six thousand pupils as school master," avowed his admiring teacher, "and no one ever surpassed him in rapidly acquiring the rudiments and rules of English Grammar." *(19)*

Some nights he worked alone, absorbed in his books until daylight. Besides grammar he studied decimal fractions, logarithms, trigonometry, the use of mathematical instruments and the scaling of maps. He caught sleep in short stretches and barely took time to eat.

Study was wearing him down. His thin features grew ghostly and gaunt; his eyes reddened and blurred. Friends thought he resembled a hard drinker out on a spree. They became worried and kept after him to take care of himself. "He was so emaciated," observed Henry McHenry, "we feared he might bring on mental derangement." *(20)*

After six weeks of serious study, Lincoln reported to Calhoun and announced that he was ready. He bought a horse, saddle and bridle on credit and acquired a compass, chain and other surveying equipment. Lincoln set out to measure and mark property lines all over Sangamon County.

"It has never been denied that his surveys were exact and just and he was so manifestly fair that he was often chosen to settle disputed questions of corners and measurements," Herndon said. *(21)*

Henry McHenry remembers an argument over the exact location of an old street corner. "After a good deal of disputing," he reported, "we agreed to send for Lincoln and to abide by his decision.

"He came with compass, flag-staff and chain . . . and surveyed the whole section. When in the neighborhood of the disputed corner by actual survey, he called for his staff and driving it in the ground at a certain spot said: 'Gentlemen, here is the corner.'

"We dug down into the ground at the point indicated and lo! There we found about six or eight inches of the original stake, sharpened at the end and beneath which was the usual piece of charcoal placed there by Rector, the surveyor who laid the ground off for the government many years before." (22)

He laid the lines for towns in New Boston, Bath, Albany and Huron. He surveyed roads and county lines. He made friends wherever he went. "Not only did his wit, kindliness and knowledge attract people, but his strange clothes and uncouth awkwardness advertised him—the shortness of his trousers causing particular remark and amusement," said Coleman Smoot. "Soon the name 'Abe Lincoln' was a household word." (23)

When he surveyed the town of Petersburg, he let one street go crooked. It was the street near Jemima Elmore's house, a widow whose husband served with Lincoln in the Black Hawk War. He drew the line to go around her property so as not to cut her house in half.

For the first time in his life, Lincoln was making a comfortable living. His salary of three dollars a day was royal in an economy where the Governor of the State earned a thousand dollars a year and decent board and lodging went for a dollar a week. But he was never allowed to enjoy the fruits of his labor. His creditors found him.

April 7, 1834. Peter Van Bergen sues Lincoln and Berry. He holds a note signed by the two principles for $379.82. Jimmy Short explains: "Radford sold out his stock of goods to W. G. Greene and Greene sold out to Lincoln and Berry. Lincoln and Berry gave their note . . . to Greene and Greene assigned it to Radford. Radford assigned it to Peter Van Bergen." (24)

The judge orders Lincoln to pay Van Bergen his share, set at $154. When Lincoln admits he can't pay, the court moves to take possession of all his personal belongings.

Lincoln was crushed. "Mr. L. was then very much discouraged and said he would let the whole thing go by the board," remembered Jimmy Short. (25) Gone were his horse, bridle, saddle and all his surveying instruments. Suddenly, after such a promising start to his career he was unable to continue.

"I did all I could to put him in better spirits," Jimmy Short said. *(26)* On the day Lincoln's wares went up for public auction, he (Jimmy Short) made sure he was there. "When the sale came off—which Mr. Lincoln did not attend—I bid on the . . . property at $120," Jimmy said. "Immediately gave it up again to Mr. L." *(27)*

Through the generosity of his friend, Lincoln was back in business. But not for long. Again he was in danger of being separated from his horse. "My father sold Lincoln the horse," recalled Tom Watkins. "My recollection is that Lincoln agreed to pay him fifty dollars for it. Lincoln was a little slow in making the payments and after he had paid all but ten dollars, my father, who was a high strung man, became impatient and sued him for the balance.

"I have always been sorry Father sued him," admitted Watkins. *(28)*

Somehow, Lincoln managed to come up with enough money to prevent the repossession of his horse.

April 19, 1834. The name Abraham Lincoln appeared in the *Sangamo Journal* once again as a candidate for the state legislature. This time, he ran as a candidate of the Whig Party along with his political mentor, John Stuart. "I have Lincoln's word for it that it was more of a hand shaking campaign than anything else," said Herndon. *(29)*

"He came to my house near Island Grove during the harvest," remembered Rowan Herndon. "There were some thirty men in the field. He got his dinner and went out in the field where the men were at work.

"I gave him an introduction and the boys said that they could not vote for a man unless he could make a hand."

"Well, boys," crowed Lincoln, "if that is all, I am sure of your votes."

Said Rowan Herndon, "He took hold of the cradle and led the way all the round with perfect ease. The boys were satisfied and I don't think he lost a vote in the crowd." *(30)*

When Doc Barrett saw Lincoln, he complained to Rowan Herndon, "Can't the party raise no better materials than that?"

"I said go tomorrow and hear all before you pronounce judgement," Rowan recalled. "When he come back, I said— 'Doc, what say you now?' "

"Why sir! He is a perfect take-in," the Doc replied. "He knows more than all of them put together." *(31)*

Election Day was August 4th. This time, Lincoln finished second, outpolling his friend John Stuart, who finished fourth, good enough to seat them both in the Illinois State Legislature.

The next session of the legislature was scheduled to begin on December 1, 1834. The new lawmaker made his preparations to leave New Salem and take his place in the government. He arranged with friend Caleb Carman to care for the two loves of his life that he would be leaving behind—Jane and Susan.

"I will tell you about Lincoln and his two cats," said Carman. "When living with me in Salem we had two kittens, Lincoln's favorite pets. He would take them up in his lap and play with them and hold their heads together to say that Jane had a better countenance than Susan had—that being their names . . . He went to Vandalia to the legislature and left very strict orders for the cats to be well taken care of." *(32)*

As an elected representative, Lincoln was showing a new-found awareness of the image he would project. He had to do something about it.

"After he was elected to the legislature, he came to my house one day," related Coleman Smoot.

"Smoot," he said. "Did you vote for me?"

"I did."

"Well," said Lincoln, "You must loan me money to buy suitable clothing. I want to make a decent appearance in the legislature."

Said Smoot, "I then loaned him $200, which he returned to me according to promise." *(33)*

Lincoln spent $60 on a fine cloth suit, the first one he ever owned. Then as November drew to a close, he boarded a stagecoach for the 75-mile journey to the state capital at Vandalia. Abraham Lincoln, now twenty-five, was ready to begin his career as a servant of the people.

* * *

"I would be much pleased to see some heroic shrewd, fully-informed, healthy-bodied, middle-aged, beard-faced American blacksmith or boatman come down from the West across the Alleghenies and walk into the Presidency, dressed in a clean suit of working attire, and with the tan all over his face, breast and arms; I would certainly vote for that sort of man. . . ." *(34)*

—*Walt Whitman, 1856*

Lincoln in Life and Literature:
A Chronology

1778   January 6. Thomas Lincoln, Abraham's father, born.

1782   Abraham Lincoln, grandfather of the President and father of Thomas Lincoln, leaves Virginia with his family and settles in Kentucky.

1784   February 5. Nancy Hanks, Abraham's mother, is born.

1786   May. Grandfather Abraham Lincoln is killed by Indians.

1788   Sarah Bush, Abraham's step-mother is born.

1799   Dennis Hanks, Abraham's cousin, is born.

1806   March 13. Sarah Bush marries Daniel Johnston.

   June 12. Thomas Lincoln marries Nancy Hanks. They settle in Elizabethtown, Kentucky.

1807   February 10. Sarah Lincoln is born.

1808   Fall. Lincoln family moves to Nolin's Creek near Hodgenville, Kentucky.

1809   February 12. Abraham Lincoln is born.

1811   Spring. Lincolns move to Knob Creek farm.

1815   Daniel Johnston dies, leaving Sarah Bush Johnston a widow with three children.

1816   December. Lincolns relocate in Indiana and build an open-faced hut near Gentryville.

1818   October 5. Nancy Hanks Lincoln dies.

   December 13. Mary Todd (Mrs. Abraham Lincoln) born in Lexington, Kentucky.

December 25. William Herndon, Lincoln's law partner and biographer, is born.

1819   December 2. Thomas Lincoln marries Sarah Bush Johnston in Elizabethtown, Kentucky.

1826   August 2. Sarah Lincoln (Abraham's sister) marries Aaron Grigsby.

1828   January 20. Sarah Lincoln Grigsby dies in childbirth.

Fall. Abraham Lincoln and Allen Gentry make flatboat trip down Mississippi River to New Orleans.

1830   March. Lincolns move from Gentryville, Indiana to Illinois near Decatur.

1831   March. Lincoln and John Hanks hired by Denton Offut to take a flatboat to New Orleans.

April 19. Lincoln's flatboat is stranded on mill dam at New Salem.

July. Lincoln returns from New Orleans and is hired as a storekeeper in New Salem by Denton Offut.

1832   March 9. Lincoln announces candidacy for Illinois State Legislature.

April. Lincoln and Rowan Herndon pilot the steamship Talisman down the Sangamon River.

April 22. Lincoln joins Illinois Militia for Black Hawk War and is elected Captain.

July 16. Lincoln discharged from military service.

August 6. Lincoln defeated in election for State Legislature.

Autumn. Herndon Brothers sell their share in store to Lincoln and William Berry.

1833   March 6. Lincoln and Berry receive license to sell liquor.

May 7. Lincoln named Postmaster of New Salem.

Spring. Lincoln-Berry store fails.

1834   April 19. Lincoln announces candidacy for Illinois State Legislature.

August 4. Lincoln elected to Illinois State Legislature.

December 1. Lincoln attends first session of legislature at Vandalia, Illinois. Meets fellow lawmaker Stephen A. Douglas for the first time.

1835   January 10. William Berry dies, leaving Lincoln solely responsible for their $1100 debt.

August 25. Ann Rutledge dies.

1836   August 1. Lincoln meets Mary Owens in New Salem and begins a lukewarm courtship.

August 1. Lincoln re-elected to State Legislature.

1837   March 1. Lincoln admitted to Illinois Bar.

April 12. Lincoln becomes law partner of John Stuart.

August 16. Lincoln writes final letter to Mary Owens, ending their brief courtship.

1838   Summer. Lincoln re-elected to State Legislature.

1839   Autumn. Lincoln meets Mary Todd at Springfield.

1840   Re-elected to State Legislature. Campaigned across Illinois for Whig Presidential candidate William Henry Harrison and engaged in direct debate with spokesman for the Democratic ticket, Stephen Douglas.

Fall. Lincoln engaged to Mary Todd.

1841   January 1. Lincoln breaks engagement with Mary Todd.

April 14. Lincoln becomes law partner of Stephen T. Logan.

1842   November 4. Lincoln marries Mary Todd. He gives her a wedding band that she wears to her dying day. Inscribed on the inside are the words: "Love is Eternal."

1843   August 1. Son Robert Todd Lincoln is born.

1844   December 9. Lincoln accepts William Herndon as law partner.

1846   March 10. Second son, Edward Baker Lincoln, is born.

April 18. Lincoln sends samples of his poetry to friend Andrew Johnston.

August 3. Lincoln is elected to U.S. House of Representatives.

September 6. Lincoln sends more original poetry to Andrew Johnston.

1849   January 13. Lincoln attempts to introduce a bill to abolish slavery in the District of Columbia.

March 4. Congressman Lincoln's term expires.

1850   February 1. Edward Lincoln, age 4, dies after illness of two weeks.

December 21. William Wallace (Willie), third son, is born.

1851   January 17. Thomas Lincoln, Abraham's father, dies.

1853   April 4. Thomas (Tad) Lincoln is born.

1855   February 8. Lincoln defeated in campaign to become U.S. Senator.

1856   May 29. Lincoln helps organize new Republican Party in Illinois.

June 19. Lincoln receives considerable support for Vice-Presidency at Republican Convention but is defeated.

1858   June 16. Receives Republican nomination to run for U.S. Senate against Stephen Douglas. Lincoln gives famous "House Divided" speech.

August-September. Lincoln and Douglas meet in series of debates across Illinois.

November 2. Democrats win election, returning Douglas to Senate.

1859   December 20. Lincoln writes brief autobiographical sketch for newspaperman Jesse Fell.

1860   February 27. Lincoln is acclaimed for his powerful speech at Cooper Union in New York City. ("Let us have faith that right makes might . . .")

May 9. John Hanks appears at Republican State Convention in Illinois with two fence rails Lincoln split thirty years before. He becomes famous as the "rail-splitter" candidate.

May 18. Republican National Convention nominates Lincoln for President of the United States.

June 1. Lincoln prepares lengthy autobiographical sketch for John Locke Scripps.

June 18. Senator Stephen A. Douglas of Illinois is nominated for President by Democrats.

June 28. John Breckinridge nominated by Southern Democrats.

July 15. Scripps' campaign biography of Lincoln appears in the Chicago Press and Tribune.

November 6. Lincoln elected President with minority of the vote. His opponents polled a million more votes than he did, yet he had the highest vote total of any candidate.

December 20. South Carolina becomes the first state to secede from the Union.

1861 January-February. Mississippi, Florida, Alabama, Georgia, Louisiana and Texas secede from the Union.

January 30. Lincoln visits step-mother, Sarah Bush Lincoln.

February 4. Delegates from secessionist states form Confederate Government.

February 18. Jefferson Davis inaugurated as President of the Confederate States of America.

March 4. Abraham Lincoln inaugurated as sixteenth President of the United States.

April 14. Union garrison at Fort Sumter surrenders to Confederate forces.

April 15. President Lincoln calls for 75,000 volunteers to preserve Union.

1862 February 20. Lincoln's son, William Wallace (Willie), dies in White House.

July 22. Lincoln presents draft of Emancipation Proclamation to his Cabinet. He decides to wait for a Union battlefield victory before announcing it.

September 17. Union army is victorious at Antietam.

September 22. Emancipation Proclamation is announced publicly.

1863   July 1-3. Battle of Gettysburg. Lee's Confederate forces are in retreat after heavy casualties on both sides.

July 13-16. Hundreds killed. Millions of dollars in property is destroyed during draft riots in New York City.

November 19. Lincoln delivers Gettysburg Address.

1864   June 8. Lincoln nominated for second term as President.

August 23. Lincoln asks Cabinet to endorse secret memorandum promising cooperation to his successor as President for the sake of preserving the Union.

November 8. Lincoln re-elected as President.

November 15. General Sherman sets Atlanta on fire, beginning his army's March of Destruction through Georgia.

1865   March 4. Abraham Lincoln inaugurated as President for the second time.

April 2. Confederate government abandons their capital at Richmond.

April 4. Lincoln walks two miles through the streets of Richmond. He sits in Jefferson Davis' chair at the former Confederate Executive Mansion.

April 9. Lee surrenders to Grant at Appomattox.

April 14. 10:20 P.M. Lincoln is shot at Ford's Theater by actor John Wilkes Booth.

April 15. 7:22 A.M. Lincoln never regains consciousness and dies of head wound.

May. William Herndon visits Petersburg, Illinois to interview former residents of New Salem who knew Lincoln as a young man in the 1830's.

June 13. Herndon meets Dennis Hanks, Lincoln's cousin, in Chicago.

September 8. Herndon meets Abraham's step-mother, Sarah Bush Lincoln.

September 14. Herndon and Lincoln's boyhood friend Nat Grigsby visit grave of Lincoln's mother, Nancy Hanks Lincoln.

1866 *The Life of Abraham Lincoln,* by Josiah Gilbert Holland, appears characterizing Lincoln as a good Christian gentleman.

1869 Sarah Bush Lincoln dies.

1871 July 15. Tad Lincoln dies after illness of several weeks.

1872 *Life of Abraham Lincoln from His Birth to His Inauguration as President,* by Ward Hill Lamon and Chauncey Black, is published. It is an unflattering account of Lincoln's life by his personal bodyguard, Lamon, and by Black, an anti-Lincoln Democrat. Lamon made liberal use of Herndon's research material.

1882 July 16. Mary Todd Lincoln dies after years of living as a recluse in a darkened room.

1885 *The Life of Abraham Lincoln,* by Isaac Arnold, an Illinois politician who served in Congress with Lincoln, is published.

1889 *Herndon's Lincoln: The True Story of a Great Life,* by William Herndon and Jesse Weik, appears. It is the most intimate, detailed and controversial biography ever to appear on Lincoln. Despite some wild allegations that were later proven false, his work is, considered the standard source on Lincoln. It is due to Herndon's diligence that we owe much of our knowledge of Lincoln as a man.

1890 *Abraham Lincoln,* by John Nicolay and John Hay. The President's personal secretaries, publish their ten-volume biography. Authorized by Robert Lincoln, who made all his father's personal papers and documents available to them, it is a detailed and knowledgeable insider's account of the Lincoln Administration during the Civil War.

1891 March 18. William Herndon dies.

1892 Dennis Hanks, nearly 93, dies after being run over by a horse-drawn carriage.

1896 *The Early Life of Abraham Lincoln,* by Ida Tarbell, is published. It is a result of a series of articles for *McClure's Magazine.* Tarbell, a professional journalist, used her skills as an investigative reporter to uncover much new information on Lincoln's early life.

1908 *Boyhood of Lincoln,* by Eleanor Atkinson, appears. It is a lengthy verbatim interview with Dennis Hanks that took place in 1889.

1926 *Abraham Lincoln: The Prairie Years,* by Carl Sandburg. Powerful, poetic panorama of the early Lincoln. Sensitive, vivid, compelling, it created an image of Lincoln that has endured to this day. However, it has been criticized for lacking historical integrity.

1928 *Abraham Lincoln 1809-1858,* by Albert Beveridge, was published unfinished after the author's death. Beveridge combined practical political experience (He was a senator from Indiana) with the trained eye of a historian (He won a Pulitzer Prize for his earlier biography of John Marshall) to produce one of the most distinguished and scholarly biographies of Lincoln ever written.

1939 *Abe Lincoln in Illinois,* Broadway play starring Raymond Massey wins Pulitzer Prize. Perpetuated many myths on Lincoln, who was depicted as a New Deal liberal.

Young Mr. Lincoln. Young Henry Fonda plays a "jack-legged lawyer" from Illinois. "I'm a Lincoln nut," said Fonda. "I've read three-quarters of the books that have been written about Lincoln."

Abraham Lincoln: The War Years, by Carl Sandburg. Companion volumes to *Prairie Years.* Together they formed a massive work of art in literature that earned Sandburg a Pulitzer Prize.

1952 *Abraham Lincoln,* by Benjamin Thomas, the first biography of Lincoln to make use of the newly available (1947) Robert Todd Lincoln Collection in the Library of Congress and the soon-to-be published *Collected Works of Abraham Lincoln,* which Thomas helped edit.

1954 *The Collected Works of Abraham Lincoln,* edited by Roy Basler, is the culmination of nearly thirty years work collecting, editing and ordering all of Lincoln's letters, speeches and documents, both public and private.

1959 *Lincoln's Youth: Indiana Years; Seven to Twenty-One, 1816-1830,* by Louis A. Warren, an exhaustively researched, annotated account of Lincoln's years in Indiana.

1960 *The Real Abraham Lincoln,* by Reinhard Luthin, a hard-nosed factual account of his life, presented by a noted Columbia University history professor.

1977 *With Malice Toward None: The Life of Abraham Lincoln,* by Stephen Oates. An artful biography in graceful prose, dramatic narration and sensitive characterization.

1984 *Lincoln,* by Gore Vidal, a fictional account of backstairs White House politics during the Civil War.

Chapter Notes

INTRODUCTION
THE FRONTIER YEARS: DIGGING UP THE STORY

1. David Donald, *Lincoln's Herndon*, Alfred A. Knopf, 1948, p. 300. (Herndon to Weik, December 21, 1885)

2. John Locke Scripps, *Life of Abraham Lincoln*, Indiana University Press, 1961, p. 13. (Reprinted from *Chicago Press and Tribune*, May 19, 1860) (Scripps to Herndon, June 24, 1865)

3. Emanuel Hertz, *The Hidden Lincoln*, The Viking Press, 1938, p. 64. (Herndon to Ward Hill Lamon, Feb. 25, 1870)

4. Hertz, 84. (Herndon to Weik, Oct. 8, 1881)

5. Hertz, 71. (Herndon to Lamon, March 6, 1870)

6. William F. Herndon, *Herndon's Lincoln*, I:ix.

7. Hertz, 29. (Herndon to Hart, Jan. 13, 1866)

8. Herndon, *Herndon's Lincoln*, Bobbs-Merrill Co., 1970, p. xiv.

9. Hertz, 440. (*Herndon Notes*, Jan. 3, 1886)

10. Donald, p. 184. (Herndon to Josiah Holland, June 8, 1865)

11. Hertz, 353. (*Herndon Notes*, Sept. 8, 1865)

12. Hertz, 84-85.

13. Hertz, 353.

14. Hertz, 357-358. (*Herndon Notes*, Sept. 14, 1865)

15. William Barton, *The Life of Abraham Lincoln*, Bobbs-Merrill, 1925. V.I p. 484. (Hanks to Herndon, April 2, 1866)

16. Eleanor Atkinson, *The Boyhood of Lincoln*, The McClure Co., 1908, p. 3. (Interview with Dennis Hanks, Jan. 1889)

17. Hertz, 94. (Herndon to Weik, April 14, 1885)

18. Donald, 308. (Herndon to Weik, May 6, 1885)

19. Hertz, 94. (Herndon to Weik, April 14, 1885)

20. ibid

21. Albert Beveridge, *Abraham Lincoln*, Houghton-Mifflin Co., 1928, p. 15. (Hanks to Herndon, Feb. 10, 1866)

22. Beveridge, 15. (Hanks to Herndon, Feb. 22, 1866)

23. Beveridge, 15. (Hanks to Herndon, Feb. 10, 1866)

24. Hertz, 276. (Statement of Hanks, June 13, 1865)

25. Beveridge, 15. (Hanks to Herndon, Feb. 10, 1866)

26. Beveridge, 5.

27. Donald, 180. (Hanks to Herndon, Dec. 12, 1865)

28. Hanks to Herndon, January 26, 1866

29. Beveridge, 5n.

30. Hertz 13.

31. Abraham Lincoln, *The Life and Writings of Abraham Lincoln*, Random House, 1940, Philip Van Doren Stern, ed; p. 564.

32. Hertz, 120.

33. Hertz, 440. (*Herndon Notes*, Jan. 8, 1886)

34. Hertz, 64.

35. Hertz, 63. (Herndon to Lamon, Feb. 25, 1870)

36. Hertz, 12.

37. Hertz, 438. (*Herndon Notes*, Jan. 8, 1886)

38. Donald, 331. (Herndon to Fowler, Aug. 15, 1889)

39. Hertz, 267. (Herndon to Bartlett, Feb. 27, 1891) Note: This was Herndon's last letter. He died March 18, 1891.

40. New York Times Book Review, *After 175 Years They Still Pursue Lincoln*, Herbert Mitgang, Feb. 12, 1984.

41. Abraham Lincoln, CW III:359-360.

42. Herndon, *Life of Lincoln*, Da Capo Press, 1983, p. 353.

43. Carl Sandburg, *The War Years*, Harcourt, Brace & World, 1939; II:306.

CHAPTER 1.

1. Albert Beveridge, *Abraham Lincoln*, Houghton-Mifflin Co., 1928, p. 8.

2. Ida M. Tarbell, *The Early Life of Abraham Lincoln*, reprinted: A. S. Barnes & Co., 1974 p. 24; original: S. S. McClure, 1896.

3. Tarbell, *The Early Life of Abraham Lincoln*, p. 23 (From records in surveyor's office, Jefferson County, KY.)

4. Beveridge, *Abraham Lincoln*, p. 24.

5. Carl Sandburg, *Abraham Lincoln, The Prairie Years:* Harcourt, Brace and Co., 1926, p. 15.

6. Emanuel Hertz, *The Hidden Lincoln*, The Viking Press, 1938, p. 275. (Letter from Dennis Hanks to William Herndon, June 13, 1865)

7. Abraham Lincoln, *The Life and Writings of Abraham Lincoln*, Philip Van Doren Stern, ed., Random House, 1940 p. 600. (Autobiographical sketch written for use in preparing a campaign biography, June 1, 1860)

8. Hertz, *The Hidden Lincoln*, p. 355. (Letter from Nat Grigsby to William Herndon, September 12, 1865)

9. Eleanor Atkinson, *The Boyhood of Lincoln*, The McClure Co., 1908, p. 11. (Interview with Dennis Hanks, January 1889)

10. Sandburg, *The Prairie Years*, p. 6.

CHAPTER 2.

1. Louis A. Warren, *Lincoln's Youth, Indiana Years, Seven to Twenty-One*, 1816-1830, Greenwood Press, reprinted 1976, p. 6. Original: Indiana Historical Society, 1959.

2. Carl Sandburg, *Abraham Lincoln, The Prairie Years and The War Years*, One Volume Edition, Harcourt, Brace, Jovanovich, 1954 p. 5.

3. Warren, p. 8. (Statement by C.H.S. Vawter, granddaughter of Sarah Mitchell in Louisville Courier-Journal, February 20, 1874.)

4. Atkinson, p. 11.

5. Hertz, p. 275. (Letter from Dennis Hanks to William Herndon, June 13, 1865.)

6. Warren, p. 240

7. Sandburg, 1954, p. 6.

8. Tarbell, 1896, reprinted 1974, p. 235. (Statement of Christopher Columbus Graham, April 13, 1882.)

9. Tarbell, p. 233.

CHAPTER 3.

1. Atkinson, p. 6.

2. Atkinson, p. 7.

3. Atkinson, p. 8.

4. Beveridge, p. 3.

5. Atkinson, p. 9.

6. Sandburg, 1954, p. 8.

7. Sandburg, 1954, p. 8.

8. Francis Marion Van Natter, *Lincoln's Boyhood*, Public Affairs Press, 1963, p. 7.

9. Van Natter, p. 14.

10. Atkinson, p. 11.

11. Beveridge, p. 29. (Burba to Herndon, May 25, 1866)

12. Atkinson, p. 13.

13. Ida M. Tarbell, *The Life of Abraham Lincoln*. McClure & Phillips and Co., 1900, Vol. I., p. 17.

14. Nicolay and Hay, *Abraham Lincoln: A History*, Vol I., p. 27.

15. Hertz, p. 276. (Hanks to Herndon, June 13, 1865)

16. John Locke Scripps, *Life of Abraham Lincoln*, reprint: Indiana

University Press, 1961 p. 32 (original: Chicago Press and Tribune, May 19, 1860)

17. Henry Rankin, *Personal Recollections of Abraham Lincoln,* 1916, p. 325.

18. Abraham Lincoln, *Collected Works of Abraham Lincoln,* Roy P. Basler, Ed., Rutgers University Press, 1953, Volume II, p. 217.

19. Tarbell, *The Early Life of Abraham Lincoln,* p. 44.

20. Tarbell, *The Early Life of Abraham Lincoln, p.* 45.

21. Beveridge, p. 31.

CHAPTER 4.

1. Keith W. Jennison, *The Humorous Mr. Lincoln,* Bonzano Books, 1965, p. 1.

2. Jennison, p. 1.

3. Abraham Lincoln, *The Life and Writings of Abraham Lincoln,* Philip Van Doren Stern, ed., p. 600.

4. Warren, p. 12.

5. Warren, p. 13.

6. Warren, p. 13.

7. William H. Herndon and Jesse W. Weik, *(Abraham Lincoln: The True Story of a Great Life)* D. Appleton & Co., 1892, p. 16.

8. Beveridge, p. 38.

9. Hertz, p. 354, (Letter from Nat Grigsby to William Herndon, September 12, 1865.)

10. Hertz, p. 278, (Letter from Dennis Hanks to William Herndon, June 13, 1865)

11. Beveridge, p. 40. (Letter from Dennis Hanks to William Herndon, March 22, 1866)

12. Abraham Lincoln, *The Life and Writings of Abraham Lincoln,* p. 565.

13. Atkinson, p. 15.

CHAPTER 5.

1. Hertz, p. 278-279. (Letter from Dennis Hanks to William Herndon, June 13, 1865.)

2. Beveridge, p. 43-44 (Letters from Hanks to Herndon, March 7 and 12, 1866)

3. Abraham Lincoln, *The Life and Writings of Abraham Lincoln,* p. 601 (Autobiographical Sketch)

4. David Turnham to Herndon, Feb. 21, 1866

5. Abraham Lincoln, *Collected Works,* Vol. I, p. 386. (From letter September 6, 1846.)

6. Abraham Lincoln, *The Life and Writings of Abraham Lincoln*, p. 600-601. (From Autobiographical Sketch)

7. Atkinson, p. 12-13

8. Van Natter, p. 5.

9. Herndon, p. 21.

10. Hertz, p. 279.

11. Atkinson, p. 37.

12. Lincoln, *The Life and Writings of Abraham Lincoln*, p. 601.

13. Herndon, p. 50-51.

14. Herndon, p. 51.

15. Herndon, p. 51.

16. Beveridge, p. 45. (Letter from Hanks and Herndon, March 12, 1866.)

17. Van Natter, p. 12.

18. Atkinson, p. 16.

19. Hertz, p. 279. (Letter from Hanks to Herndon, June 13, 1865.)

20. Warren, p. 54.

21. Atkinson, p. 16.

22. Atkinson, p. 16.

23. Warren, p. 55.

24. Atkinson, p. 17.

25. Warren, p. 56.

26. Hertz, p. 73 (Herndon to Lamon, March 6, 1870)

27. Hertz, p. 279. (Hanks to Herndon, June 13, 1865.)

CHAPTER 6.

1. Beveridge, p. 57. (Hanks to Herndon, March 22, 1866)

2. Atkinson, p. 19.

3. Henry B. Rankin, *Personal Recollections of Abraham Lincoln*, G. P. Putnam's Sons, 1916, p. 320.

4. Atkinson, p. 19.

5. Atkinson, p. 19-20.

6. Warren, p. 63.

7. Herndon, p. 26. (Haycraft to Herndon, Dec. 7, 1866)

8. Sandburg, *Abraham Lincoln, The Prairie Years*, p. 26.

9. Atkinson, p. 20.

10. Atkinson, p. 21.

11. Beveridge, p. 59. (Harriet A. Chapman to Herndon, Dec. 17, 1865)

12. Hertz, p. 350. (Mrs. Lincoln to Herndon, Sept. 8, 1865)

13. Atkinson, p. 22.

14. Hertz, p. 281. (Hanks to Herndon, June 13, 1865)

15. Atkinson, p. 22.
16. Atkinson, p. 21.
17. Atkinson, p. 22-23.
18. Atkinson, p. 21.
19. Hertz, p. 351-352. (Mrs. Lincoln to Herndon, Sept. 8, 1865)
20. Warren, p. 194.

CHAPTER 7.

1. Sandburg, *Abraham Lincoln, The Prairie Years*, p. 26.
2. Atkinson, p. 35.
3. Warren, p. 143.
4. Beveridge, p. 87.
5. Warren, p. 142.
6. Warren, p. 153.
7. Warren, p. 153.
8. Warren, p. 154.
9. Warren, p. 249.
10. Hertz, p. 360.
11. Hertz, p. 363. (William Wood to Herndon, Sept. 15, 1865)
12. Beveridge, p. 61.
13. Hertz, p. 363. (Joseph Richardson to Herndon)
14. Atkinson, p. 40.
15. Warren, p. 197.
16. Herndon, p. 43-44.
17. Beveridge, p. 93.
18. Herndon, p. 43-44.
19. Beveridge, p. 94.
20. Hertz, p. 355. (Grigsby to Herndon, Sept. 12, 1865)
21. Warren, p. 210.
22. Atkinson, p. 35-36.
23. Herndon, p. 22. (David Turnham to Herndon)
24. Sandburg, p. 29-30.

CHAPTER 8.

1. Atkinson, p. 17.
2. Sandburg, p. 23.
3. Leonard Swett, *Reminiscences of Abraham Lincoln*, Allen Thorndike Rice, ed., North American Publishing Co., 1886, p. 458.
4. Abraham Lincoln, *Collected Writings*, III p. 512. (Lincoln to J. W. Fell, Dec. 20, 1859).
5. Hertz, p. 276. (Hanks to Herndon, June 13, 1865)
6. Atkinson, p. 18-19.

7. Beveridge, p. 28.

8. Swett, p. 458.

9. Warren, p. 11.

10. Atkinson, p. 17.

11. Hertz, p. 354. (Grigsby to Herndon, Sept. 12, 1865)

12. Scripps, p. f28. (Grigsby to Herndon, Sept. 4, 1865)

13. Hertz, p. 354.

14. Herndon, p. 32.

15. Beveridge, p. 70.

16. Warren, p. 133. (David Turnham to Herndon, Sept. 15, 1865)

17. Herndon, p. 31-32. (Burba to Herndon, March 31, 1866)

18. Warren, p. 169.

19. Mrs. Allen Gentry to Herndon, Sept. 17, 1865, H-W Collection.

20. Herndon, p. 35

21. Mrs. Allen Gentry to Herndon, Sept. 17, 1865, H-W Collection.

22. Daniel 3:1, 11, 12.

23. Warren, p. 83. (Lincoln to Sen. Henderson of Missouri)

24. Van Natter

25. Warren, p. 102.

26. Warren, p. 243.

27. Warren, p. 128.

28. Abraham Lincoln, *The Life and Writings of Abraham Lincoln*, Van Doren Stern, ed., p. 601.

29. Mrs. Allen Gentry, Sept. 17, 1865, H-W Collection.

CHAPTER 9.

1. Atkinson, p. 26-27.

2. Hertz, p. 360.

3. Beveridge, p. 68.

4. Warren, p. 46.

5. Sandburg, *The War Years*, Vol. II, p. 309.

6. Atkinson, p. 24.

7. Atkinson, p. 23-24.

8. Atkinson, p. 25.

9. *The Arabian Nights*, Grosset & Dunlap, 1946, p. 13.

10. *The Arabian Nights*, p. 93.

11. *The Autobiography of Benjamin Franklin*, The Spencer Press, 1936, p. 8.

12. Franklin, p. 13.

13. Franklin, p. 14.

14. Hertz, p. 346.

15. Hertz, p. 365-66.

16. Mason Locke Weems, *A History of the Life and Death, Virtues and Exploits of General George Washington,* The World Publishing Co., 1965 (Reprint—original 1809), p. 21-25.

17. Warren, p. 110-111.

18. Beveridge, p. 83.

CHAPTER 10.

1. Atkinson, p. 28-29.

2. Beveridge, p. 79.

3. Hertz, p. 351. (Mrs. Lincoln to Herndon, Sept. 8, 1865)

4. Atkinson, p. 35.

5. Sandburg, p. 42.

6. Atkinson, p. 37-38.

7. Hertz, p. 347.

8. Hertz, p. 351.

9. Elizabeth Crawford to Herndon, April 19, 1866, Herndon-Weik Collection.

10. Atkinson, p. 29-32.

11. Warren, p. 171-172.

12. Atkinson, p. 23.

13. Atkinson, p. 27.

14. Hertz, p. 351. (Mrs. Lincoln to Herndon, Sept. 8, 1865)

15. Herndon, p. 40.

16. Hertz, p. 351.

17. Herndon, p. 40.

18. Hertz, p. 351.

19. Hertz, p. 351.

20. Warren, p. 130-132.

21. Tarbell, p. 32.

22. Hertz, p. 351.

23. Beveridge, p. 78.

24. Beveridge, p. 78.

25. Warren, p. 245.

26. Beveridge, p. 91.

CHAPTER 11.

1. Hertz, p. 347.

2. Hertz, p. 355. (Nat Grigsby to Herndon, Sept. 12, 1865)

3. ibid.

4. Tarbell, *The Early Life of Abraham Lincoln,* p. 67.

5. Hertz, p. 294. (Elizabeth Crawford to Herndon, May 3, 1866)
6. ibid.
7. Beveridge, p. 79. (Nat Grigsby to Herndon, Oct. 25, 1865)
8. Hertz, p. 357. (Nat Grigsby to Herndon, Sept. 12, 1865)
9. Beveridge, p. 87. (Hanks to Herndon, March 22, 1866)
10. Herndon, p. 35.
11. Warren, p. 154.
12. Warren, p. 157.
13. Warren, p. 155.
14. Beveridge, p. 80.
15. Beveridge, p. 80. (David Turnham to Herndon, Dec. 17, 1866)
16. Sandburg, p. 460.
17. Tarbell I:26. (Lincoln to T. W. S. Kidd, editor, "The Morning Monitor," Springfield, Illinois)
18. Hertz, p. 155. (Herndon to Weik, Jan. 8, 1887)
19. Hertz, p. 362.
20. Hertz, p. 155.
21. Hertz, p. 362.
22. ibid.
23. Hertz, p. 287. (Samuel Crawford to Herndon, Jan. 8, 1866)
24. Warren, p. 196.
25. Hertz, p. 356. (Nat Grigsby to Herndon, Sept. 12, 1865)
26. Hertz, p. 367-8. (Elizabeth Crawford to Herndon, Sept. 16, 1865)
27. Nat Grigsby to Herndon, Jan. 21, 1866, H-W Collection.
28. Hertz, p. 287.
29. Hertz, p. 285-287. (S. A. Crawford to Herndon, Jan. 4, 1866)

CHAPTER 12.

1. Sandburg, *The Prairie Years*, p. 266.
2. Hertz, p. 361.
3. Hertz, p. 314 (R. B. Rutledge to Herndon, Oct. 1866)
4. Herndon, p. 39.
5. Warren, p. 174.
6. Herndon, p. 38.
7. ibid.
8. CW I: 378. (Lincoln to Andrew Johnston, April 18, 1846)
9. ibid
10. Warren, p. 173.
11. ibid.
12. ibid.
13. ibid.

14. CW I: 384. (Lincoln to Andrew Johnston, Sept. 6, 1846)
15. CW I: 385.

CHAPTER 13.

1. Warren, p. 145.
2. ibid.
3. ibid.
4. Tarbell, *The Early Life of Abraham Lincoln*, p. 64.
5. Leonard Swett, *Reminiscences of Abraham Lincoln*, North American Publishing Co., 1886; Allen Thorndike Rice, ed., p. 458.
6. Warren, p. 146.

CHAPTER 14.

1. Warren, p. 176.
2. ibid.
3. ibid p. 179-180.
4. Lincoln, CW IV, p. 62.
5. ibid.
6. ibid.
7. Rice, p. 462
8. Warren, p. 181.
9. Warren, p. 185.
10. Atkinson, p. 39.
11. ibid.
12. Beveridge, p. 89. (Wood to Herndon, Sept. 15, 1865)

CHAPTER 15.

1. Hertz, p. 364. (Wood to Herndon, Sept. 15, 1865)
2. ibid.
3. Atkinson, p. 41.
4. Hertz, p. 347.
5. Herndon, p. 78.
6. Sandburg, p. 55.
7. Tarbell, *Life of Lincoln*, 45.
8. Warren, p. 204.
9. ibid.
10. Atkinson, p. 41.
11. Warren, p. 207.
12. Barton, p. 129.
13. ibid.
14. Warren, p. 207.
15. ibid.

16. Beveridge, p. 103f. (Hanks to Herndon, April 1866)
17. Atkinson, p. 41.
18. Warren, p. 208.
19. Lincoln to Scripps, June 1, 1860, CW IV, p. 63.
20. Warren, p. 266f.
21. Warren, p. 208.
22. ibid.
23. David Turnham to Herndon, Feb. 21, 1866
24. Atkinson, 41-42.
25. Herndon, p. 59.
26. Tarbell, *Life of Lincoln*, p. 48.
27. Sandburg, p. 57.
28. CW IV, p. 63. (Lincoln to Scripps, June 1, 1860)
29. Tarbell, *The Early Life of Abraham Lincoln*, p. 99-100.
30. Hertz, p. 347.
31. Atkinson, p. 42.
32. CW IV, p. 63. (Lincoln to Scripps, June 1, 1860)
33. Hertz, p. 347.
34. Atkinson, p. 42.
35. CW IV, p. 63. (Lincoln to Scripps, June 1, 1860)
36. Atkinson, p. 42.
37. CW IV, p. 63. (Lincoln to Scripps, June 1, 1860)
38. ibid.
39. Tarbell, *Life of Lincoln*, p. 53.

CHAPTER 16.

1. Herndon, p. 72.
2. ibid.
3. Beveridge, p. 109. (James Short to Herndon, July 7, 1865)
4. Hertz, p. 348.
5. ibid.
6. CW IV: 63. (Lincoln to Scripps, June 1, 1860).
7. Hertz, p. 348.
8. CW IV:63. (Lincoln to Scripps, June 1, 1860)
9. Hertz, p. 348.
10. Caleb Carman to Herndon, Nov. 30, 1866. H-W Collection.
11. Sandburg, p. 59.
12. Tarbell, *Life of Lincoln*, p. 52.
13. Tarbell, p. 53.
14. Hertz, p. 348.
15. Caleb Carman to Herndon Oct. 12, 1866, H-W Collection.

16. Caleb Carman to Herndon Nov. 30, 1866, H-W Collection.
17. Tarbell, p. 53-55.

CHAPTER 17.

1. Lincoln to Scripps, Scripps p. 53f.
2. Herndon, p. 66.
3. Coleman Smoot to Herndon, May 7, 1866, H-W Collection.
4. Herndon, p. 65.
5. Scripps, p. 53f.
6. Herndon, p. 66.
7. Hertz, p. 348.
8. William Greene to Herndon, May 30, 1865.
9. Herndon, p. 65.
10. Coleman Smoot to Herndon, May 7, 1866, H-W Collection.
11. ibid.
12. Hertz, p. 349.
13. Herndon, p. 66.
14. Sandburg, p. 60.
15. ibid.
16. ibid.
17. ibid.
18. ibid.
19. ibid.
20. Hertz, p. 349.
21. Herndon, p. 66-67.
22. CW II:183 (Lincoln to Joshua Speed, Aug. 24, 1855)
23. CW XI:56 (Lincoln speech to Indiana Regiment, March 17, 1865)
24. Hertz, p. 349.
25. Sandburg, p. 59.
26. ibid.
27. ibid.
28. Hertz, p. 347-348.
29. Atkinson, p. 43.

CHAPTER 18.

1. Lincoln, *Life and Writings*, p. 603. (Lincoln to Scripps, June 1, 1860)
2. Herndon, p. 68.
3. Hertz, p. 313 (R. B. Rutledge to Herndon, Oct. 1866)
4. Hertz, p. 311.

5. Benjamin P. Thomas, *Lincoln's New Salem*, Alfred A. Knopf, New York, 1954; p. 41.

6. Thomas, p. 42.

7. Sandburg, p. 97-98.

8. Herndon, p. 69.

9. ibid.

10. Herndon, p. 68.

11. Lincoln, *Life and Writings*, p. 603. (Lincoln to Scripps, June 1, 1860)

12. Herndon, p. 70.

13. Barton, p. 161.

14. Mentor Graham to Herndon, August 29, 1865, H-W Collection.

15. Lincoln, *Life and Writings*, p. 603 (Lincoln to Scripps, June 1, 1860)

16. Herndon, p. 70-71f (J. R. Herndon to Herndon, July 2, 1865)

CHAPTER 19.

1. Hertz, p. 311 (R. B. Rutledge to Herndon, October 1866)

2. Herndon, p. 72.

3. ibid.

4. ibid.

5. William Greene to Herndon, May 30, 1865, H-W Collection.

6. Herndon, p. 72.

7. Sandburg, p. 78.

8. Herndon, p. 73.

9. Beveridge, p. 110.

10. Herndon, p. 73.

11. ibid.

12. ibid.

13. James Short to Herndon, July 7, 1865, H-W Collection.

14. Hertz, p. 315 (R. B. Rutledge to Herndon, October 1866)

15. James Short to Herndon, July 7, 1865, H-W Collection.

16. Henry McHenry to Herndon, Oct. 10, 1866, H-W Collection.

17. I. G. Greene to Herndon, Oct. 5, 1866, H-W Collection.

18. James Short to Herndon, July 7, 1865, H-W Collection.

19. Henry McHenry to Herndon, Oct. 10, 1866, H-W Collection.

20. ibid.

21. ibid.

22. Hertz, p. 315.

23. Henry McHenry, Oct 10, 1866, H-W Collection.

24. Hertz, p. 315, R. B. Rutledge, October 1866.

25. James Short to Herndon, July 7, 1865, H-W Collection.

26. J. M. Rutledge to Herndon, November 18, 1866, H-W Collection.

27. Hertz, p. 315-316, R. B. Rutledge to Herndon, October 1866.

28. Henry McHenry to Herndon, October 10, 1866, H-W Collection.

29. J. M. Rutledge to Herndon, November 18, 1866, H-W Collection.

30. Sandburg, p. 79.

31. Hertz, p. 369.

32. Hertz, p. 316 (R. B. Rutledge to Herndon, October 1866)

33. Sandburg, p. 106.

34. Hertz, p. 316 (R. B. Rutledge to Herndon, October 1866)

35. Beveridge p. 112. (J. R. Herndon to Wm. Herndon, May 28, 1865)

36. ibid.

37. Hertz, p. 369.

38. Hertz, p. 315 (R. B. Rutledge to Herndon, October 1866)

39. ibid.

40. Tarbell, *Life of Lincoln*, p. 64-65.

CHAPTER 20.

1. Herndon, p. 104-105.

2. Herndon, p. 105.

3. Herndon, p. 120.

4. Herndon, p. 105-106.

5. Sandburg, p. 30.

6. Warren, p. 245.

7. Stephen B. Oates, *With Malice Toward None*, Mentor Books, New American Library, 1977.

8. Herndon, 75.

9. ibid.

10. Graham to Herndon, Aug. 29, 1865, H-W Collection.

11. ibid.

12. ibid.

13. ibid.

14. Herndon, p. 75.

15. Hertz, p. 314.

16. Thomas, p. 69.

17. Hertz, p. 314.

18. ibid.

19. Lincoln, *Life and Writings*, p. 604.

20. Beveridge, p. 116.
21. Lincoln CWI, p. 5.

CHAPTER 21.

1. Herndon, p. 78.
2. Herndon, p.79.
3. Herndon, p. 81.
4. Herndon, p. 81.
5. ibid.
6. Lincoln, *Life and Writings*, p. 603.
7. Herndon, p. 76.
8. Thomas, p. 61.
9. Herndon, p. 77.
10. Scripps, p. 51.
11. Barton, p. 169.

CHAPTER 22.

1. Tarbell, *Life of Lincoln*, p. 75.
2. Beveridge, p. 120.
3. Tarbell, *Life of Lincoln*, p. 74.
4. Barton, p. 174.
5. Tarbell, *Life of Lincoln*, p. 74.
6. Herndon, p. 84.
7. Rice, p. 464.
8. Tarbell, *Life of Lincoln*, p. 76.
9. Sandburg, *The Prairie Years*, p. 90.
10. Rice, p. 465.
11. Lincoln, *Life and Writings*, p. 566.
12. Rice, p. 464.
13. Tarbell, *Life of Lincoln*, p. 86.
14. Herndon, p. 85.
15. Rice, p. 218-219.
16. Herndon, p. 87.
17. Sandburg, *The Prairie Years*, p. 91.
18. Beveridge, p. 121.
19. William Greene to Herndon, May 30, 1865, H-W Collection.
20. Herndon, p. 87.
21. ibid.
22. William Greene to Herndon, May 30, 1865, H-W Collection.
23. ibid.
24. Beveridge, p. 121.
25. William Greene to Herndon, May 30, 1865, H-W Collection.

26. ibid.
27. ibid.
28. Sandburg, *The Prairie Years*, p. 92.
29. Sandburg, *The Prairie Years*, p. 93.

CHAPTER 23.

1. Tarbell, *Life of Lincoln*, p. 79.
2. ibid., p. 86.
3. Herndon, p. 89.
4. Sandburg, *Abraham Lincoln, The Prairie Years and The War Years*, p. 31.
5. Herndon, p. 91.
6. Beveridge, p. 123.
7. Sandburg, *Abraham Lincoln, The Prairie Years and The War Years*, p. 31.
8. Tarbell, *Life of Lincoln*, p. 90.
9. Sandburg, *The Prairie Years*, p. 89.
10. Lincoln, CW I:509-510, (Speech in U.S. House of Representatives, July 27, 1848).

CHAPTER 24.

1. J. R. Herndon to Herndon, May 28, 1865, H-W Collection.
2. James Herndon to Herndon, May 29, 1865, H-W Collection.
3. J. R. Herndon to Herndon, June 21, 1865, H-W Collection.
4. J. R. Herndon to Herndon, May 28, 1865, H-W Collection.
5. Herndon, p. 95.
6. ibid.
7. Thomas, p. 86.
8. ibid.
9. J. R. Herndon to Herndon, May 28, 1865, H-W Collection.
10. ibid.
11. ibid.
12. Lincoln, *Life and Writings*, p. 566 (Lincoln to Fell, Dec. 20, 1859).
13. Lincoln, *Life and Writings*, p. 604 (Lincoln to Scripps, June 1, 1860).
14. J. R. Herndon to Herndon, May 28, 1865, H-W Collection.
15. Herndon, Herndon's Life of Lincoln, Da Capo. Paperback, 1983, p. 146.
16. Lincoln, *Life and Writings*, p. 604. (Lincoln to Scripps, June 1, 1860).
17. Herndon, p. 97.

18. ibid.

19. ibid.

20. J. R. Herndon to Herndon, May 28, 1865, H-W Collection.

21. Herndon, p. 98.

22. Lincoln, *Life and Writings*, p. 604 (Lincoln to Scripps, June 1, 1860).

CHAPTER 25.

1. Thomas P. Reep, *The Lincoln Reader*, Paul Angle, ed., Rutgers University Press, 1947, p. 52.

2. Reep, p. 52-54.

3. George Spears to Herndon, Oct. 17, 1866, H-W Collection.

4. Caleb Carman to Herndon, Dec. 8, 1866, H-W Collection.

5. Herndon, p. 106.

6. R. B. Rutledge to Herndon, Nov. 30, 1866, H-W Collection.

7. Herndon, p. 104.

8. R. B. Rutledge to Herndon, Nov. 30, 1866, H-W Collection.

9. Tarbell, p. 93-94.

10. Herndon, p. 102.

11. Herndon, p. 99.

12. Lincoln, *Life and Writings*, p. 604.

13. ibid.

14. Herndon, p. 100.

15. Reep, p. 54.

16. Tarbell, p. 105.

17. ibid.

CHAPTER 26.

1. Herndon, p. 119-120.

2. James Short to Herndon, July 7, 1865, H-W Collection.

3. Hertz, p. 312.

4. G. W. Miles to Herndon, March 23, 1866, H-W Collection.

5. J. R. Herndon to Herndon, July 3, 1865, H-W Collection.

6. W. G. Greene to Herndon, Jan. 23, 1866, H-W Collection.

7. Herndon, p. 119.

8. Graham to Herndon, April 2, 1866, H-W Collection.

9. Herndon, p. 121.

10. Hertz, p. 312.

11. Herndon, p. 122.

12. Hertz, p. 312.

13. Herndon, p. 123.

14. Herndon, p. 124.

15. Herndon, p. 123.
16. Hertz, p. 312.
17. McNamar to Herndon, May 5, 1866, H-W Collection.
18. Hertz, p. 312.
19. Herndon, p. 125-126.
20. Herndon, p. 127.
21. Hertz, p. 312.
22. Herndon, p. 128.
23. James Short to Herndon, July 7, 1865, H-W Collection.
24. Mentor Graham to Herndon, April 2, 1866, H-W Collection.
25. Hertz, p. 312.
26. Herndon, p. 129.
27. Hertz, p. 319. (R. B. Rutledge to Herndon, Nov. 21, 1866).
28. John McNamar to Herndon, May 5, 1866.
29. Hertz, p. 313.
30. Herndon, p. 129.
31. Herndon, p. 129. (John Rutledge to Herndon, Nov. 25, 1866).
32. Herndon, p. 129.
33. John Jones to Herndon, Oct. 22, 1866.
34. Hertz, p. 313.
35. G. W. Miles to Herndon, March 23, 1866, H-W Collection.
36. Herndon, p. 130.
37. G. W. Miles to Herndon, March 23, 1866, H-W Collection.
38. Herndon, p. 131.
39. A. Y. Ellis to Herndon, Sept. 19, 1866, H-W Collection.
40. Lincoln, CW I: 378 (Lincoln to Andrew Johnston, April 18, 1846).
41. A. Y. Ellis to Herndon, Sept. 19, 1866, H-W Collection.
42. Sandburg, p. 197-199.

CHAPTER 27.

1. Herndon, p. 109.
2. ibid.
3. Abraham Lincoln, *Life and Writings*, p. 604, June 1, 1860.
4. ibid.
5. Herndon, p. 114.
6. ibid.
7. Thomas, p. 96.
8. Thomas, p. 96-97.
9. Thomas, p. 97.
10. ibid.
11. Herndon, p. 110.

12. Abraham Lincoln, *Life and Writings*, p. 604, June 1, 1860.
13. W. G. Greene to Herndon, June 7, 1865, H-W Collection.
14. Hertz, p. 314.
15. Graham to Herndon, Aug. 29, 1865, H-W Collection.
16. Herndon, p. 111.
17. Graham to Herndon, Aug. 29, 1865, H-W Collection.
18. Herndon, p. 112.
19. Graham to Herndon, Aug. 29, 1865, H-W Collection.
20. Henry McHenry to Herndon, Oct. 5, 1865, H-W Collection.
21. Herndon, p. 112.
22. Herndon, p. 113.
23. Thomas, p. 112.
24. Jimmy Short to Herndon, July 7, 1865, H-W Collection.
25. ibid.
26. ibid.
27. ibid.
28. Tarbell, *Life of Lincoln*, p. 104.
29. Herndon, p. 117.
30. J. R. Herndon to Herndon, May 28, 1865, Herndon Collection.
31. ibid.
32. Caleb Carman to Herndon, Nov. 30, 1866, Herndon Collection.
33. Coleman Smoot to Herndon, May 7, 1866, Herndon Collection.
34. Walt Whitman, *The Eighteenth Presidency*, unpublished manuscript, 1856.

Bibliography

Angle, Paul. Editor. *The Lincoln Reader*. Rutgers University Press, 1947.

Atkinson, Eleanor. *The Boyhood of Lincoln*. The McClure Co., 1908.

Barton, William E. *The Life of Abraham Lincoln*. Two Vols. Bobbs-Merrill, 1925.

Basler, Roy P., Editor. *Collected Works of Abraham Lincoln*. 9 Vols. Rutgers University Press, 1953.

Beveridge, Albert. *Abraham Lincoln, 1809-1858*. Two Vols. Houghton-Mifflin Co., 1928.

Current, Richard N. *The Lincoln Nobody Knows*. Hill and Wang, 1958.

Donald, David. *Lincoln's Herndon*. Alfred A. Knopf, 1948.

Franklin, Benjamin. *The Autobiography of Benjamin Franklin*. The Spencer Press, 1936.

Herndon, William H. Collected Papers, Library of Congress.

Herndon, William H. and Weik, Jesse W. *Abraham Lincoln: The True Story of a Great Life*. Two Vols. D. Appleton & Co., 1892.

Herndon, William H. and Weik, Jesse W. *Herndon's Lincoln*, David Freeman Hawke, ed. Bobbs-Merrill, 1970.

Herndon, William H. and Weik, Jesse W. *Herndon's Life of Lincoln*. Da Capo Press, 1984.

Hertz, Emanuel. *The Hidden Lincoln*. Viking Press, 1938.

Hertz, Emanuel. *Lincoln Talks*. Viking Press, 1939.

Jennison, Keith W. *The Humorous Mr. Lincoln*. Bonzano Books, 1965.

Luthin, Reinhold. *The Real Lincoln*. New York, 1960.

Neely, Mark E. *The Abraham Lincoln Encyclopedia*. McGraw-Hill, 1982.

Nicolay, John G., and Hay, John. *Abraham Lincoln: A History*. Ten Vols. Century Co., 1890.

Oates, Stephen B. *With Malice Toward None*. New American Library, 1977.

Oates, Stephen B. *Abraham Lincoln: The Man Behind the Myths*. New American Library, 1984.

Rankin, Henry B. *Personal Recollections of Abraham Lincoln*. G. P. Putnam's Sons, 1916.

Rice, Allen Thorndike, Editor. *Reminiscences of Abraham Lincoln*. North American Publishing Co., 1886.

Sandburg, Carl. *Abraham Lincoln: The Prairie Years.* Two Vols. Harcourt Brace and Co., 1926.

Sandburg, Carl. *Abraham Lincoln: The War Years.* Four Vols. Harcourt Brace and Co., 1939.

Sandburg, Carl. *Abraham Lincoln: The Prairie Years and The War Years.* One Vol. Harcourt Brace Jovanovich, 1954.

Scripps, John Locke. *Life of Abraham Lincoln.* Chicago Press and Tribune, May 19, 1860. Reprint: Indiana University Press, 1961.

Stern, Philip Van Doren. Editor. *The Life and Writings of Abraham Lincoln.* Random House, 1940.

Tarbell, Ida M. *The Early Life of Abraham Lincoln.* McClure Co., 1896. Reprint: A. S. Barnes & Co., 1974.

Tarbell, Ida M. *The Life of Abraham Lincoln.* Two Vols. McClure & Phillips and Co., 1900.

Thomas, Benjamin P. *Lincoln's New Salem.* Alfred A. Knopf, 1934.

Thomas, Benjamin P. *Abraham Lincoln.* Alfred A. Knopf, 1952.

Van Natter, Francis Marion. *Lincoln's Boyhood.* Public Affairs Press. 1963.

Warren, Louis A. *Lincoln's Youth, Indiana Years, Seven to Twenty-One, 1816-1830.* Indiana Historical Society, 1959.

Weems, Mason Locke. *A History of the Life and Death, Virtues and Exploits of General George Washington.* The World Publishing Co., Reprint: 1965. Original: 1809.

Index

Elliot, Andrew, 117
Ellis, A. Y., 141, 167, 174, 180, 182
Elmore, Jemima, 189

Fink, Mike, 97
Frontier living, 12; childrearing, 17; drinking, 130; family, 17; social life, 78, 80–81, 82, 128–29, 130

Gentry, Allen, 49, 102–106
Gentry, James, 49, 52, 53, 102, 111
Gentry, James, II, 103
Gentry, Joseph, 49, 53
Gentry, Matthew, 49, 92–95
Gentryville, Ind., 49, 107, 131
Godby, Russell, 175
Gollaher, Austin, 26–27
Graham, Mentor, 130, 131, 143, 145, 178, 180, 187–88
Grass, Alfred, 103
Greene, Bowling, 133, 182
Greene, L. M., 178
Greene, William (Bill, Billy), 133–34, 143, 172–73, 178, 187; in militia, 155, 156, 157
Greene, William, Sr., 173
Grigsby, Aaron, 78–80, 82, 92
Grigsby, Betsy, 84
Grigsby, Charles, 82–87, 109
Grigsby, Nancy, 91, 109–10
Grigsby, Nat (Nattie), 4, 49, 54, 58–59, 69, 78–79, 80, 81, 84–85
Grigsby, R. D., 84
Grigsby, Redmond, 53, 111
Grigsby, Reuben, 49–50
Grigsby, Reuben, Jr., 82–87
Grigsby, William, 53, 82, 110
Grigsby family, 49–50, 82–84, 110

Hall, Levi, 2
Hall, Squire, 78, 98, 109, 110
Hall family, 108, 110
Hanks, Dennis, 4–6, 13, 14, 25, 39, 70–71, 72, 73, 77, 98, 107, 125, 126; childhood, 18, 21–22, 23, 26; life with Lincoln family, 31, 33, 36, 37, 40, 41, 42, 43–44, 45, 46, 50, 54, 56, 57, 63, 65; mar-riage, 78; move to Illinois, 109, 110, 111, 112, 114
Hanks, John, 67, 71, 78, 108, 109, 113, 114, 116–17, 118; trip to New Orleans, 121–22, 123–24
Hanks, Joseph, 15
Hanks, Lucy. See Sparrow, Lucy Hanks
Hanks, Nancy. See Lincoln, Nancy Hanks (mother of AL)
Hanks family, 5, 6, 108, 110
Haycraft, Samuel, 44, 58
Hazel, Caleb, 58
Head, Jesse, 19
Herndon, J. R., 132
Herndon, James, 166, 169–70
Herndon, Rowan, 137, 149, 166–67, 168–69, 170, 178, 190–91
Herndon, William (Billy), 1–2, 38, 41, 109, 112, 116, 130, 134, 135, 140, 142–43, 148, 156, 174, 175, 176, 185, 187; on AL and A. Rutledge, 178, 179, 180, 181, 182; biographical study of AL, 2–8, 82–83, 85, 89, 124, 177; early acquaintance with AL, 169–70; Herndon's Lincoln, 7–8
Hill, Samuel, 169, 179, 185
Hoskins, John, 62
Hoskins, William, 110
Hughes Station, Ky., 12
Hunting, 33–36

Illinois, 108–15
Indiana, 29, 30, 34, 49; statehood, 31
Indians, 11, 12–13, 14, 17, 25, 50, 152–55, 160–61, 162, 164

Jackson, Andrew, 144, 164, 185
Johnston, Daniel, 3, 14, 44
Johnston, Elizabeth (step-sister of AL; later Mrs. Dennis Hanks), 46, 47, 78, 109, 110
Johnston, J. D., 110
Johnston, John (step-brother of AL), 46, 47, 48, 53, 81, 82, 110; trip to New Orleans, 116–17, 122, 124–25

B
LINCOLN Kigel, Richard

The frontier years
of Abe Lincoln

$15.95

DATE			
SEP 15 '88	OCT 6 '93		
NOV 28 '88	DEC 1 '93		
FEB 24 '89	JAN 3 '94		
MAR 23 '89	JAN 03 '95		
OCT 19 '90	APR 2 4 1997		
JAN 3 '91	2 3 1998		
FEB 22 '91	DEC 0 4 1998		
OCT 9 '91	MAR 2 3 2002		
NOV 12 '91	122002		
JAN 6 '92			
JAN 21 '92			
SEP 22 '93			

© THE BAKER & TAYLOR CO.